MICHAEL DRESSEL

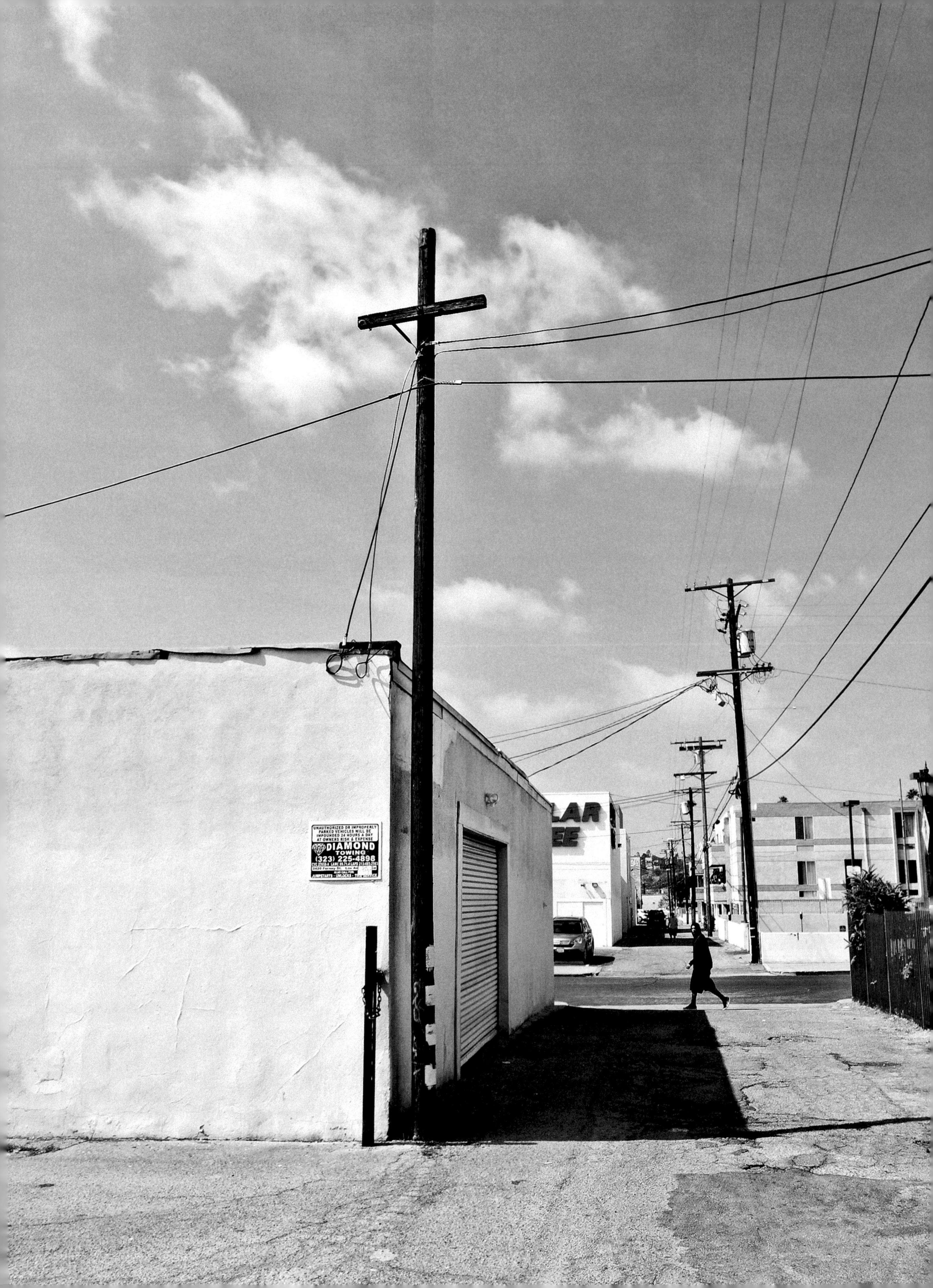
UNAUTHORIZED OR IMPROPERLY PARKED VEHICLES WILL BE IMPOUNDED 24 HOURS A DAY AT OWNERS RISK & EXPENSE
DIAMOND
TOWING
(323) 225-4898

MICHAEL DRESSEL

LOST ANGELES

GINGKO PRESS
HARTMANN BOOKS

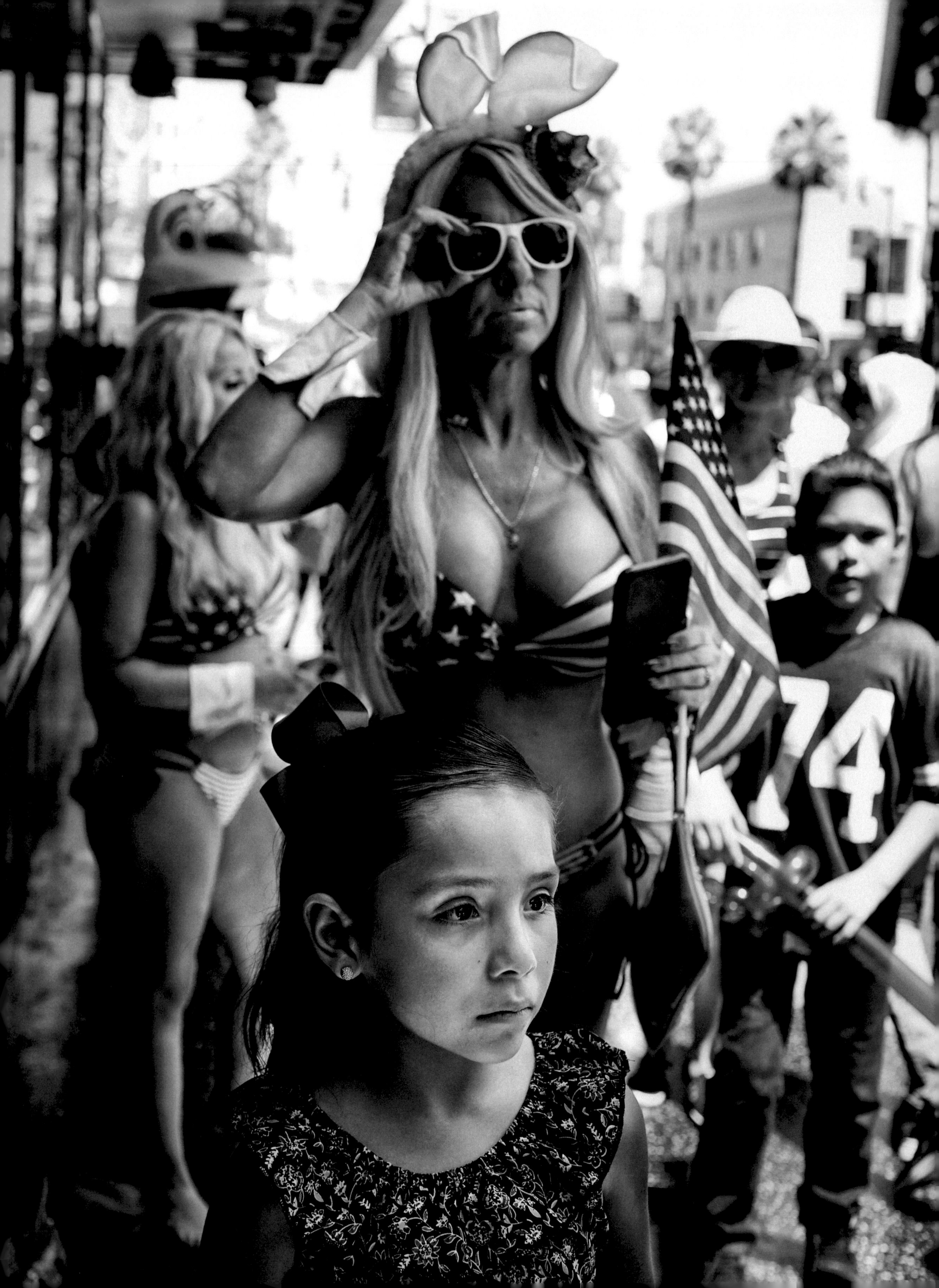
74

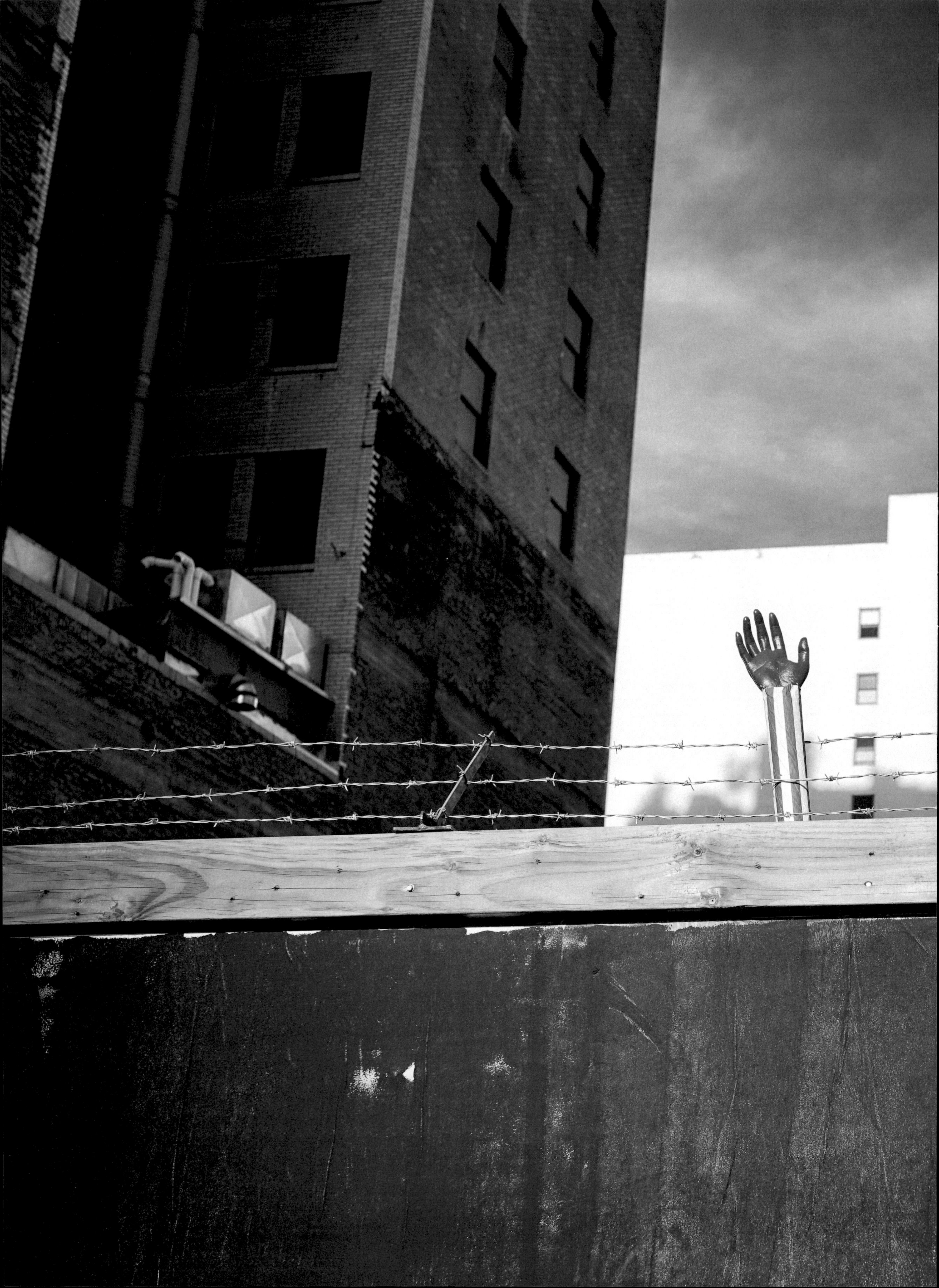

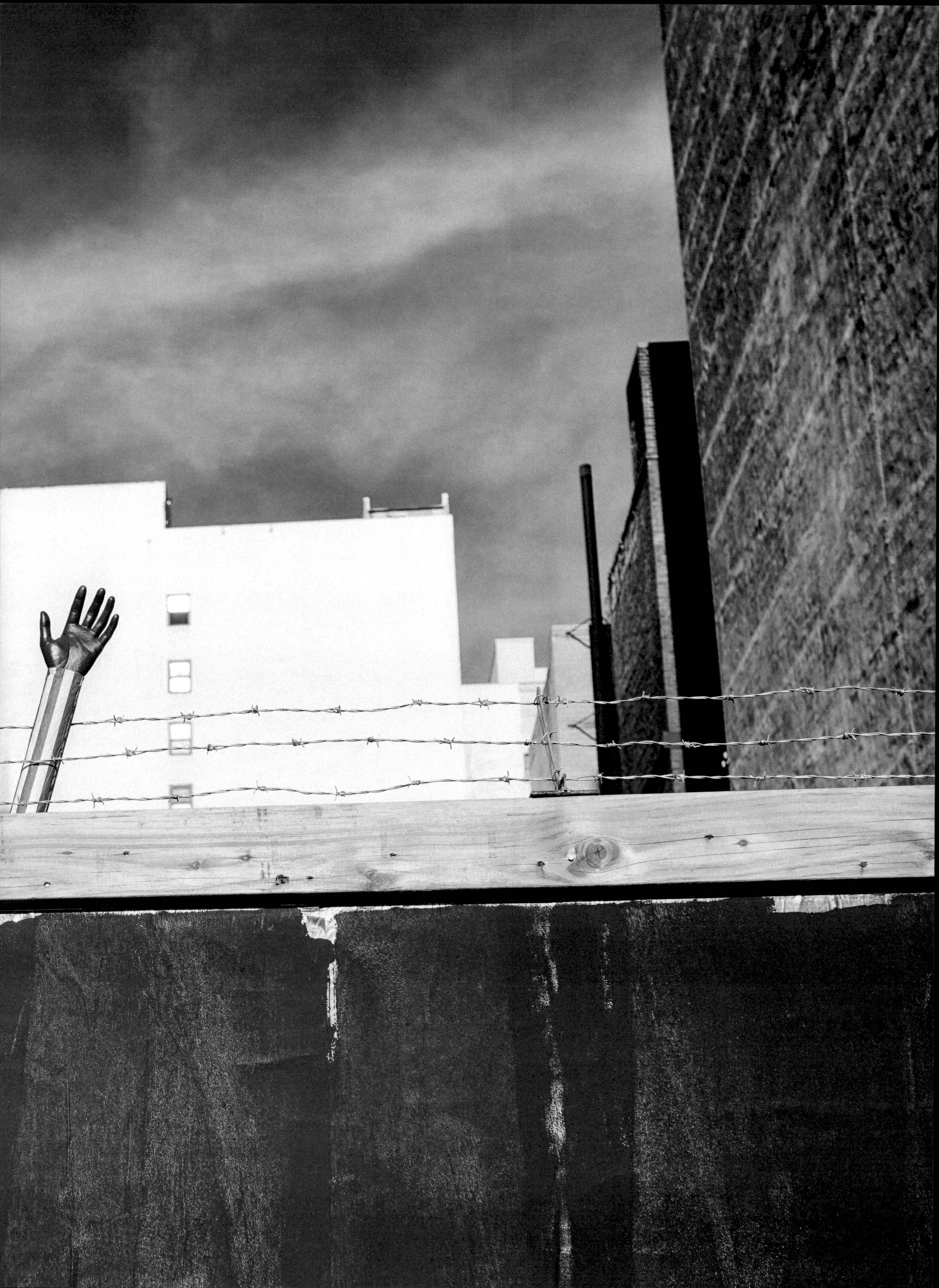

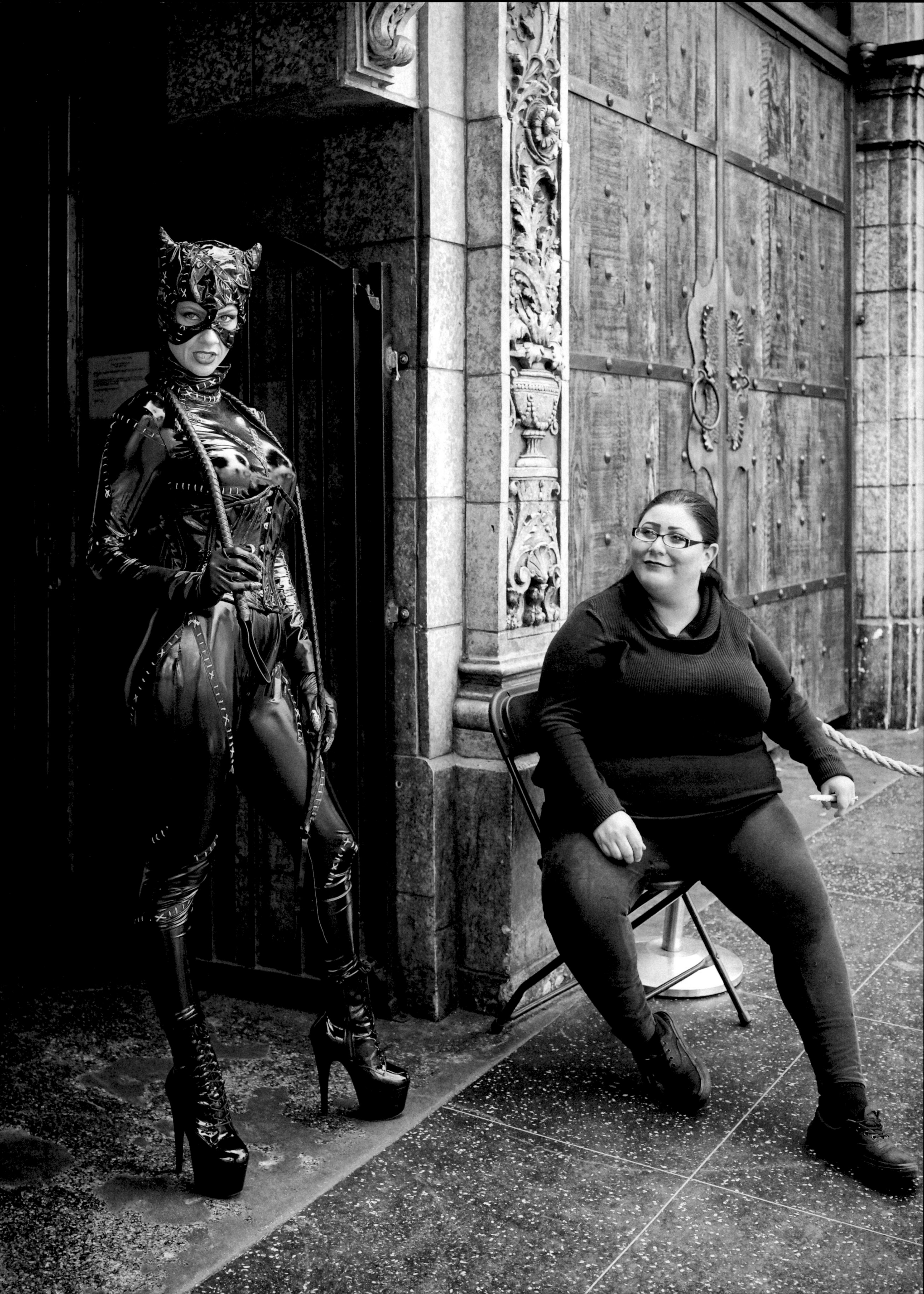

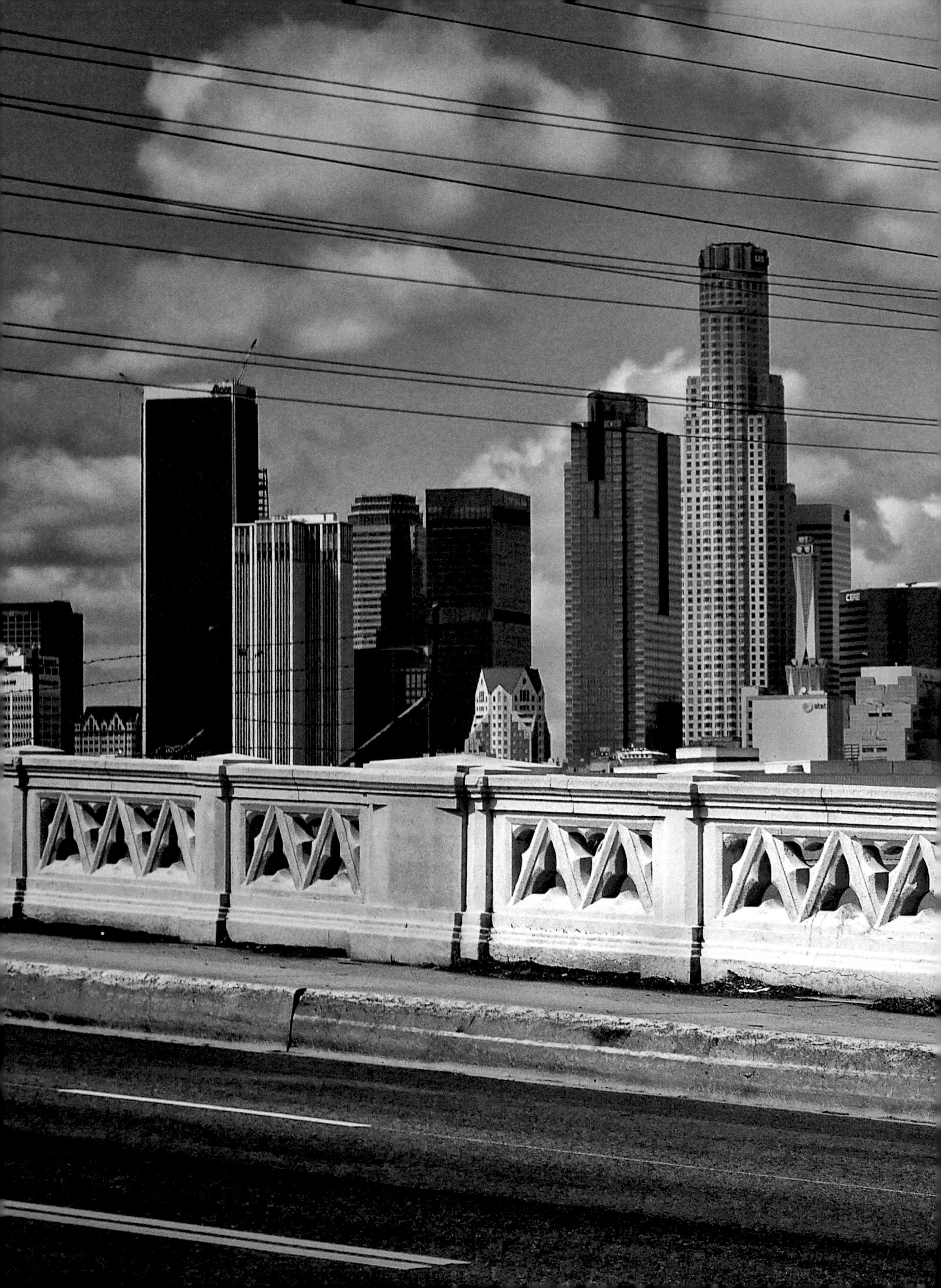

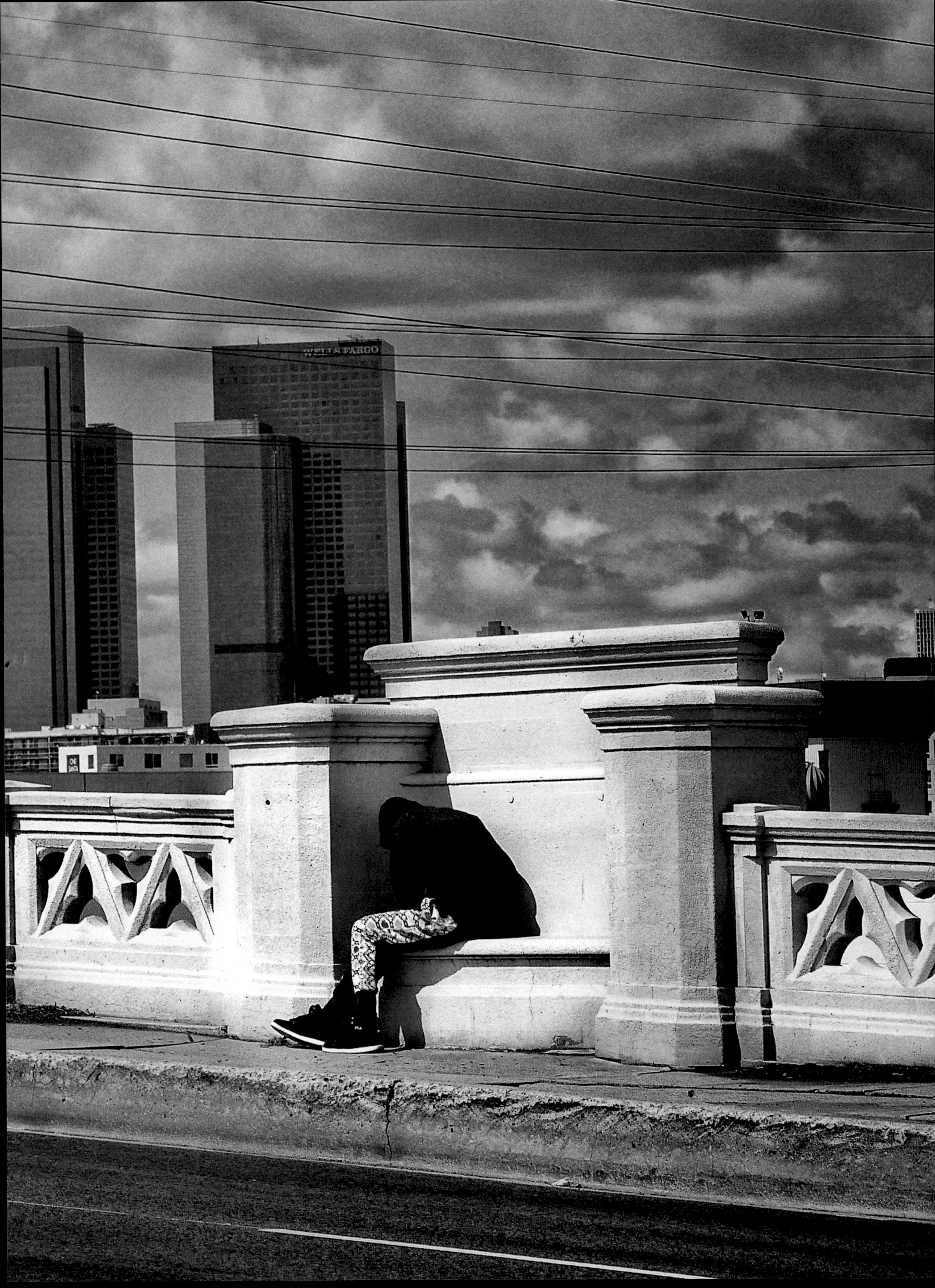
WELLS FARGO

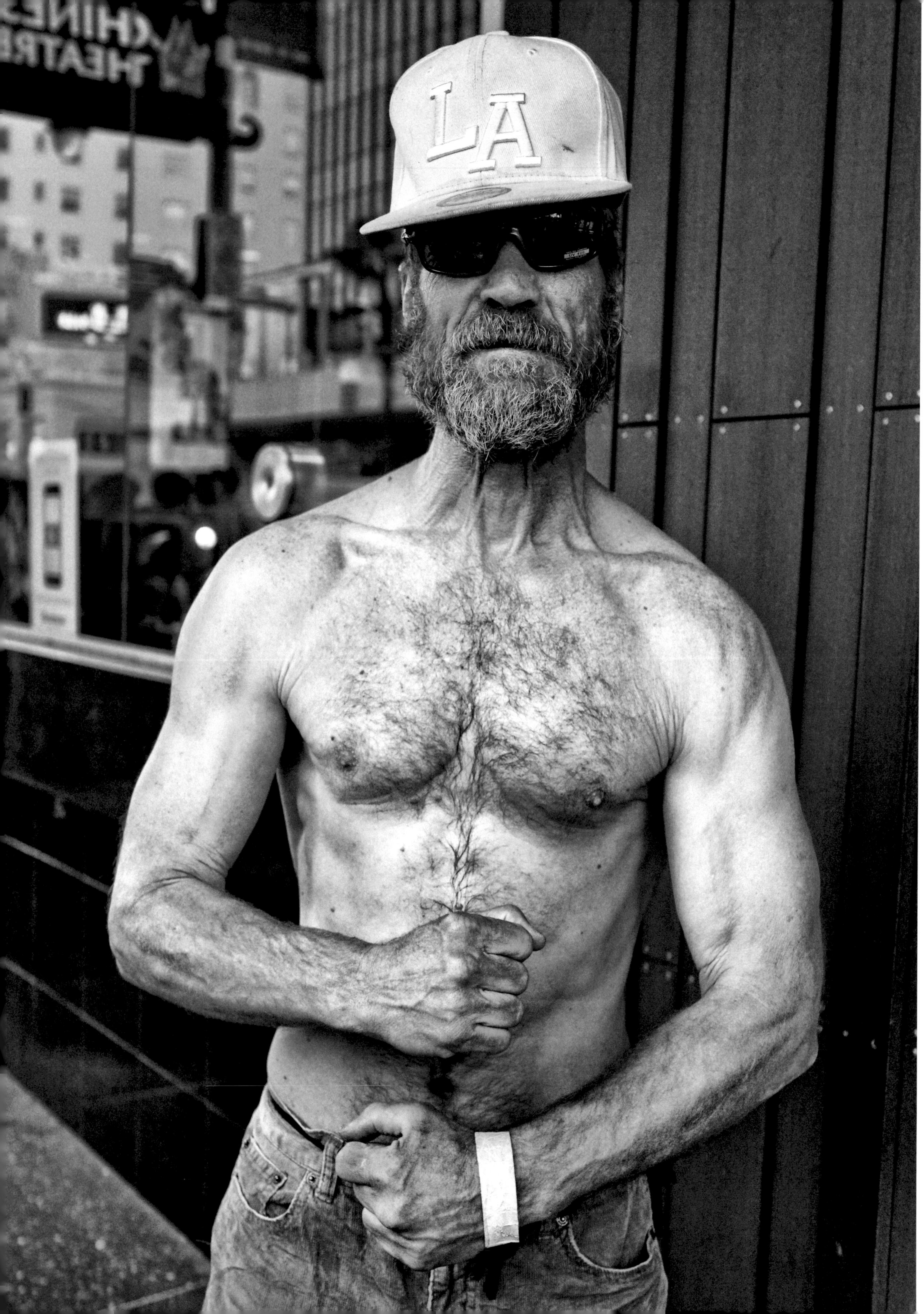
LA

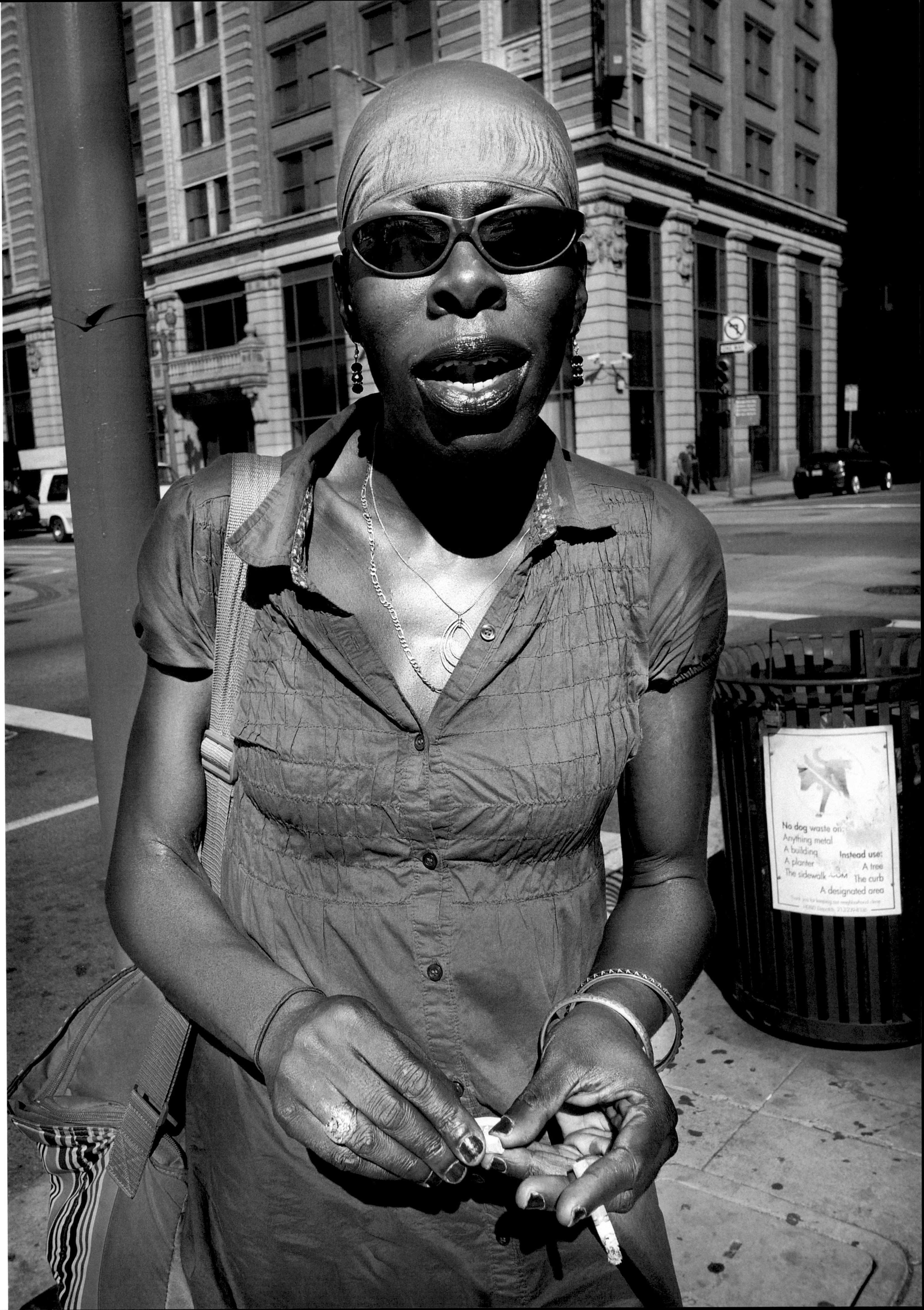
No dog waste on:
Anything metal
A building
A planter
The sidewalk
Instead use:
A tree
The curb
A designated area

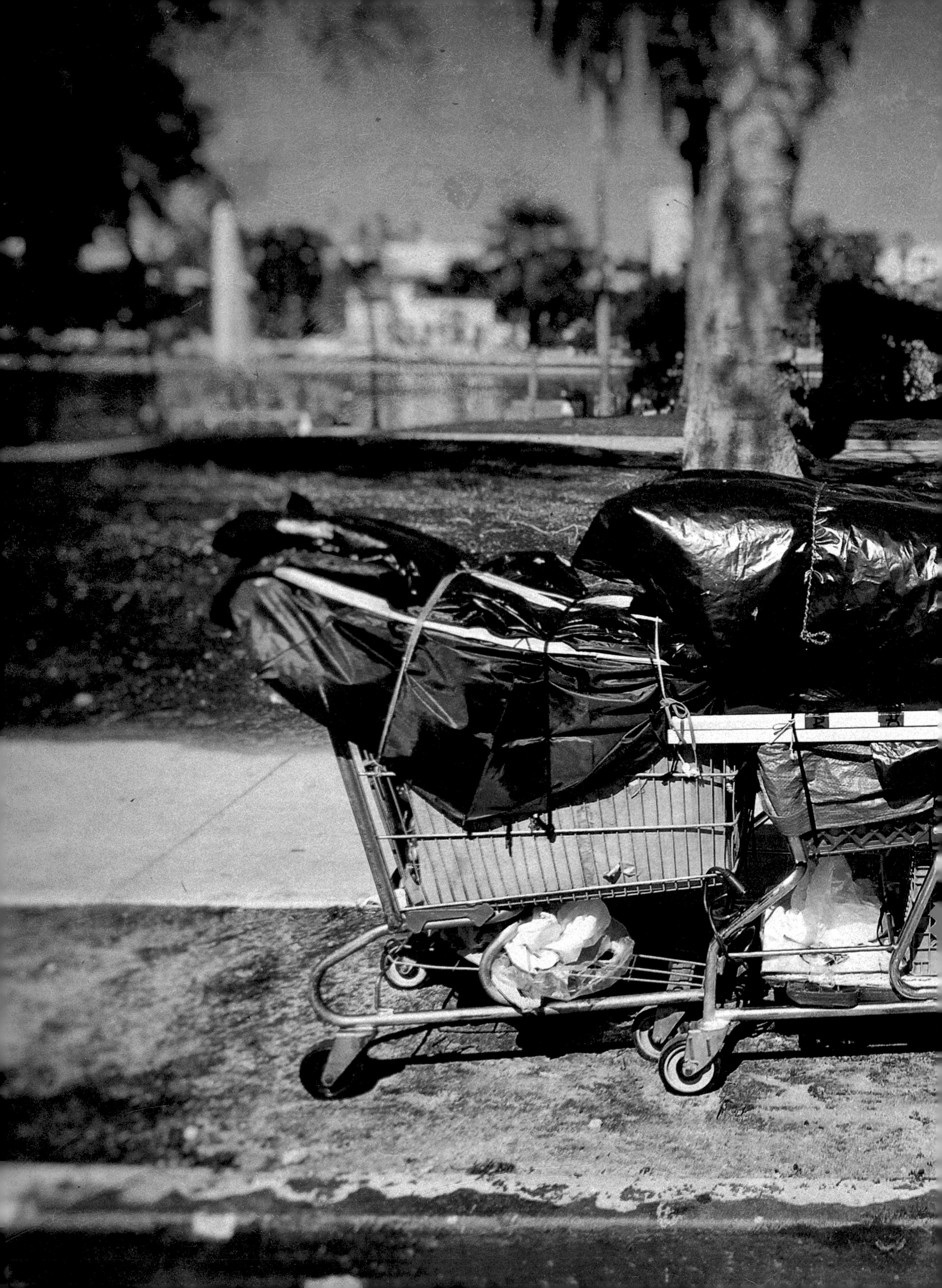

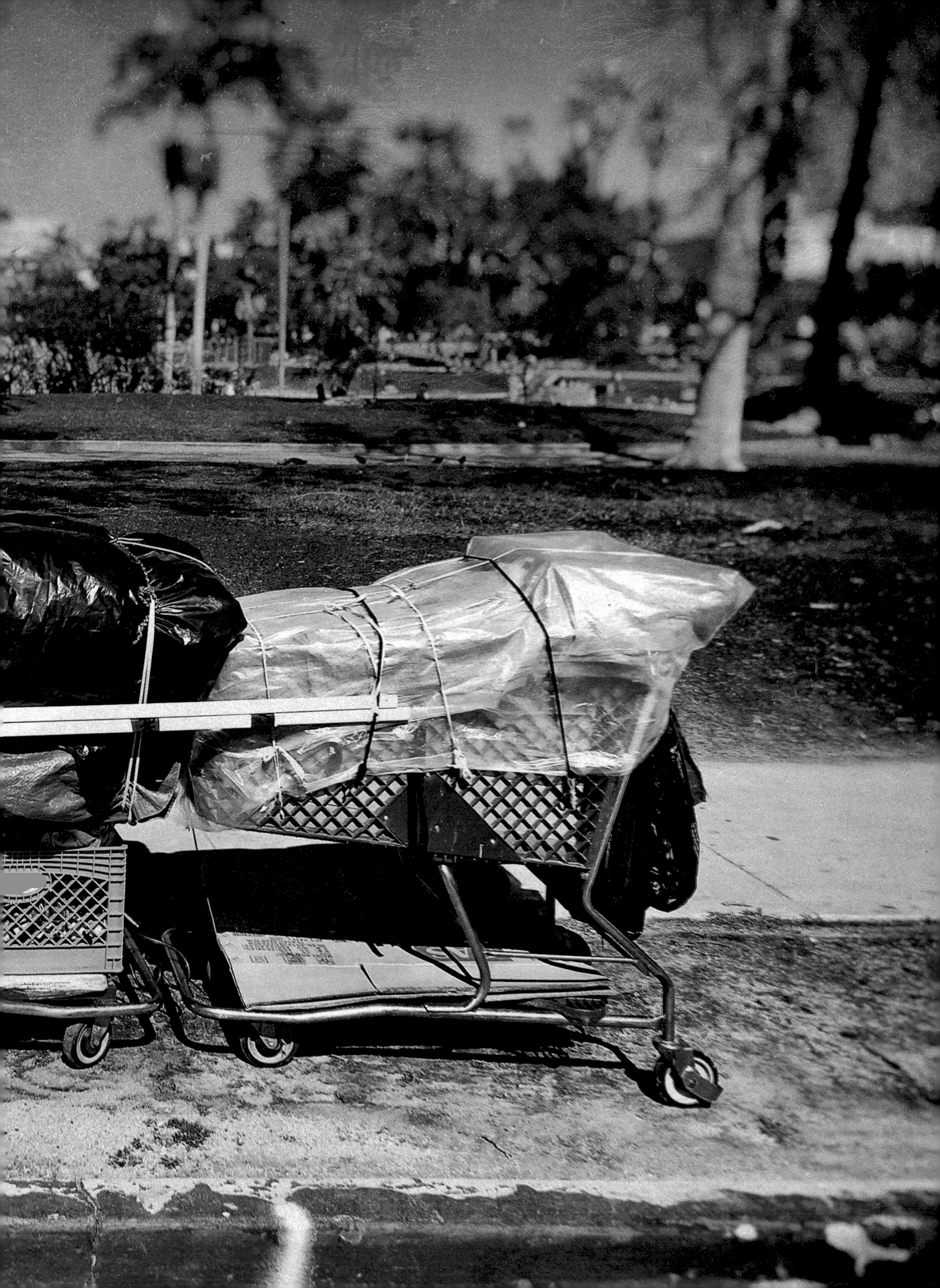

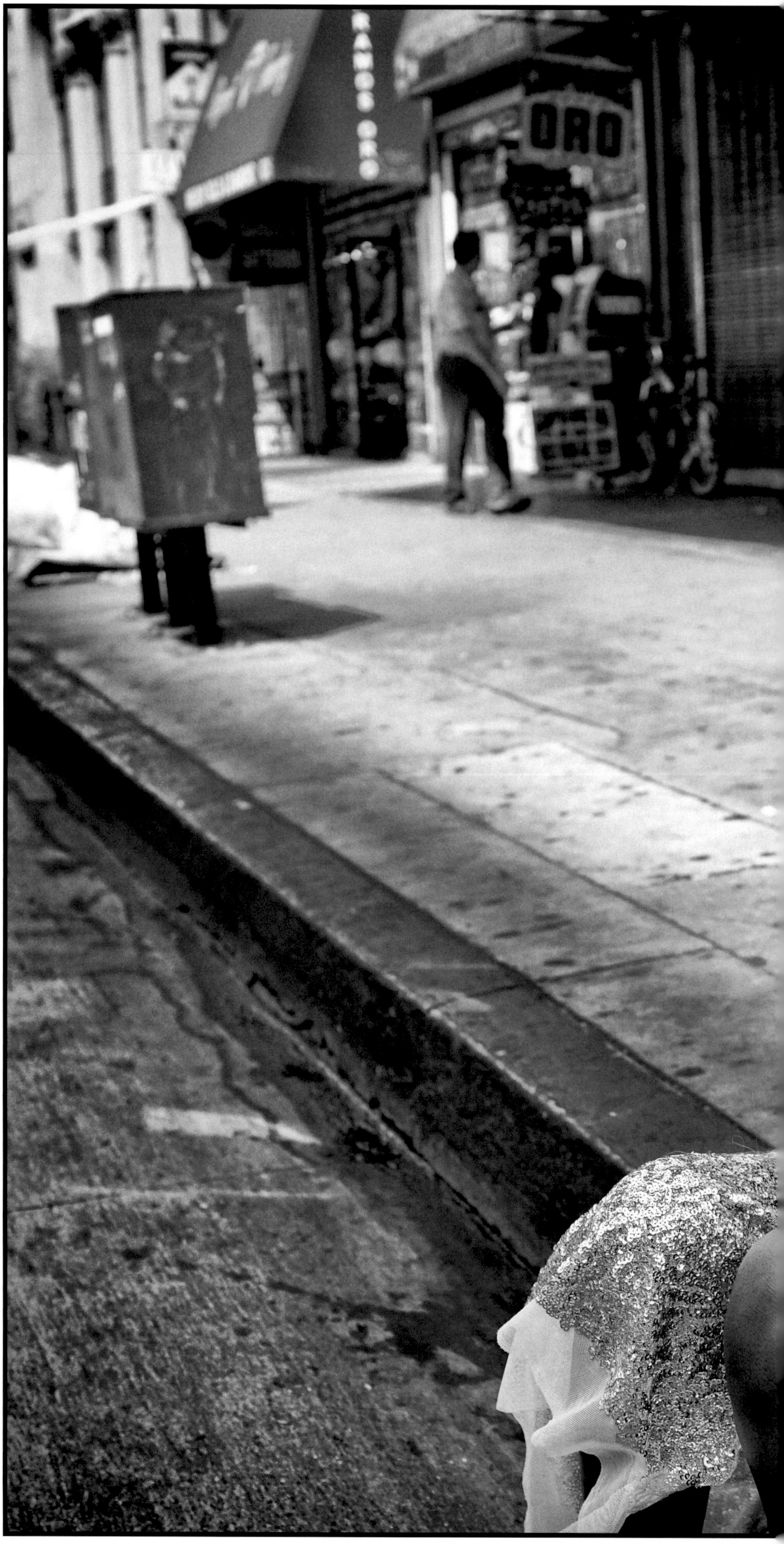
ORO

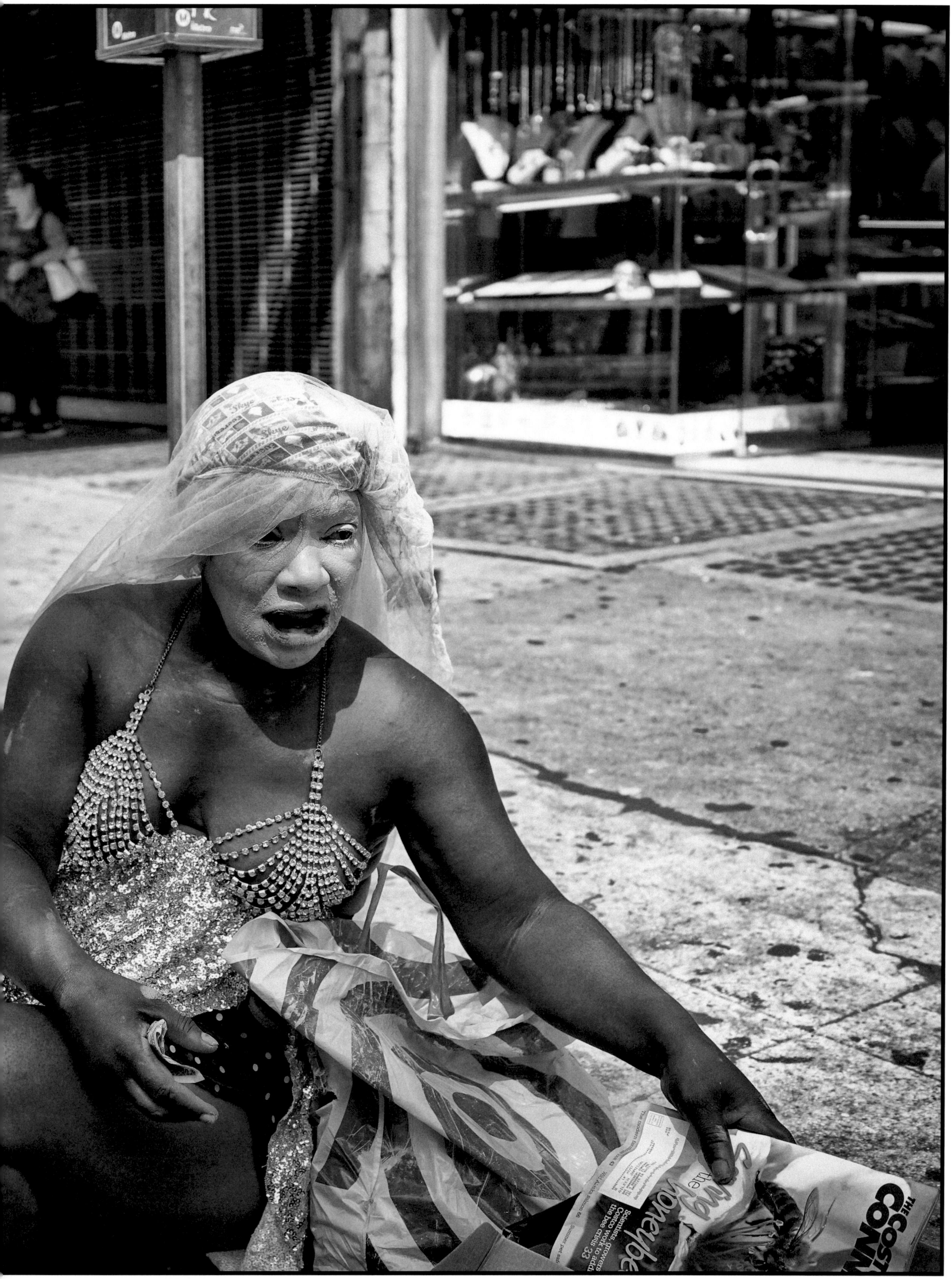

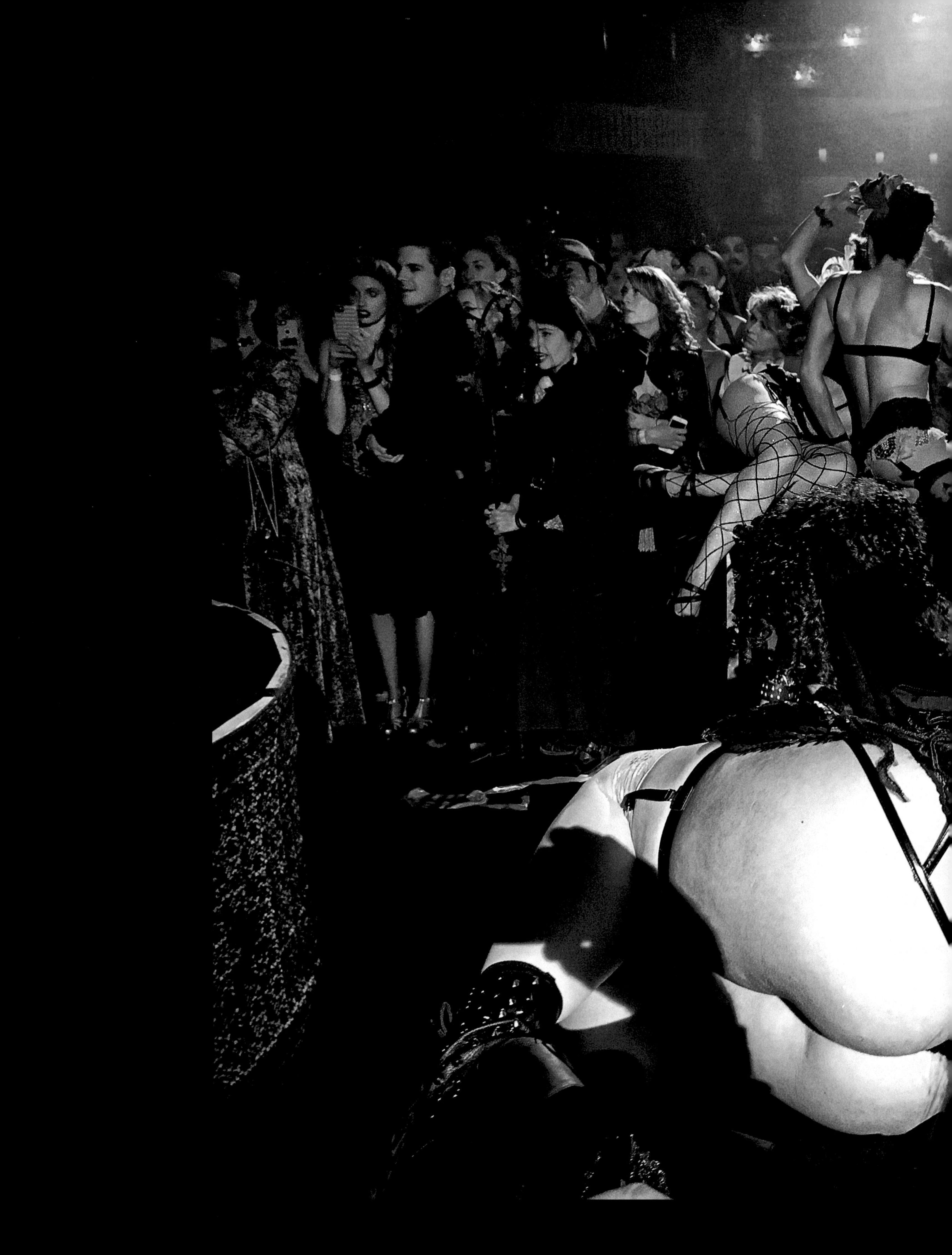

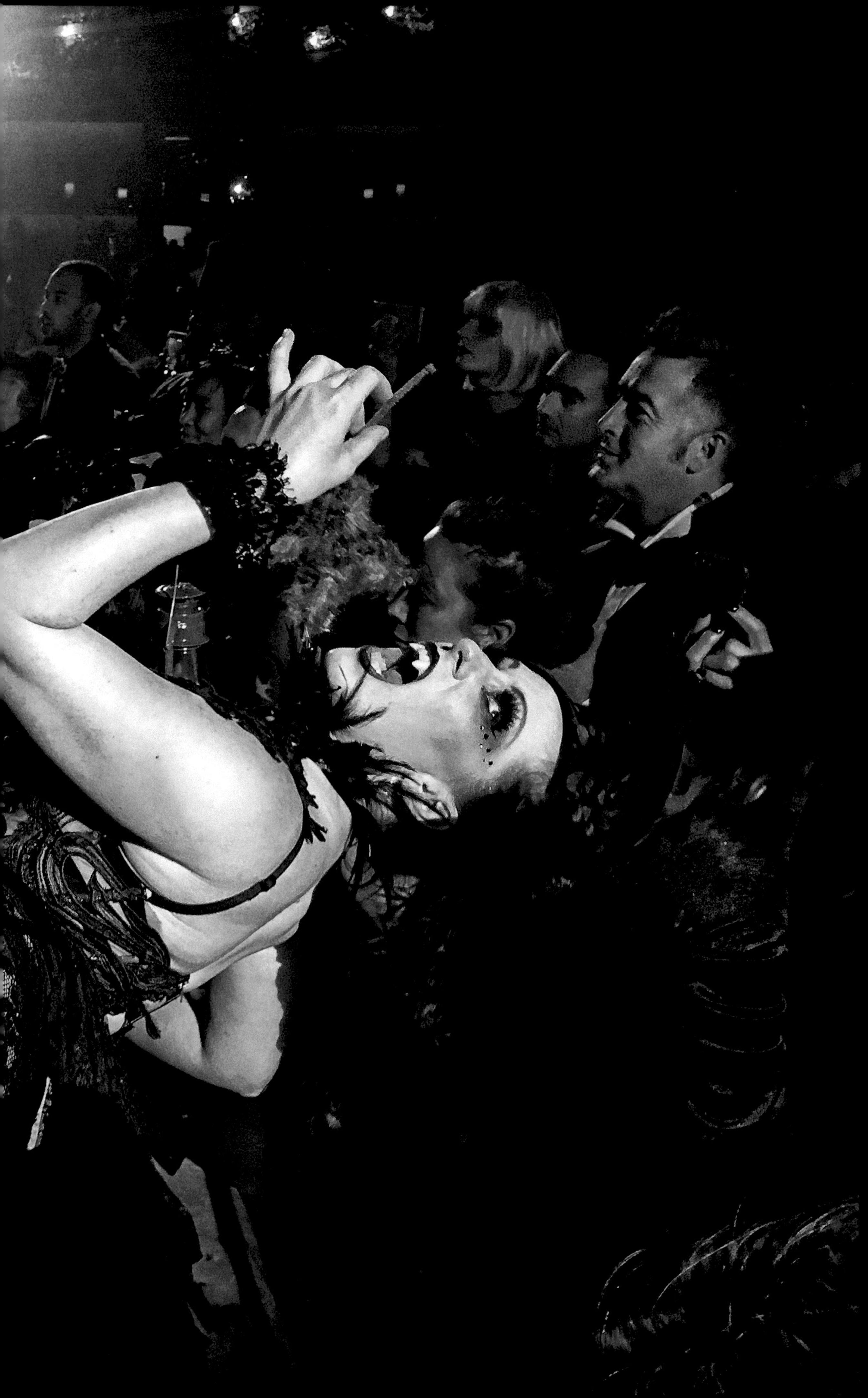

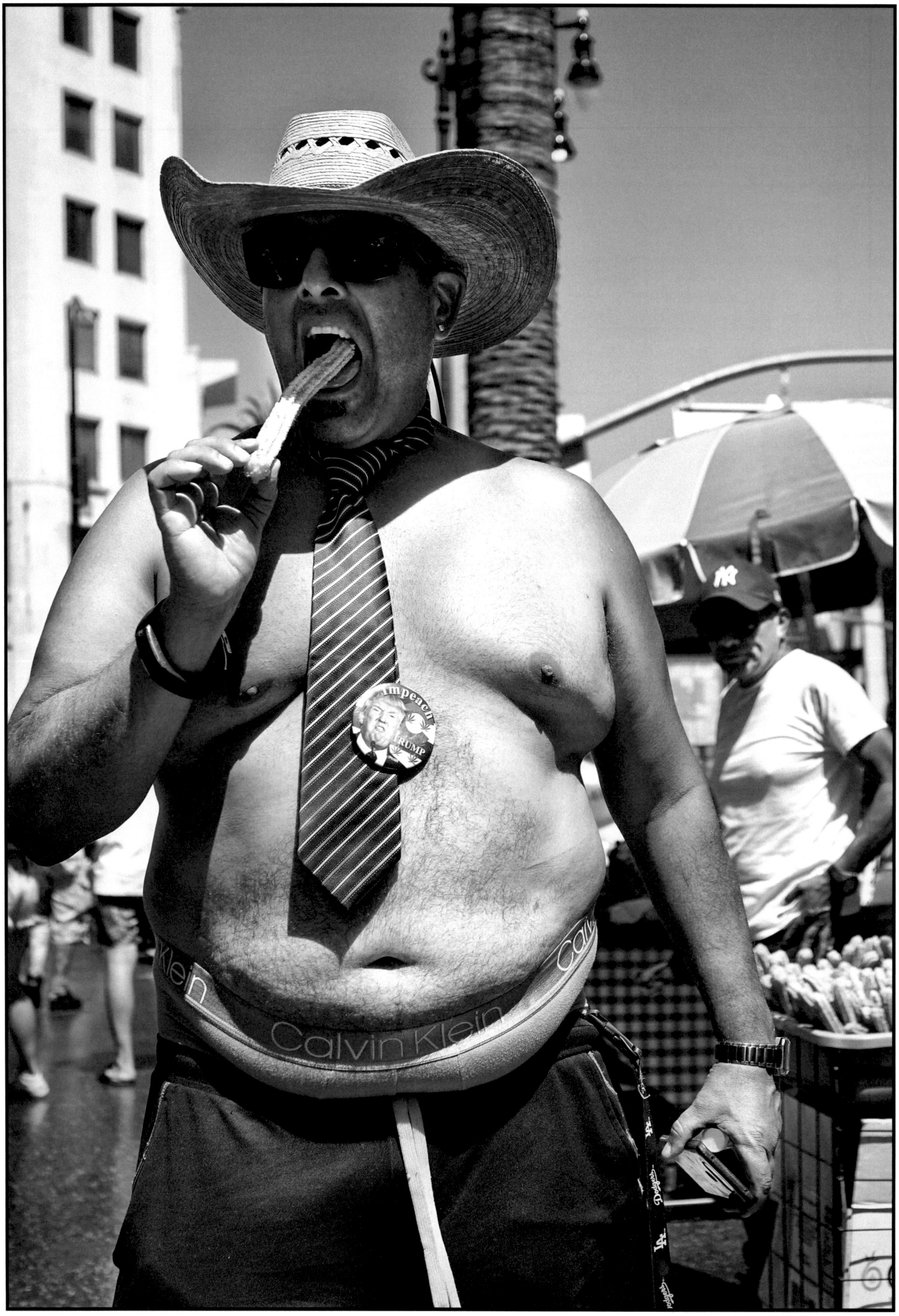
Impeach
TRUMP
Calvin Klein
Dodgers

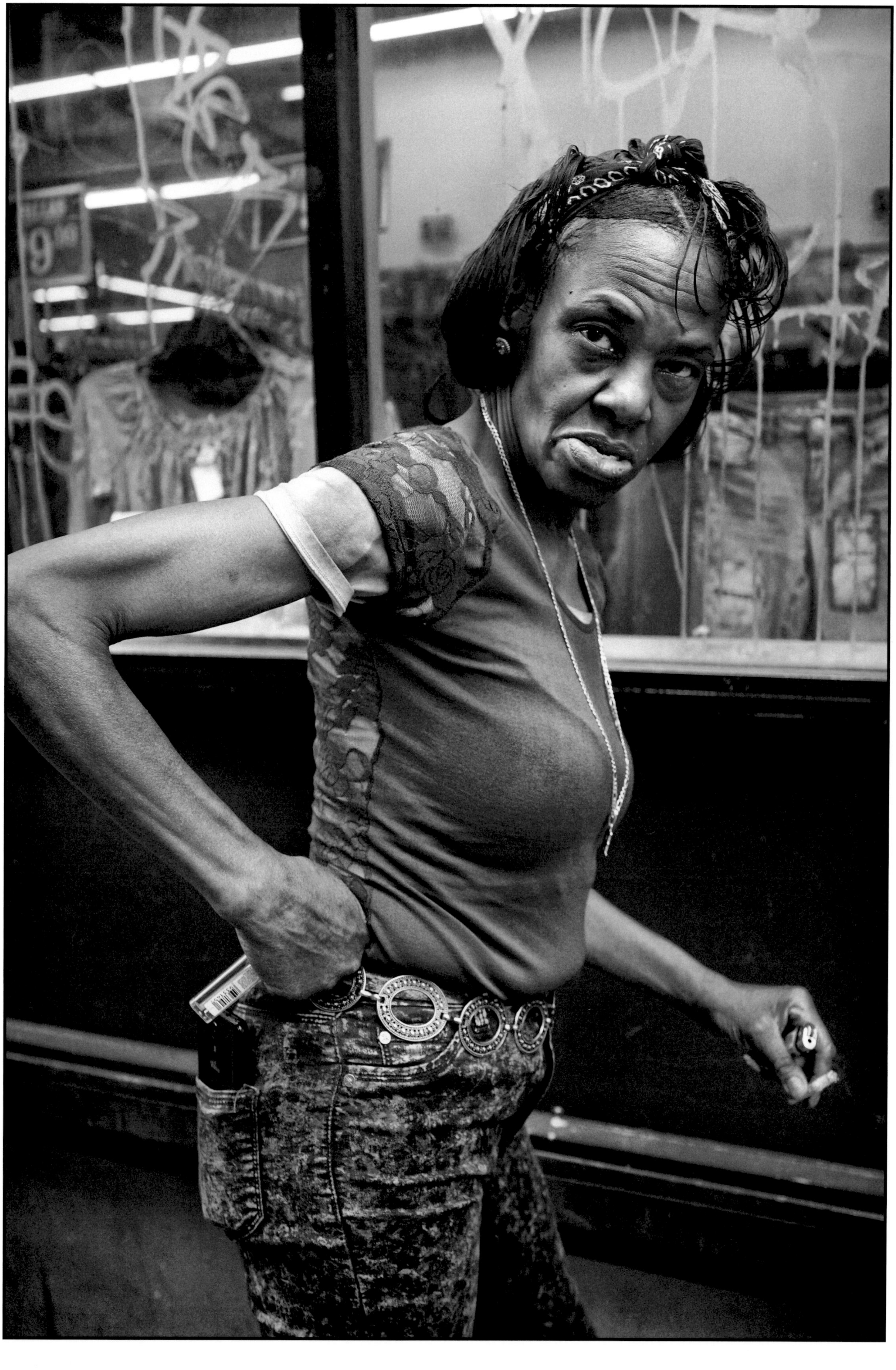

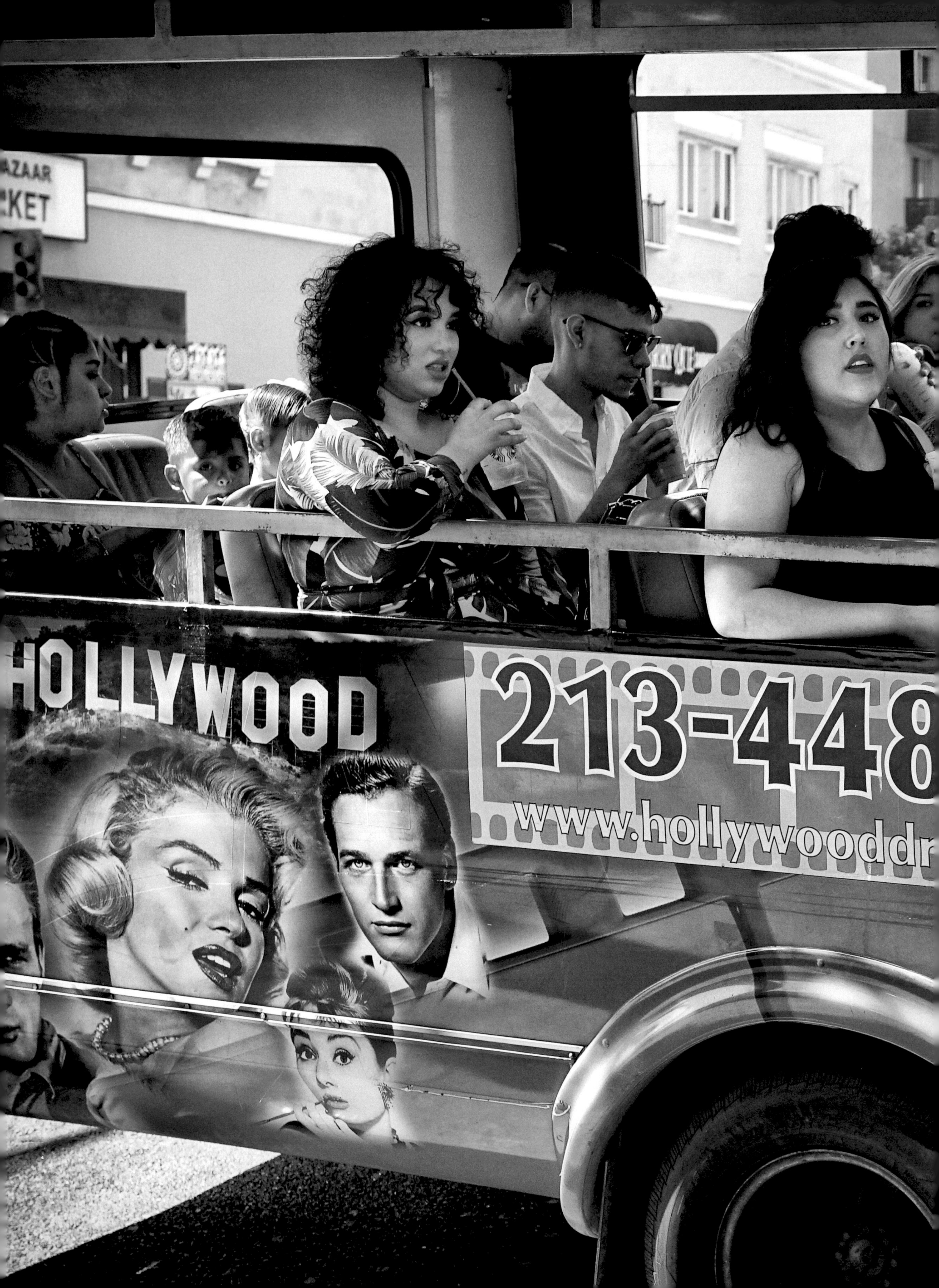
HOLLYWOOD
213-448
www.hollywooddr

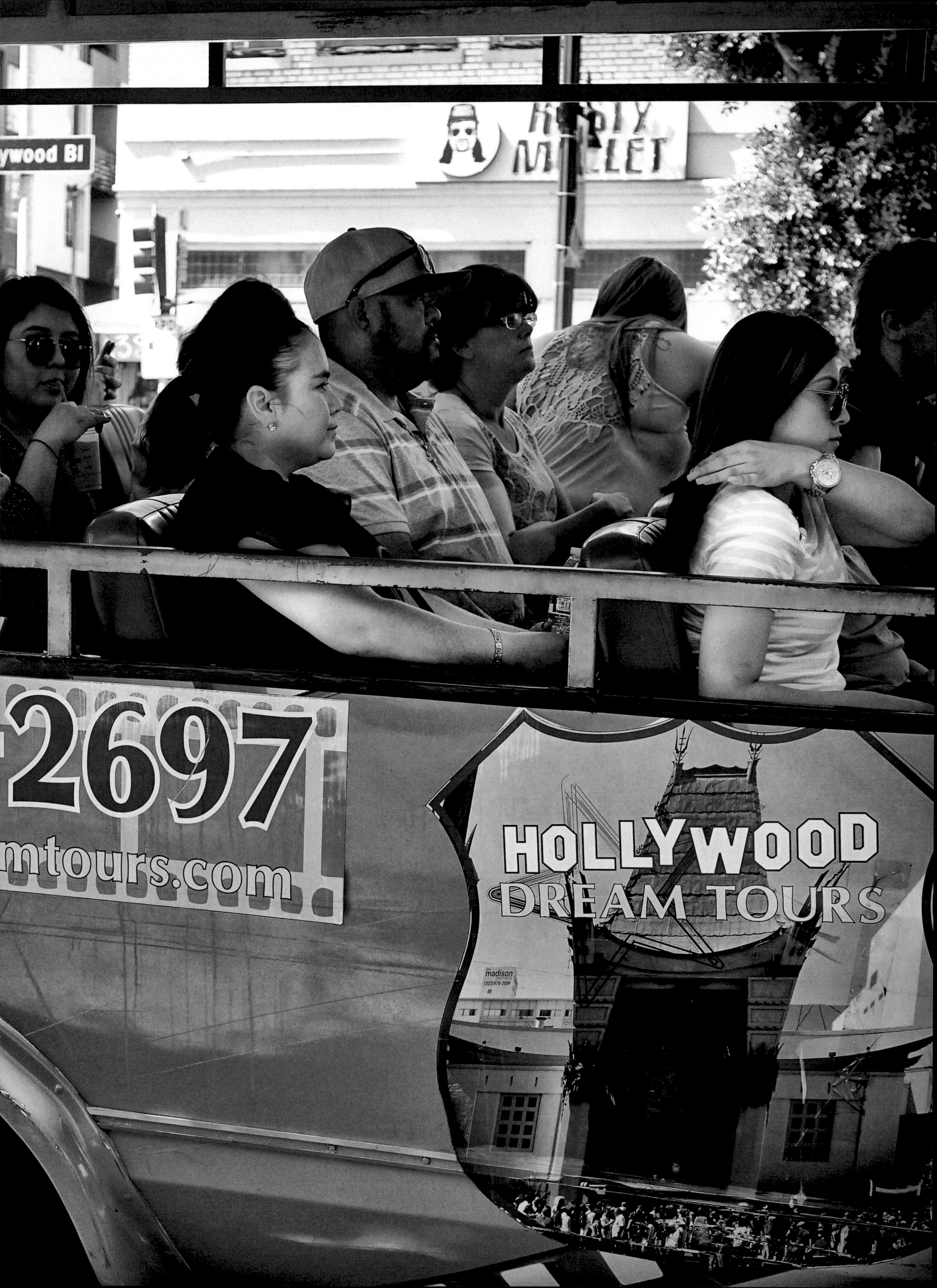
2697
HOLLYWOOD
DREAM TOURS

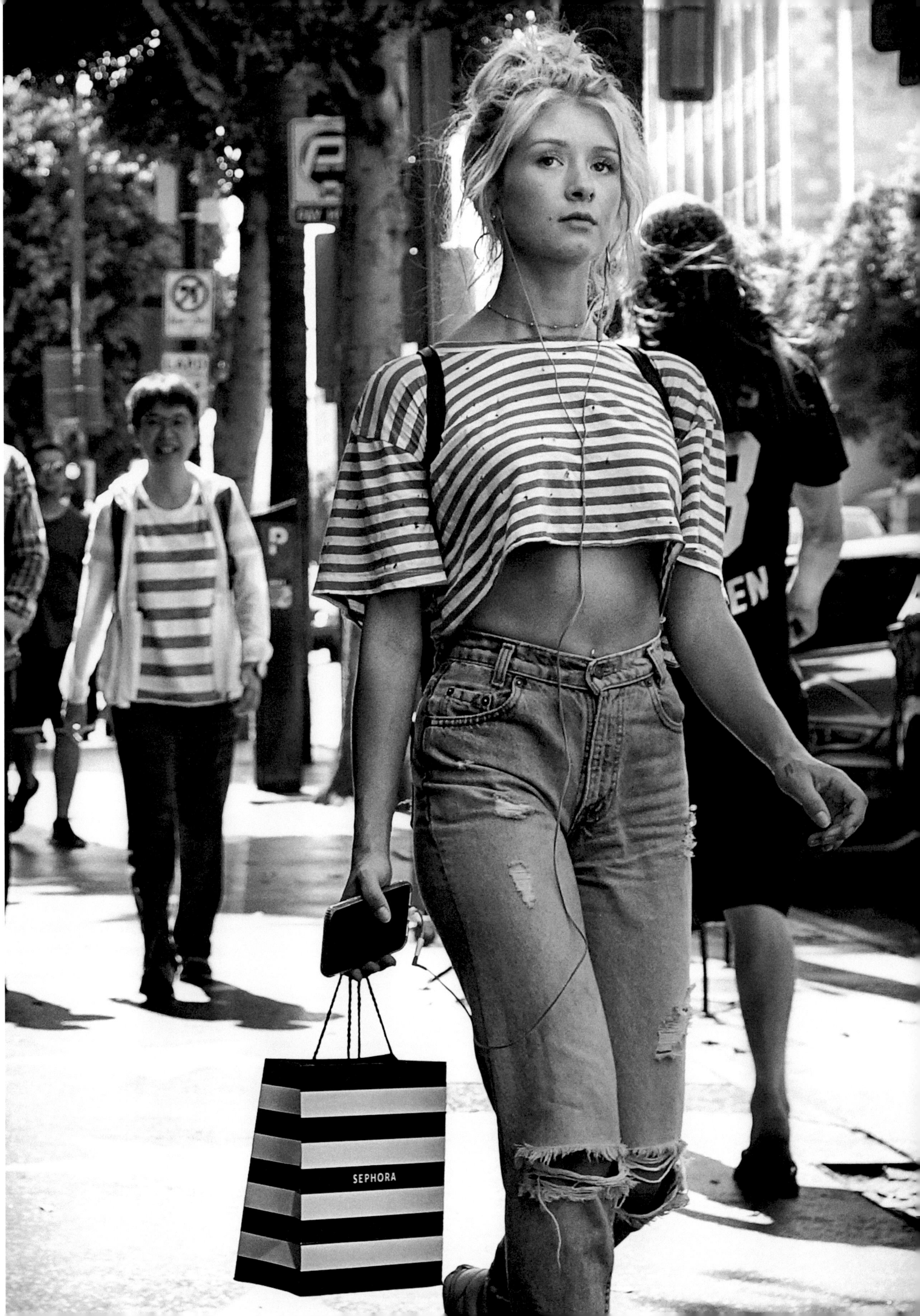
SEPHORA

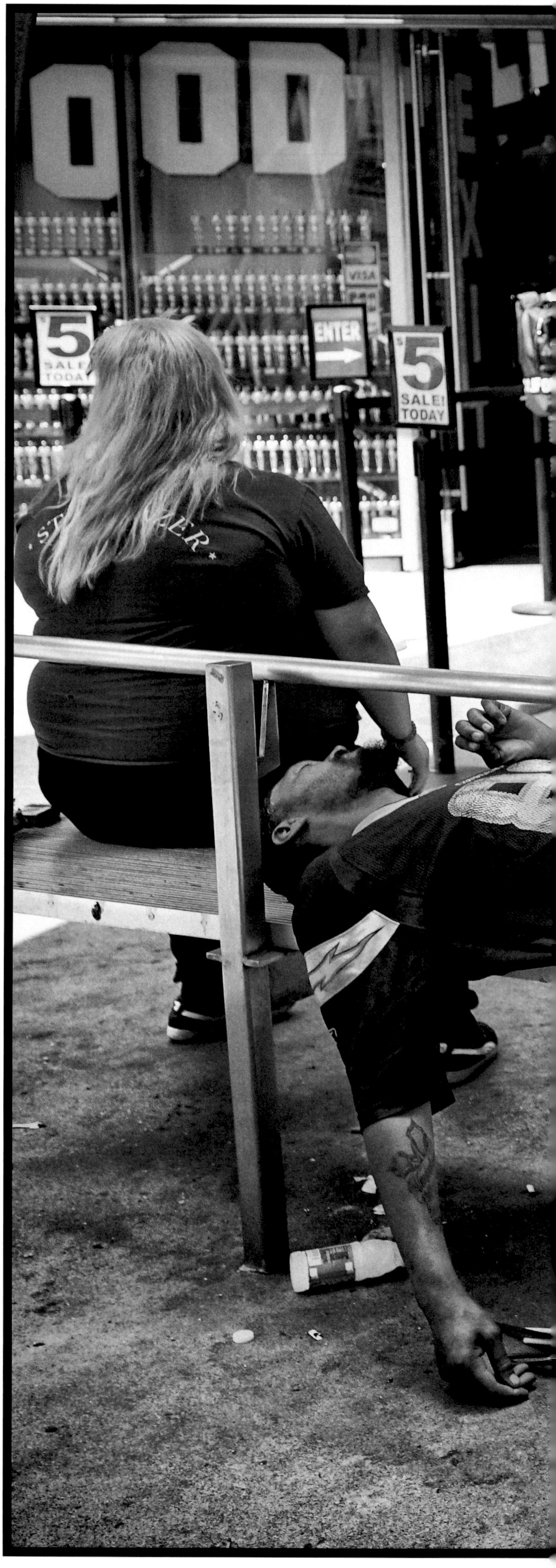
OOD
$5 SALE! TODAY
ENTER
VISA

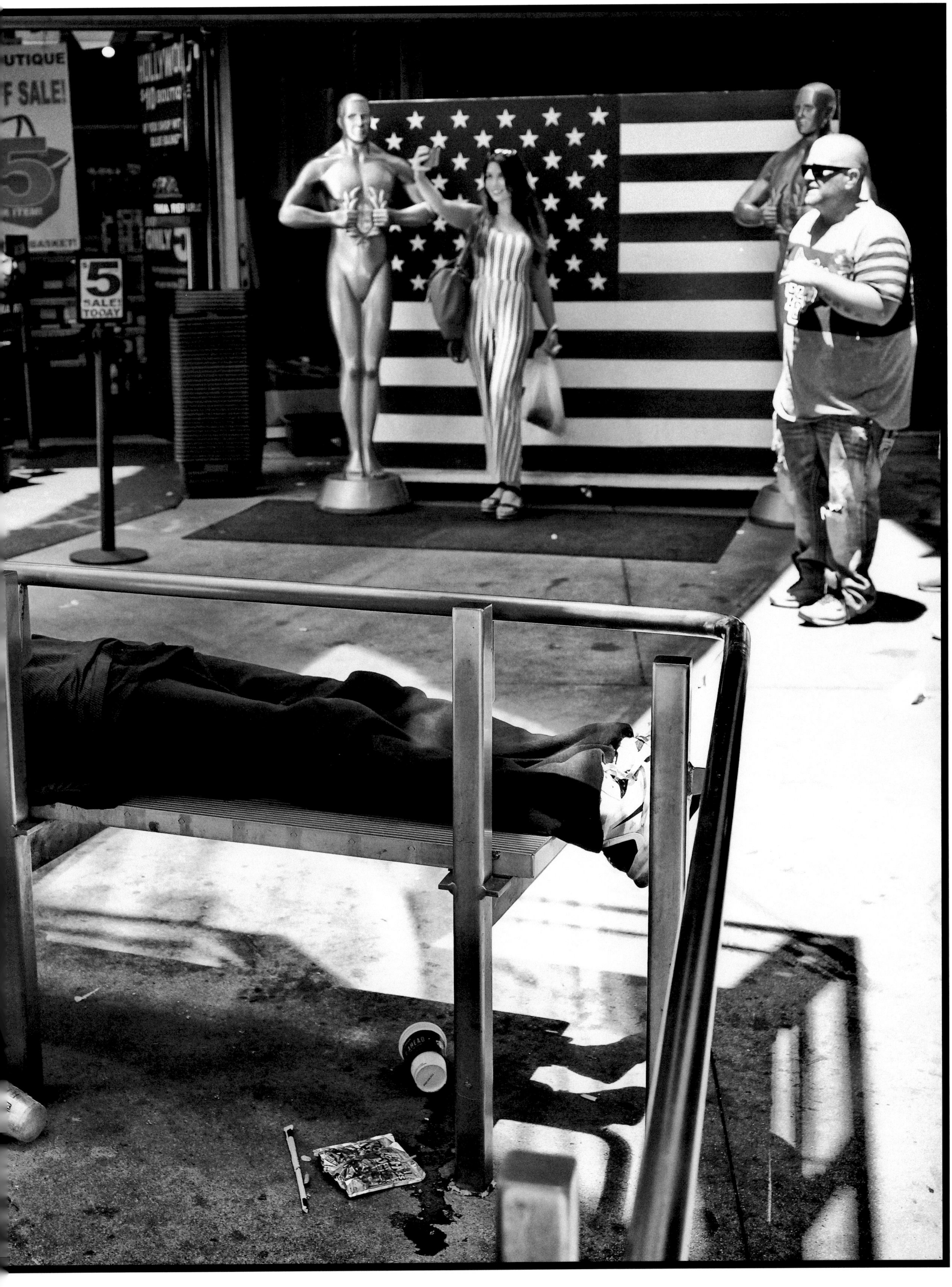
$5
SALE!
TODAY

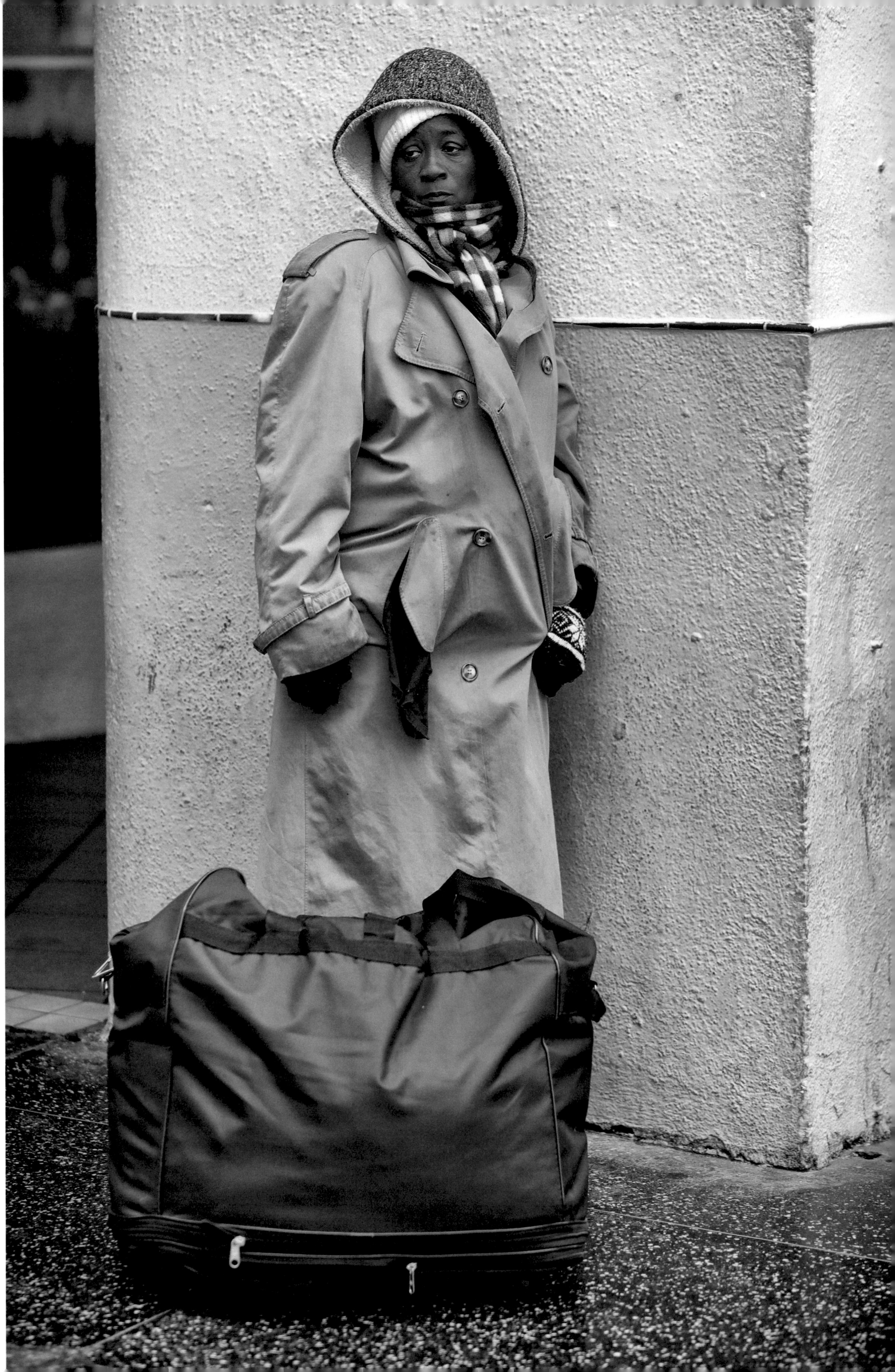

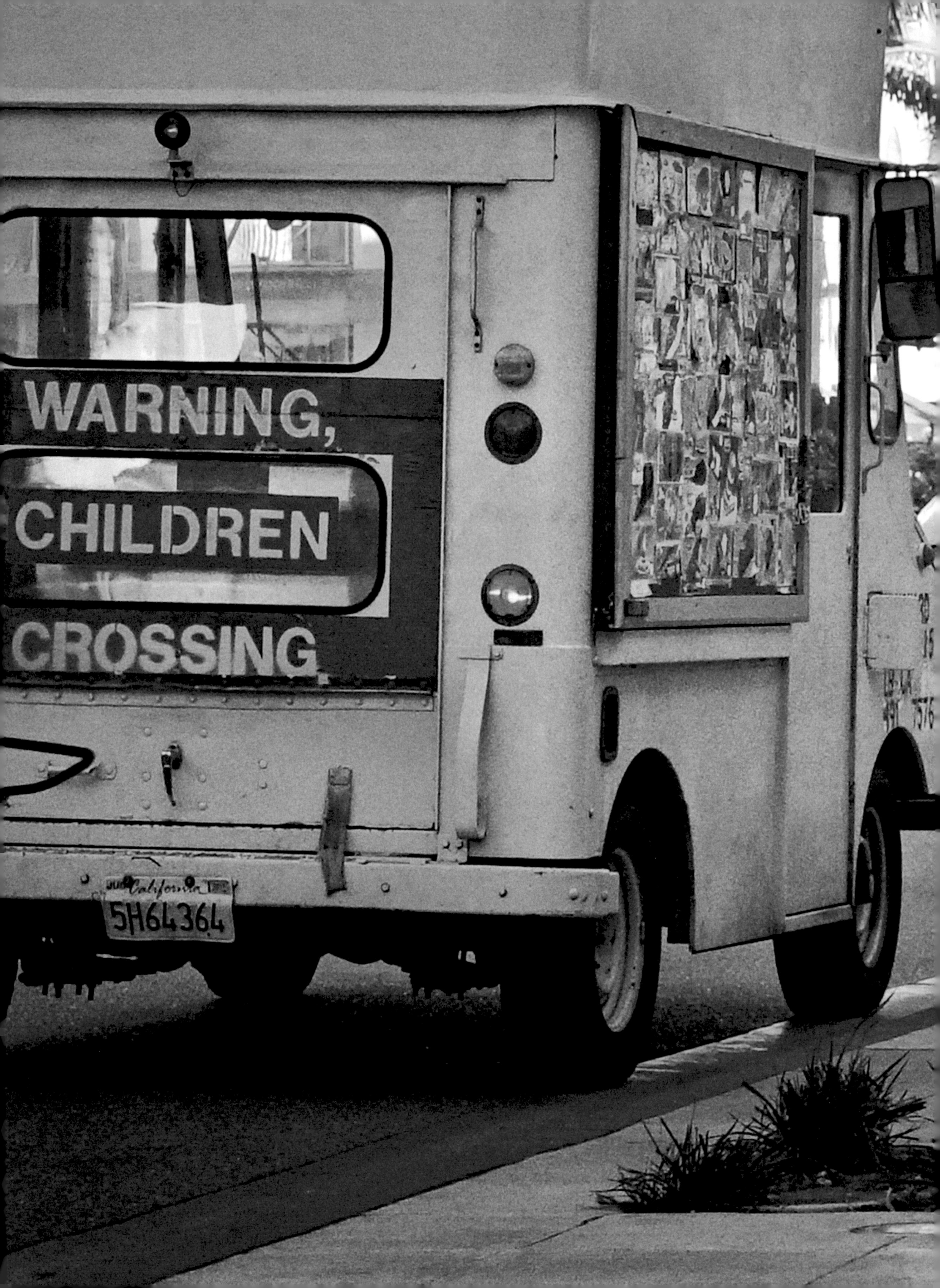
WARNING,
CHILDREN
CROSSING
California
5H64364

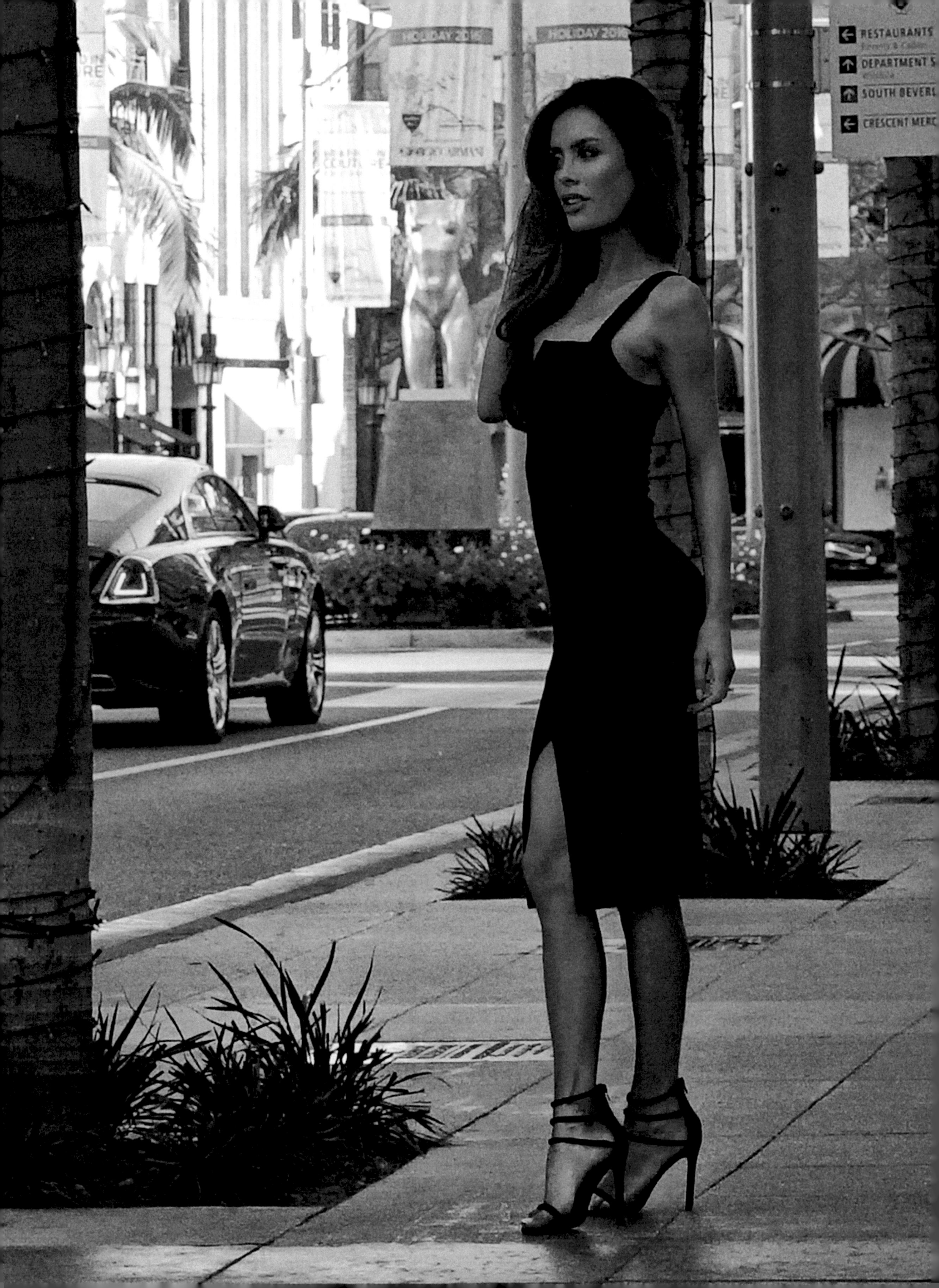
RESTAURANTS

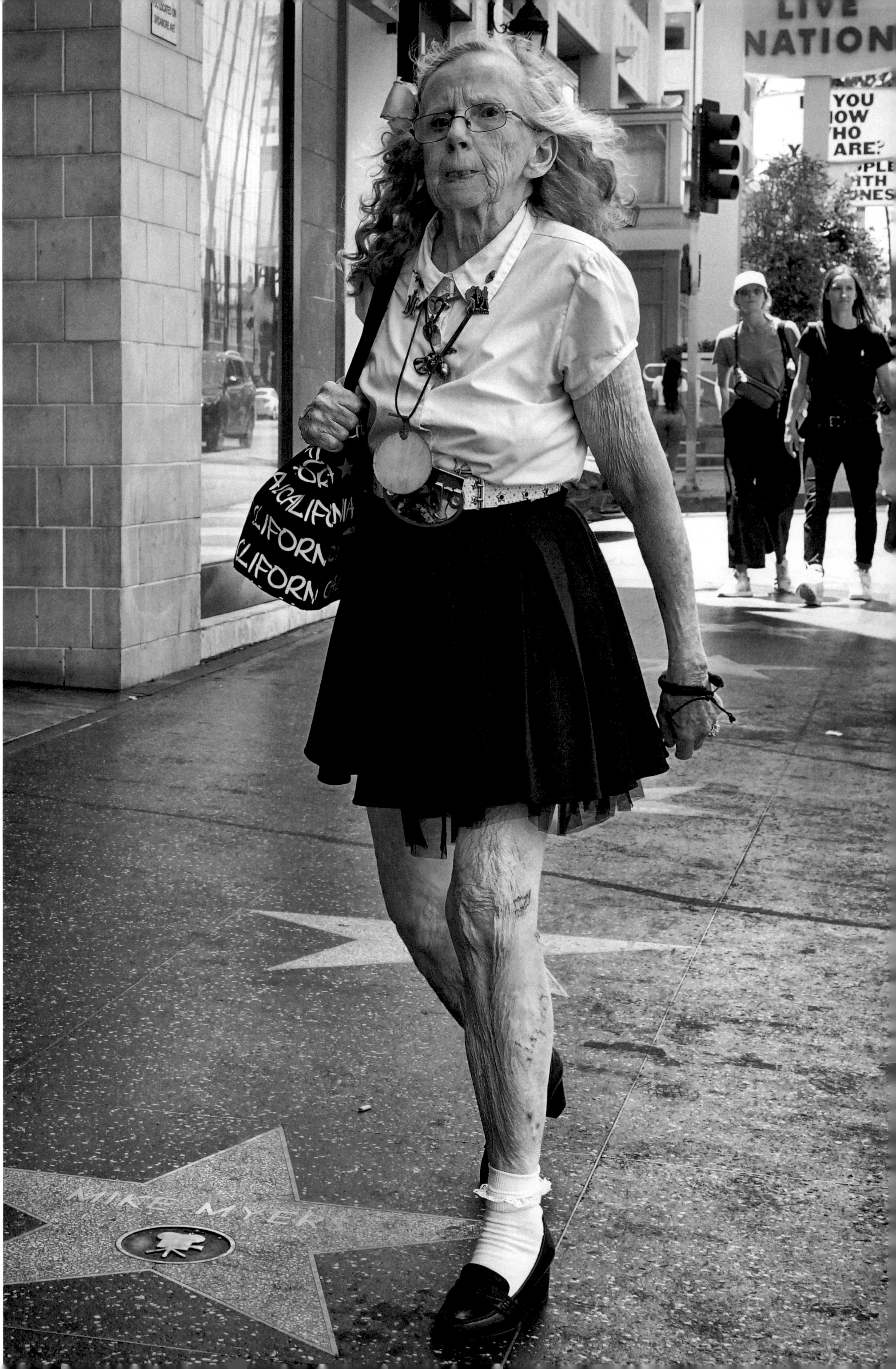
LIVE
NATION
CALIFORNIA

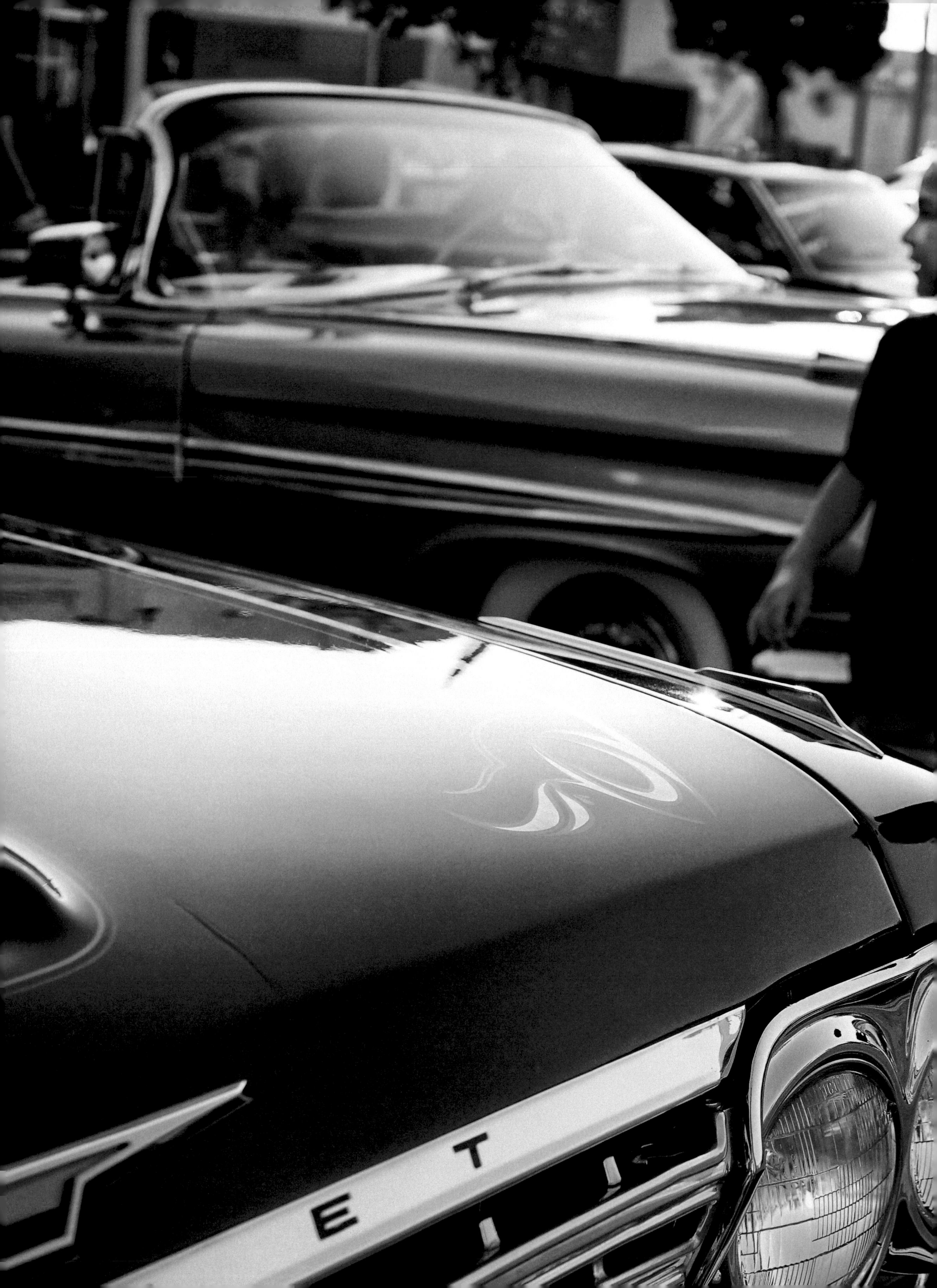
E T

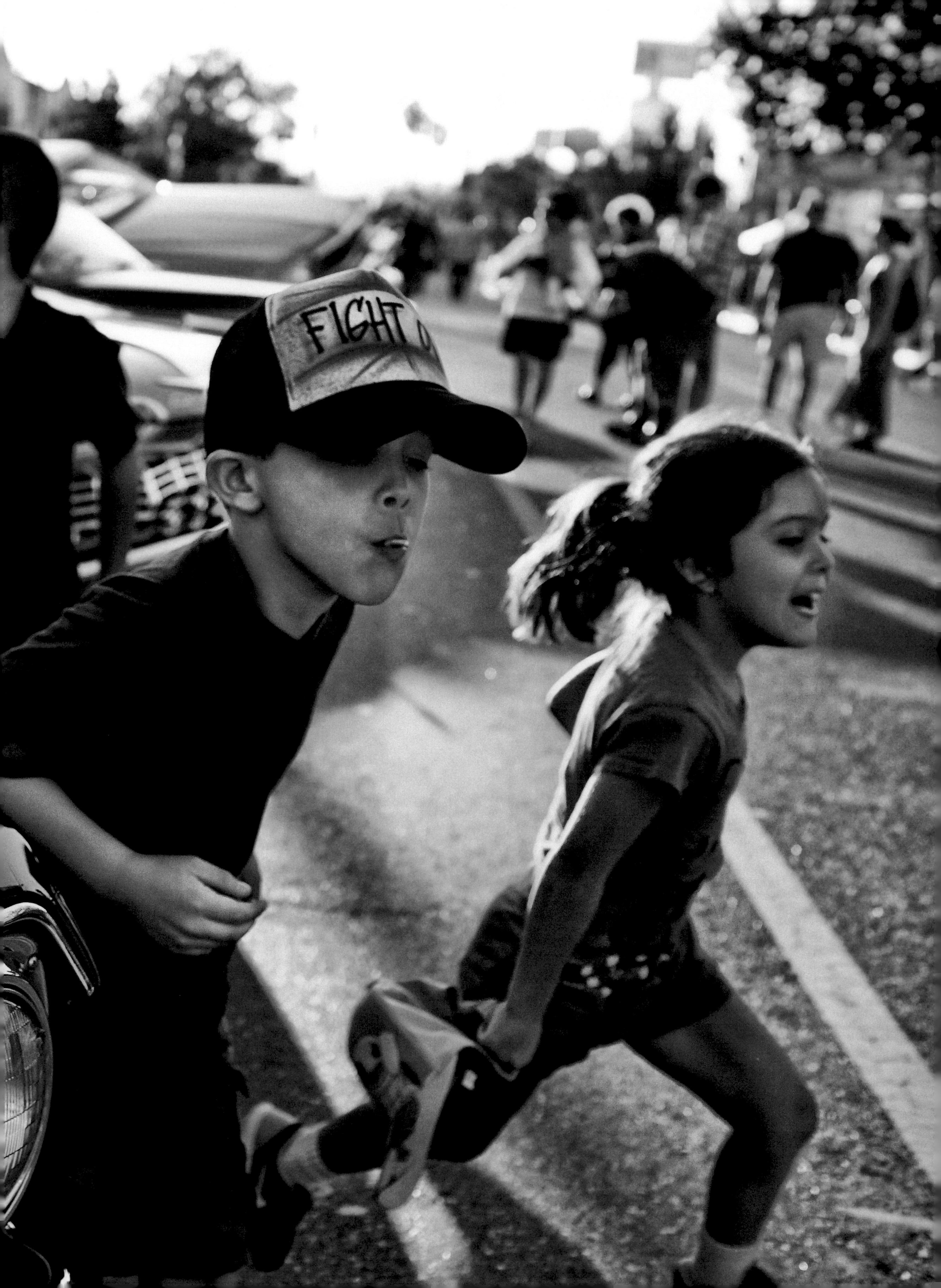
FIGHT

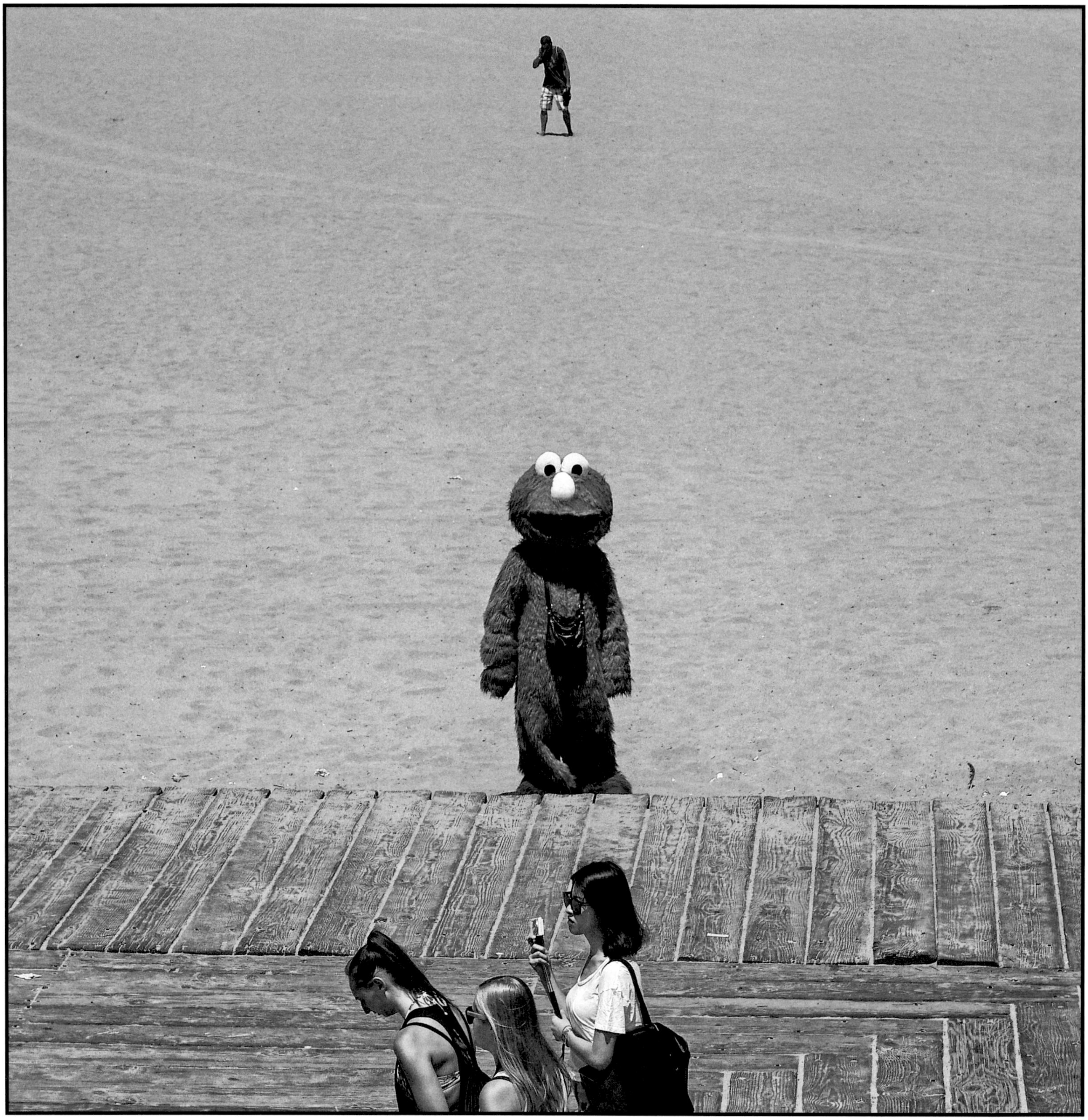

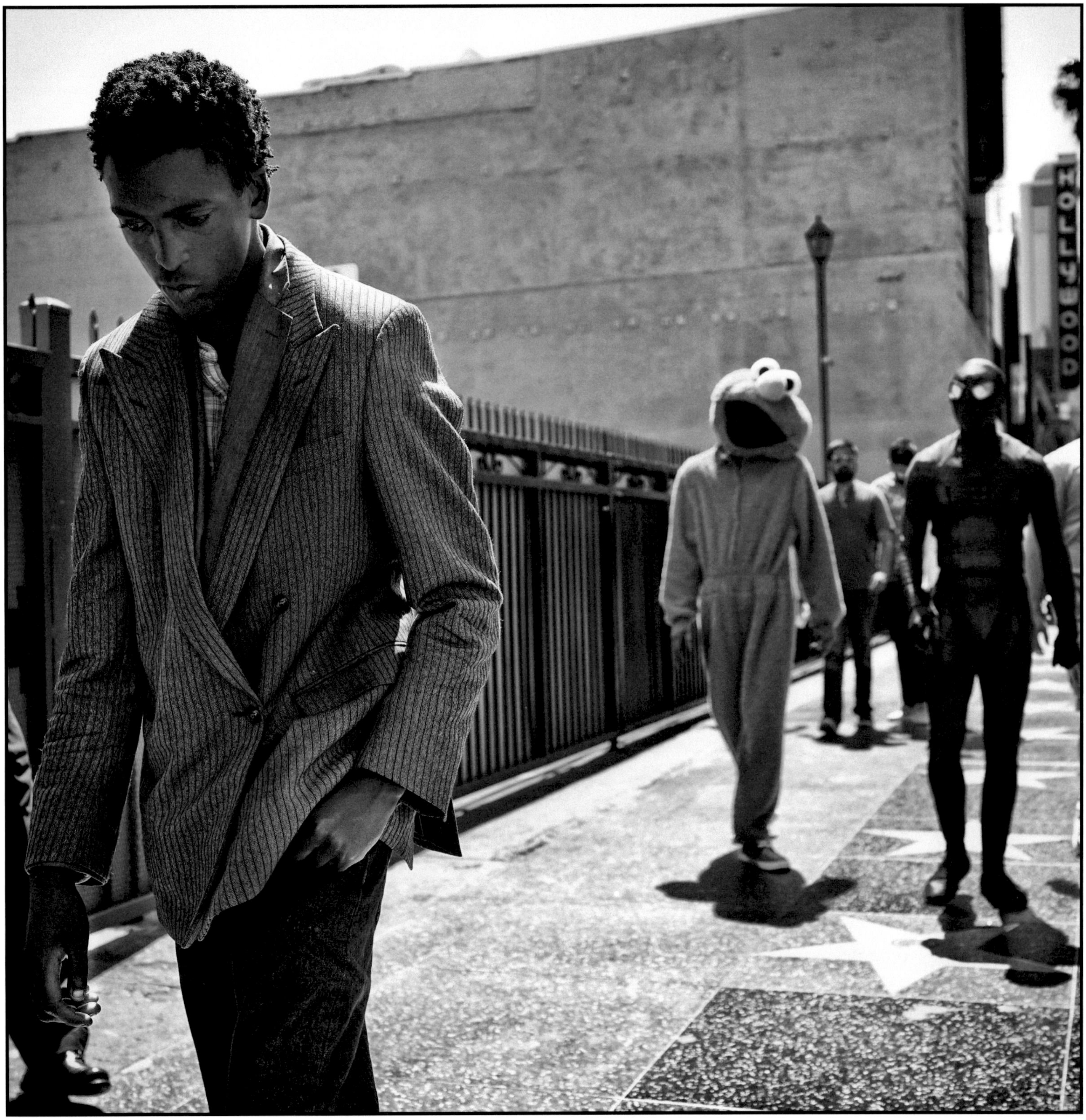
HOLLYWOOD

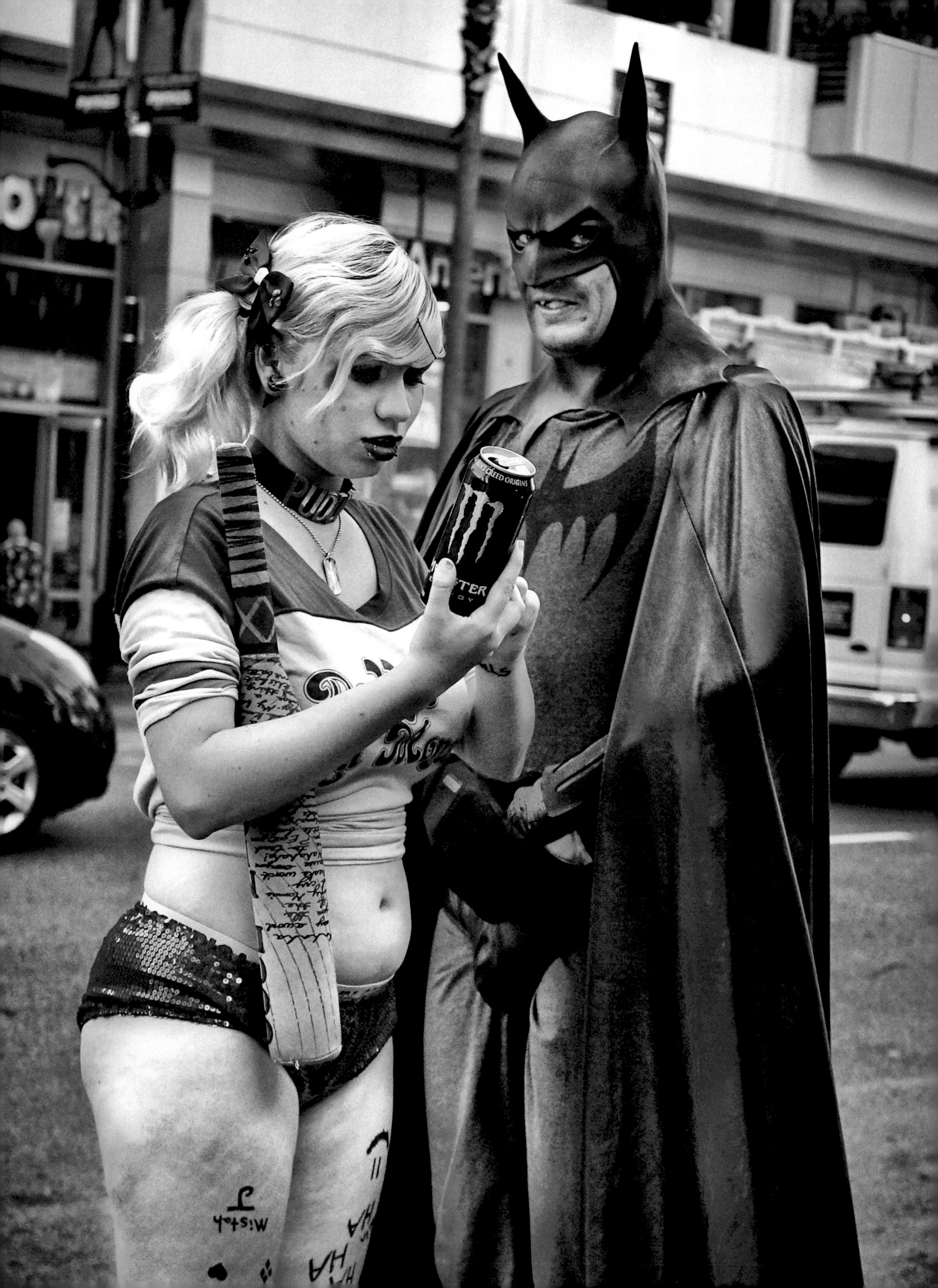

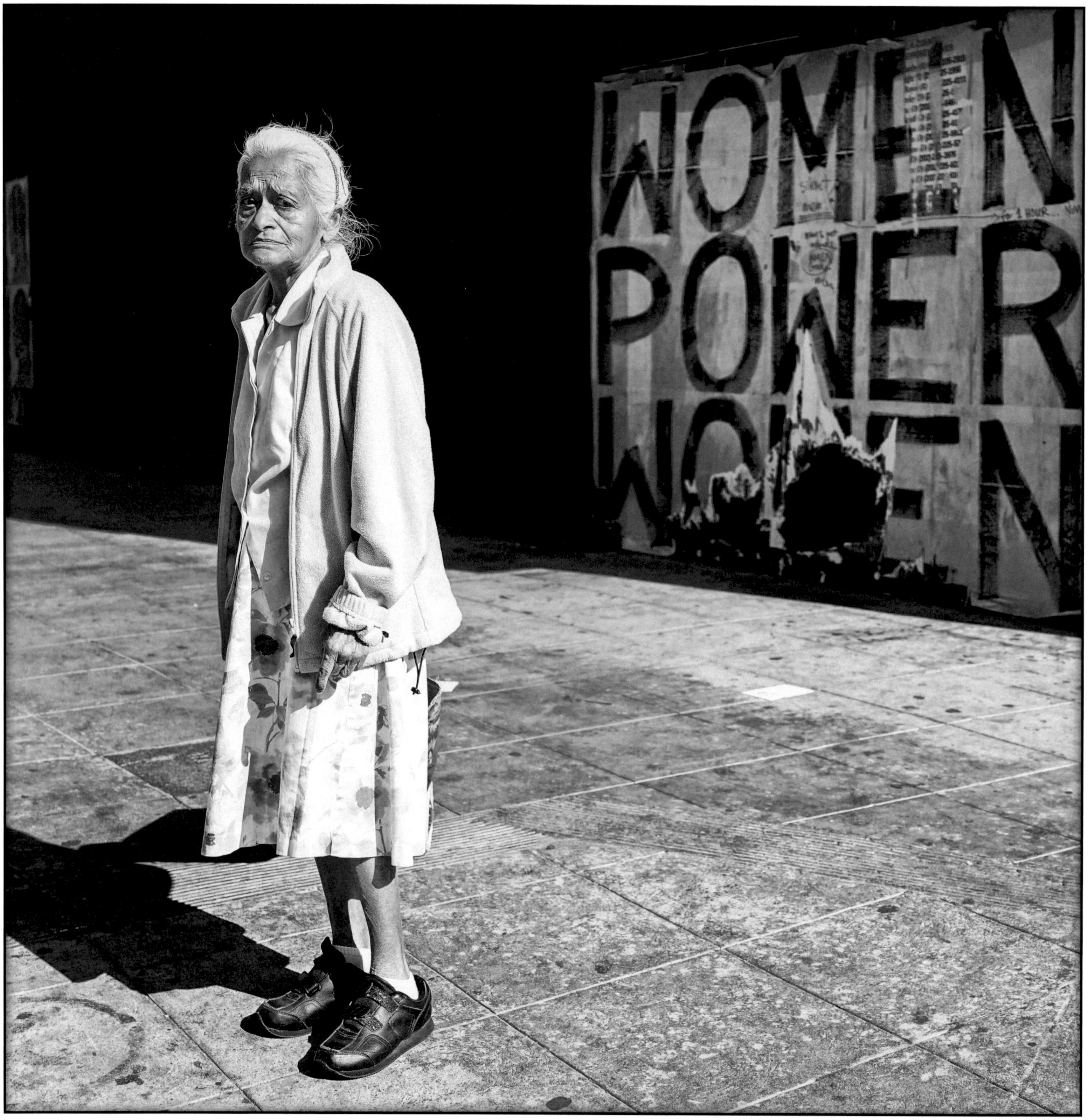
WOMEN
POWER

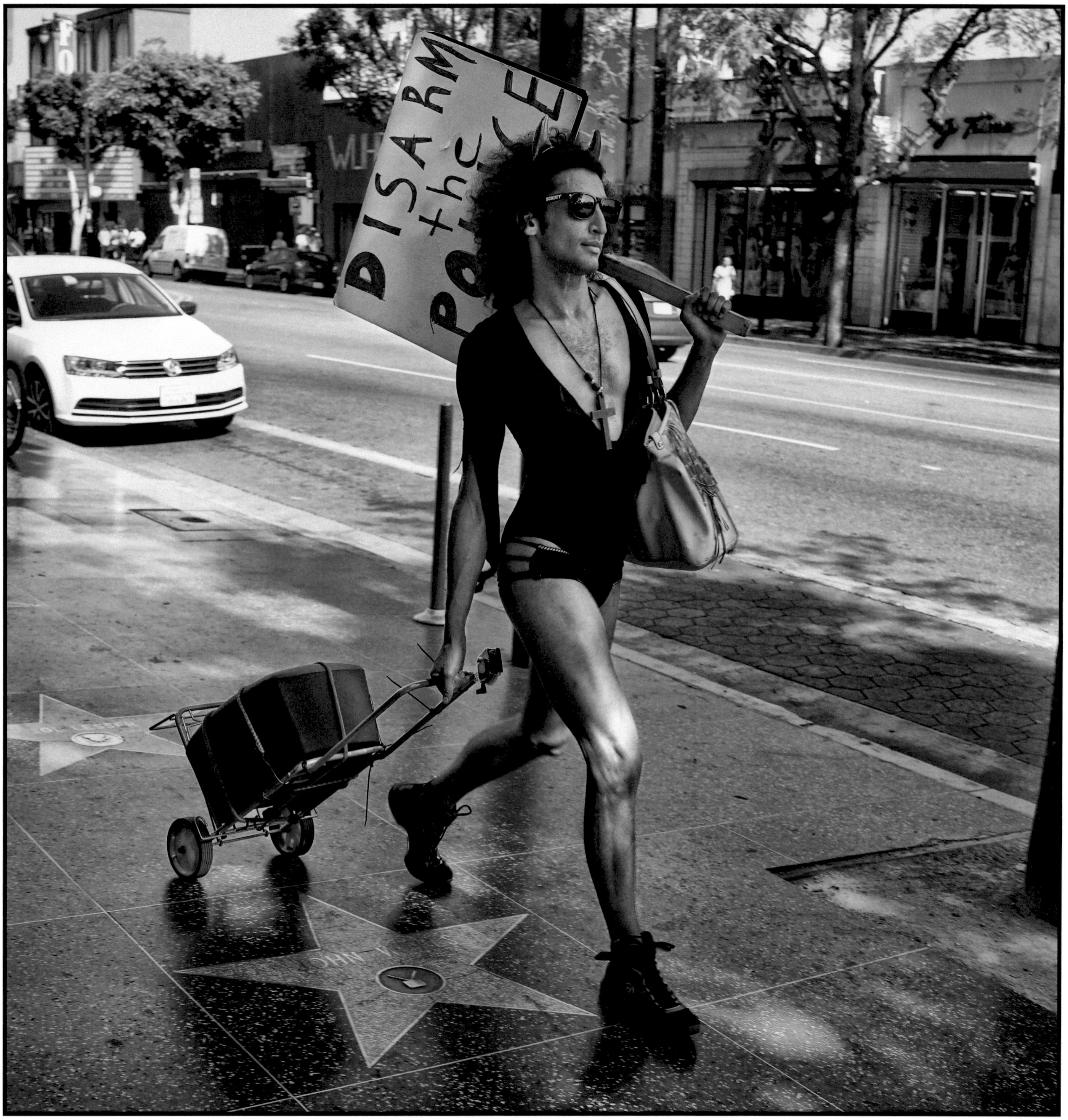
DISARM
the

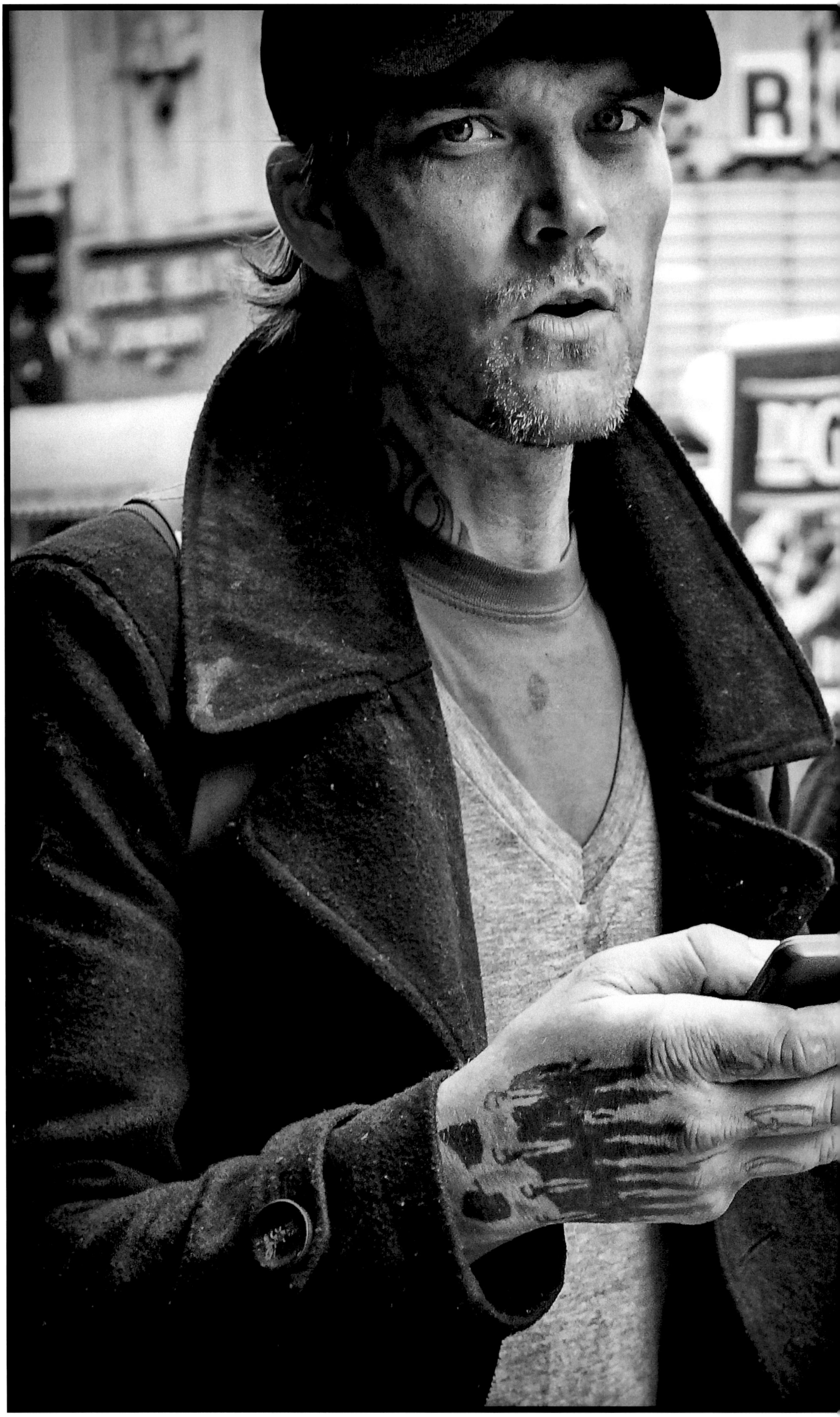

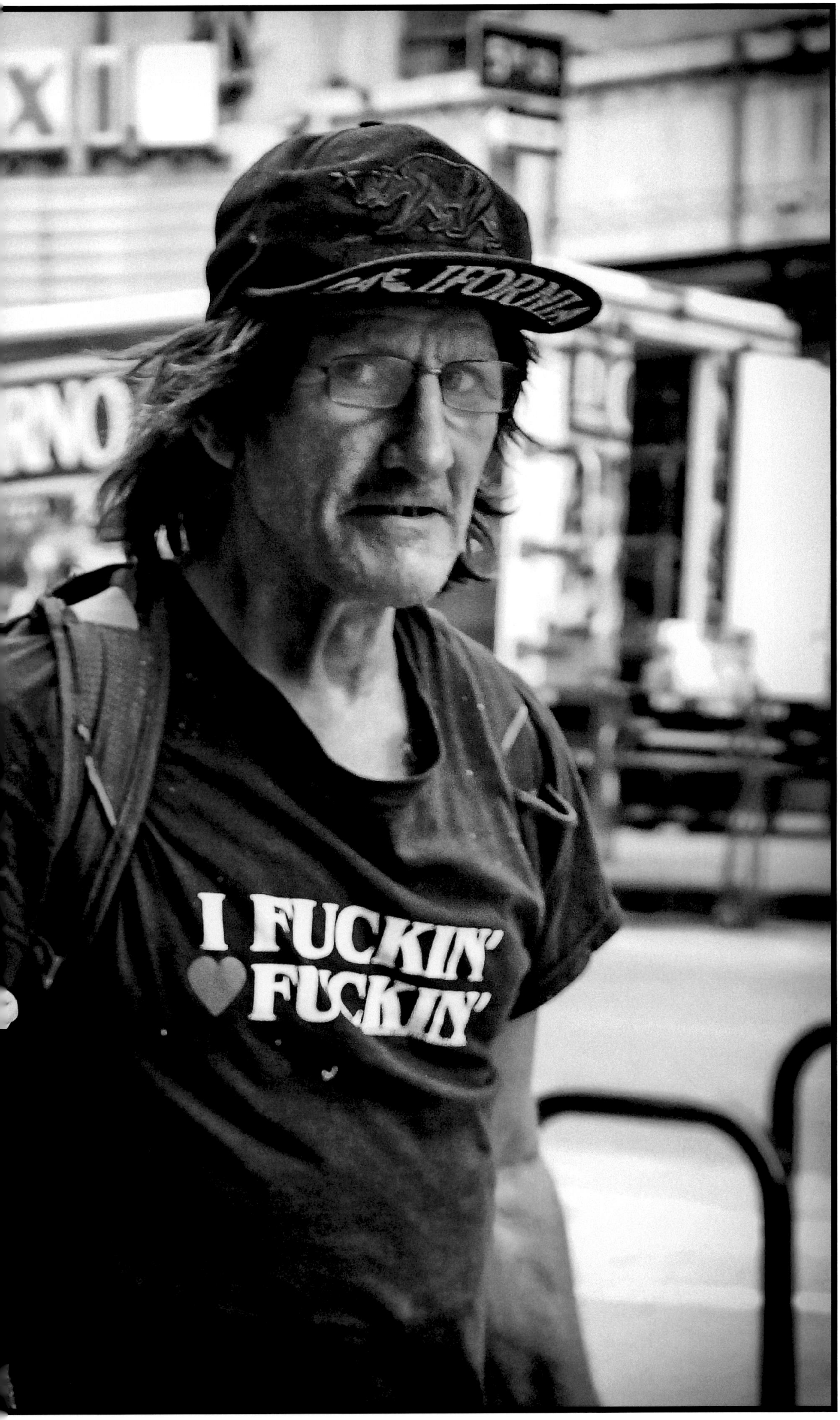
I FUCKIN'
♥ FUCKIN'

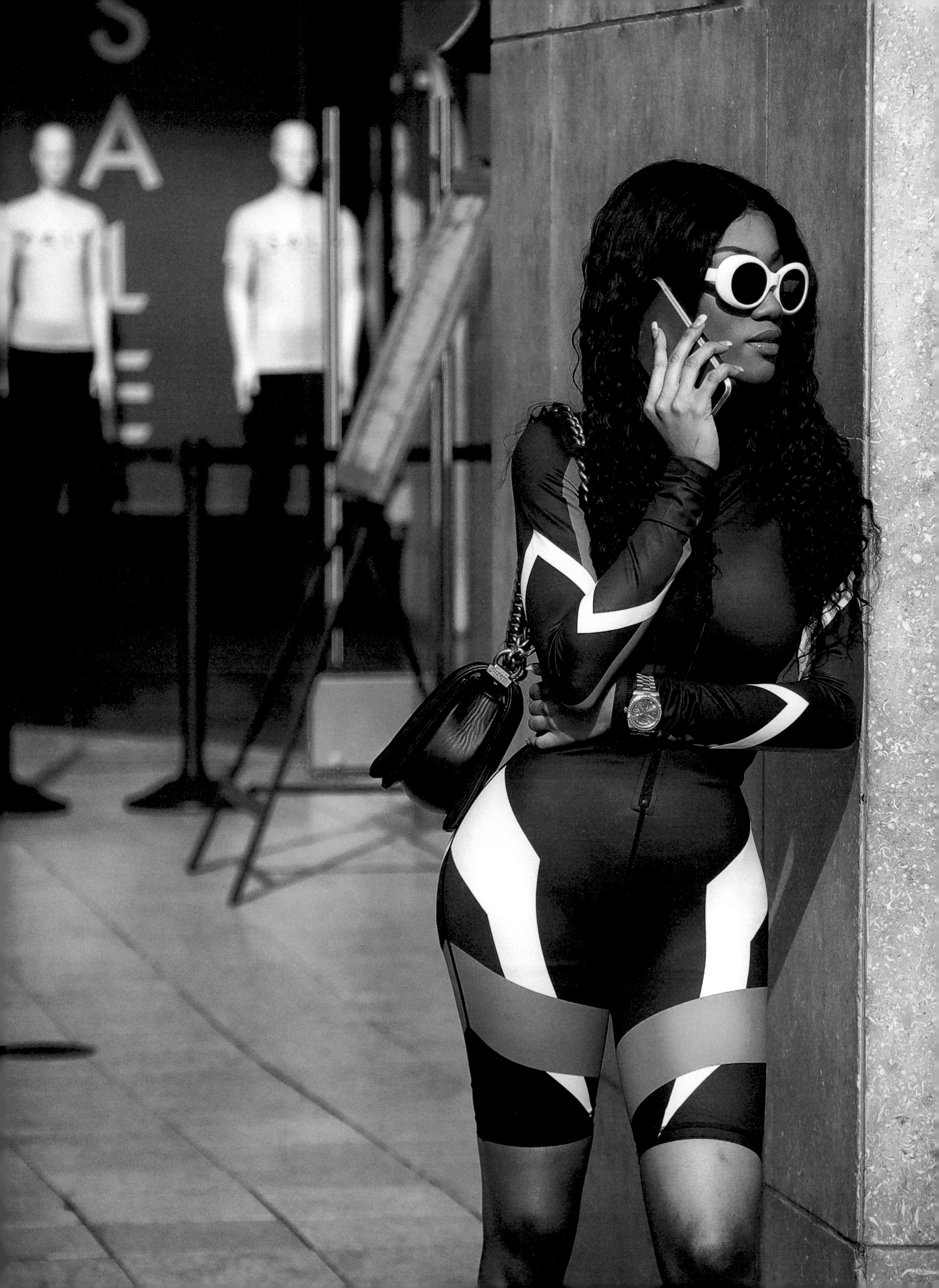
S
A
L

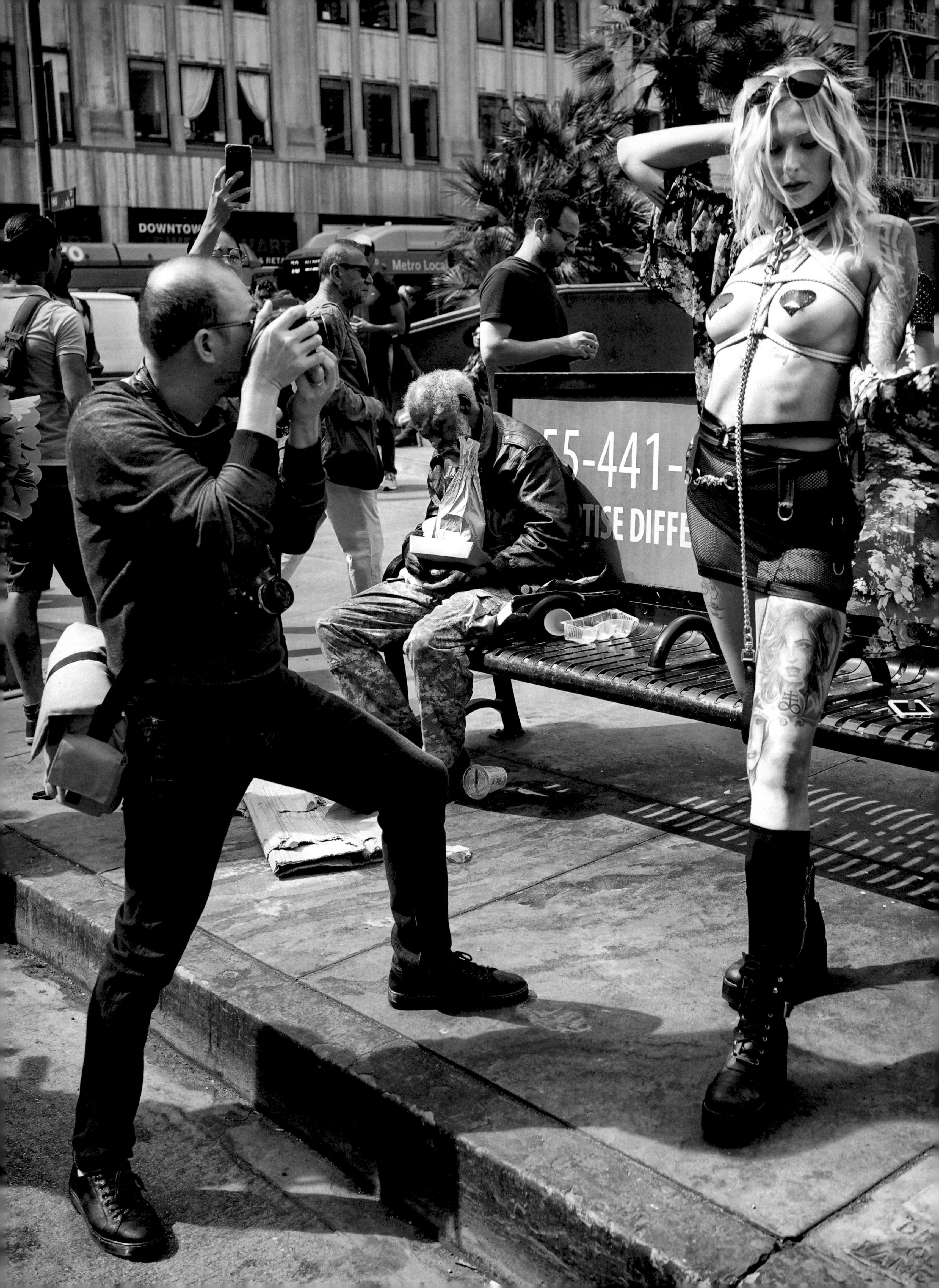
DOWNTOW
Metro Local
55-441-
TISE DIFFE

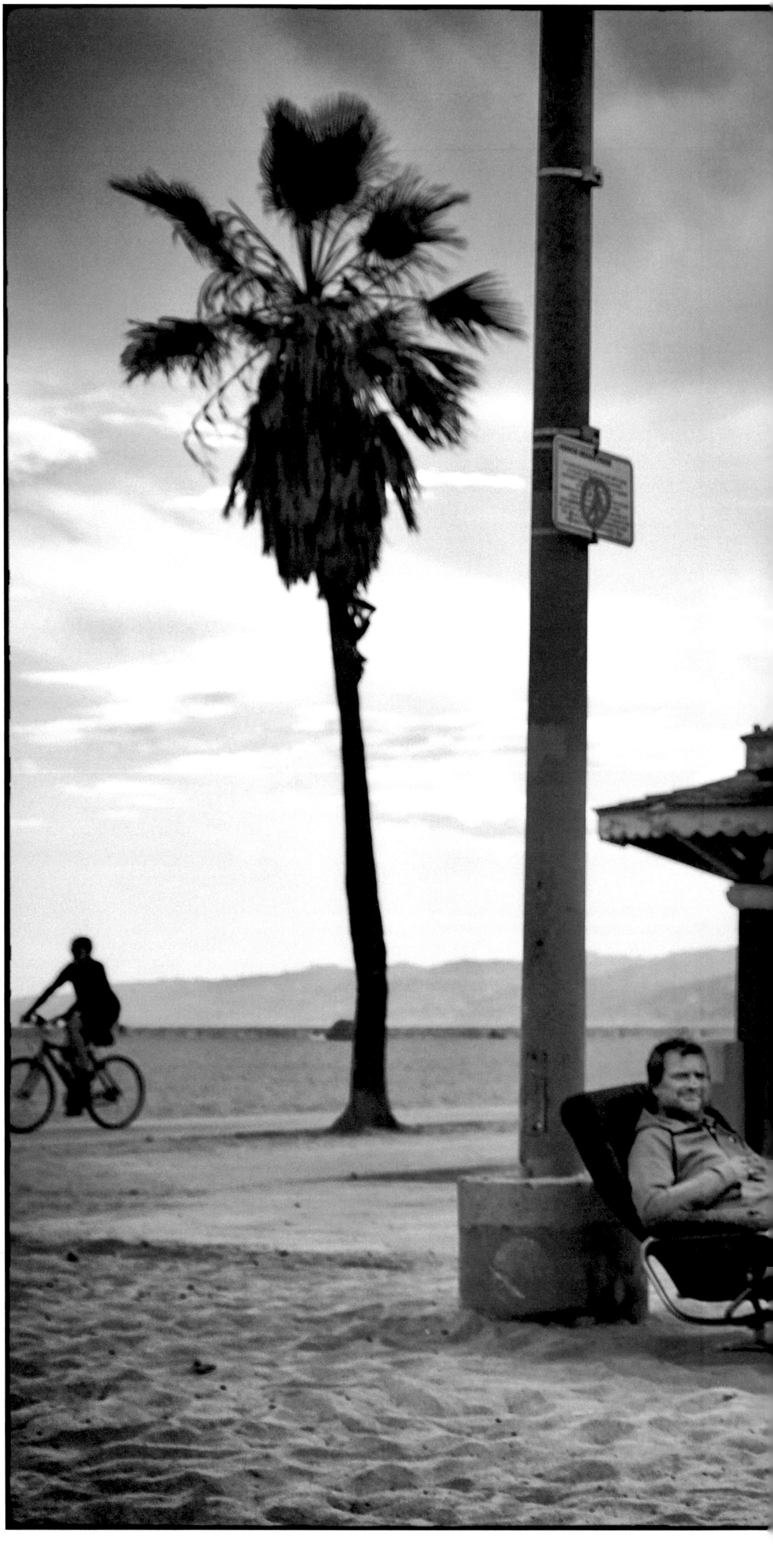

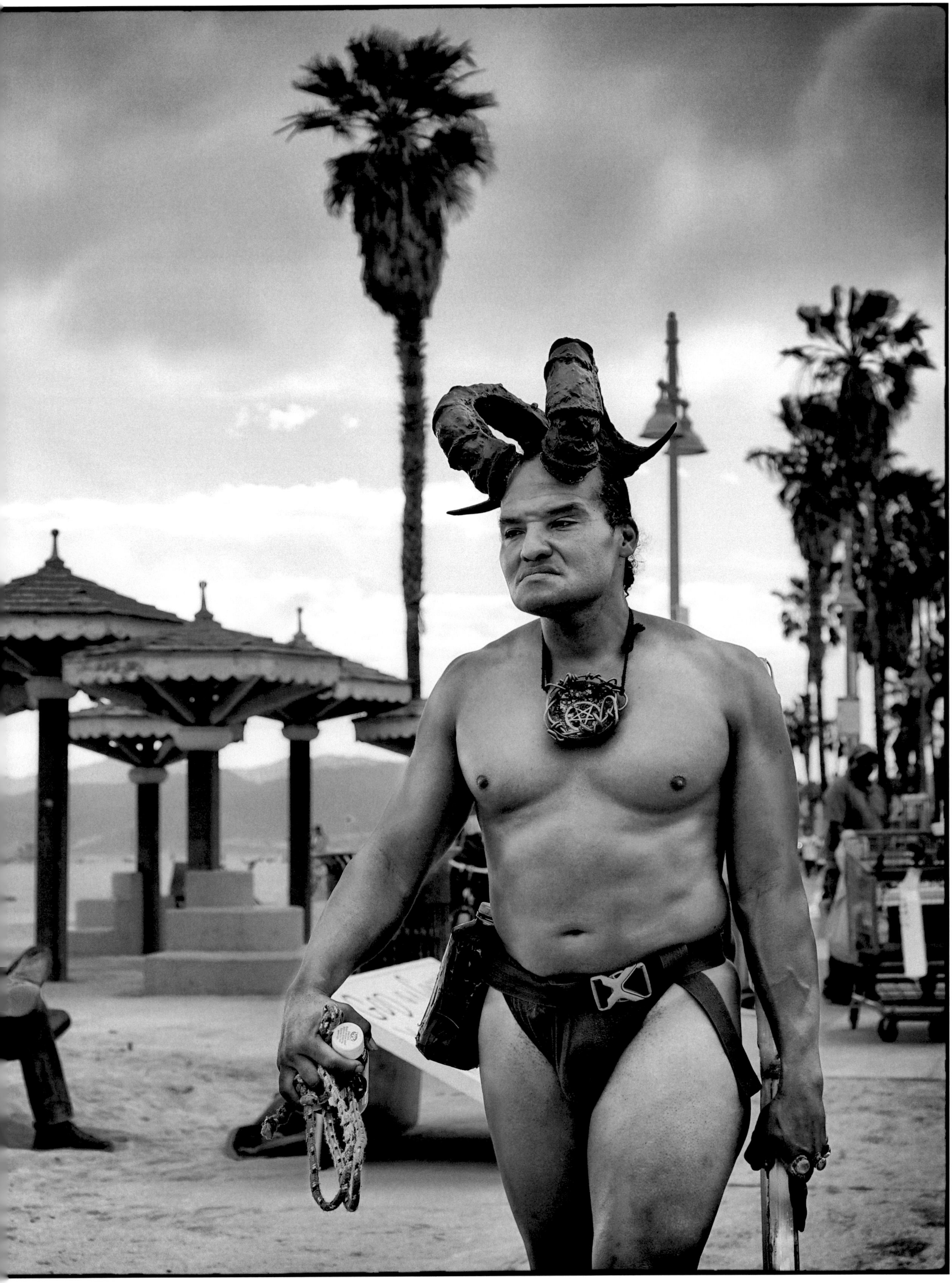

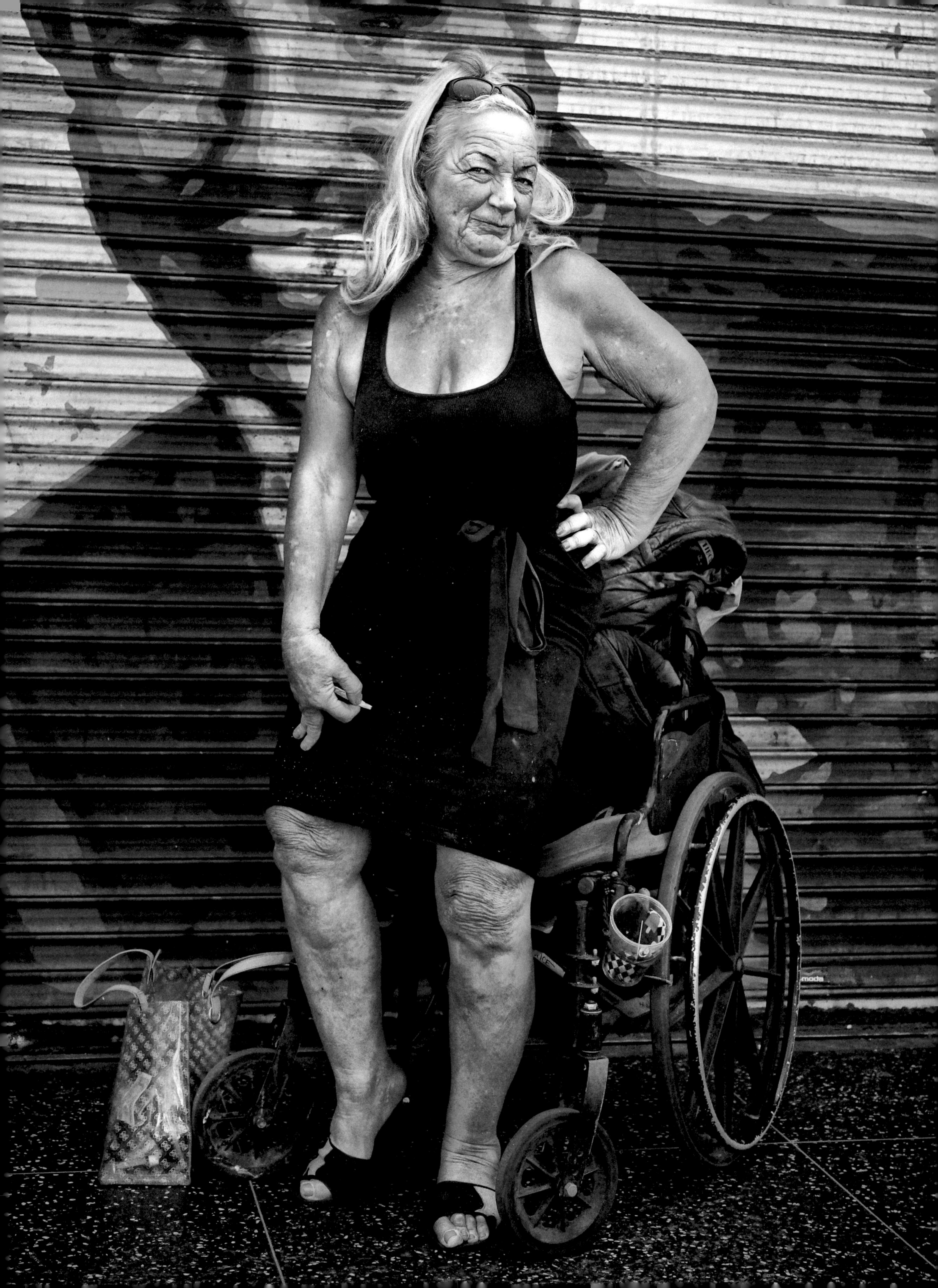

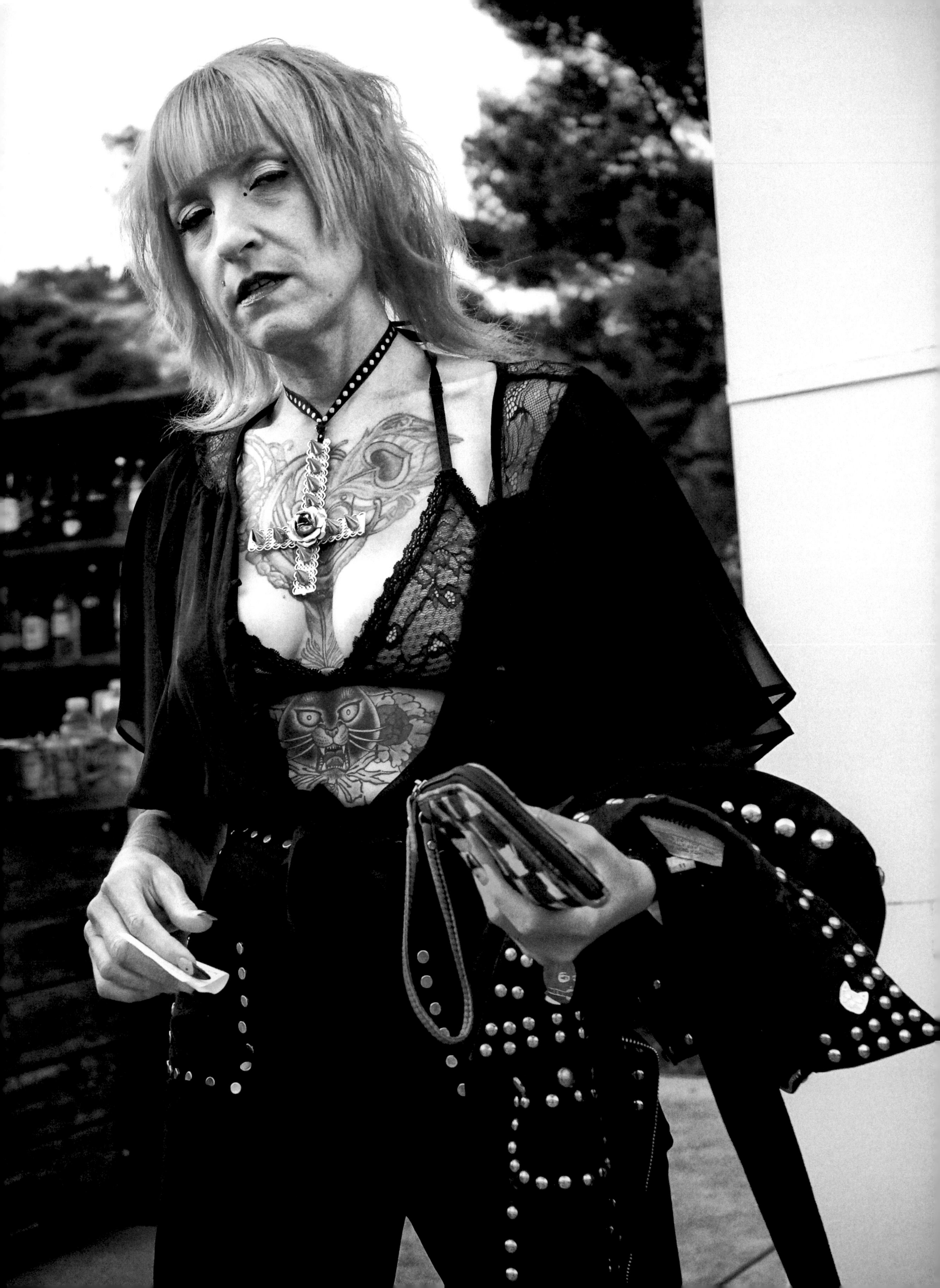

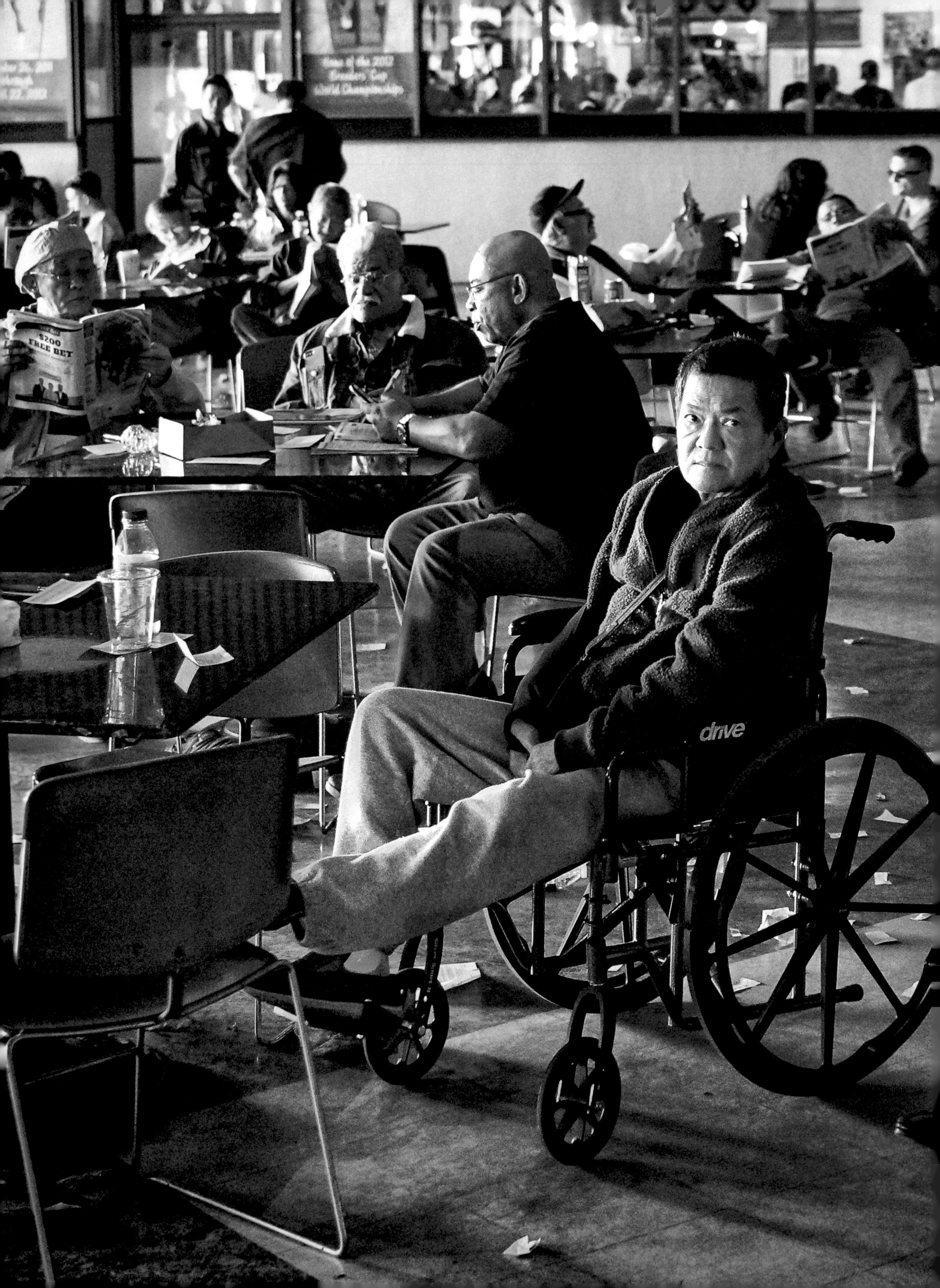
$200
FREE BET
drive

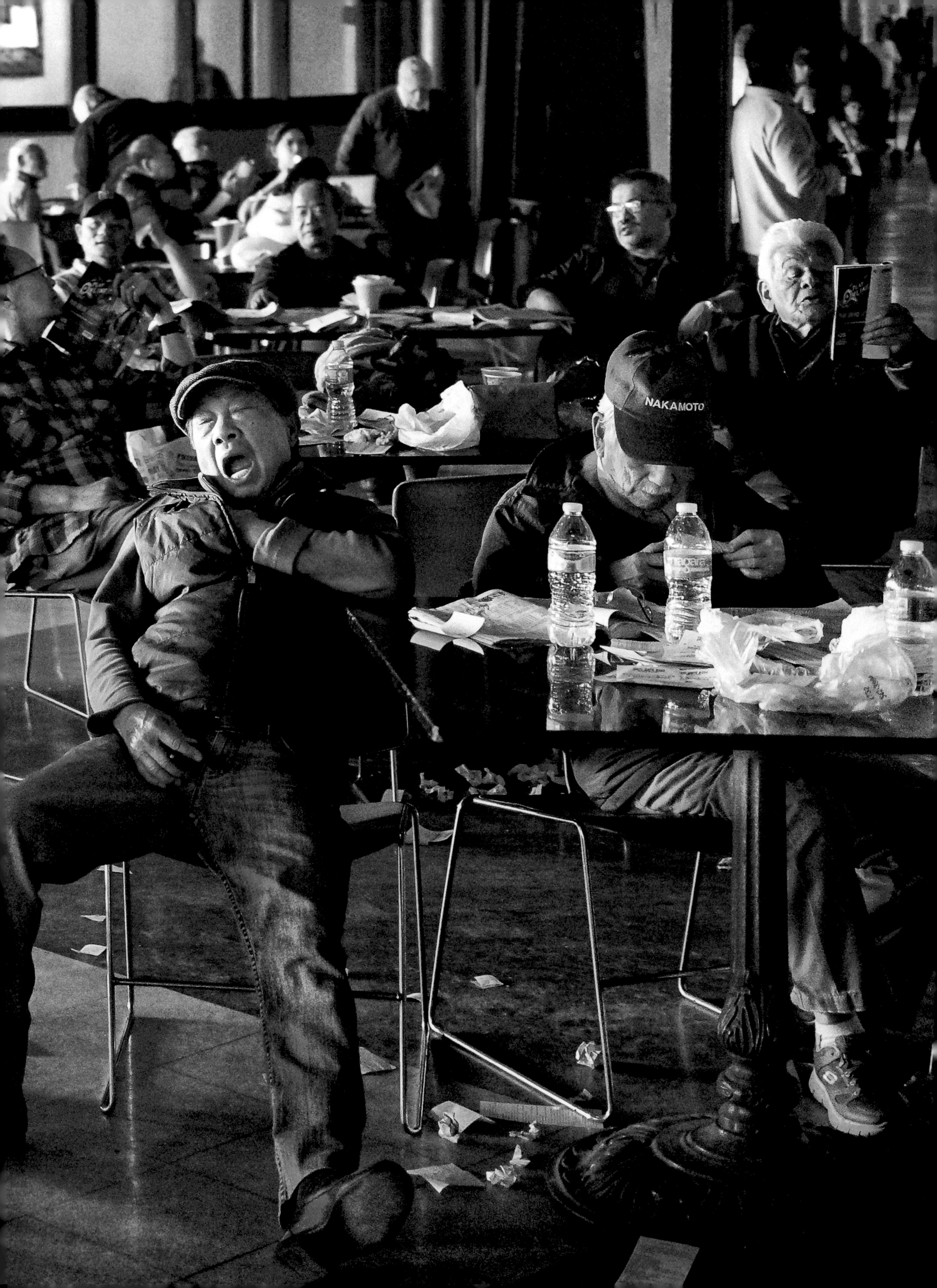
NAKAMOTO
niagara

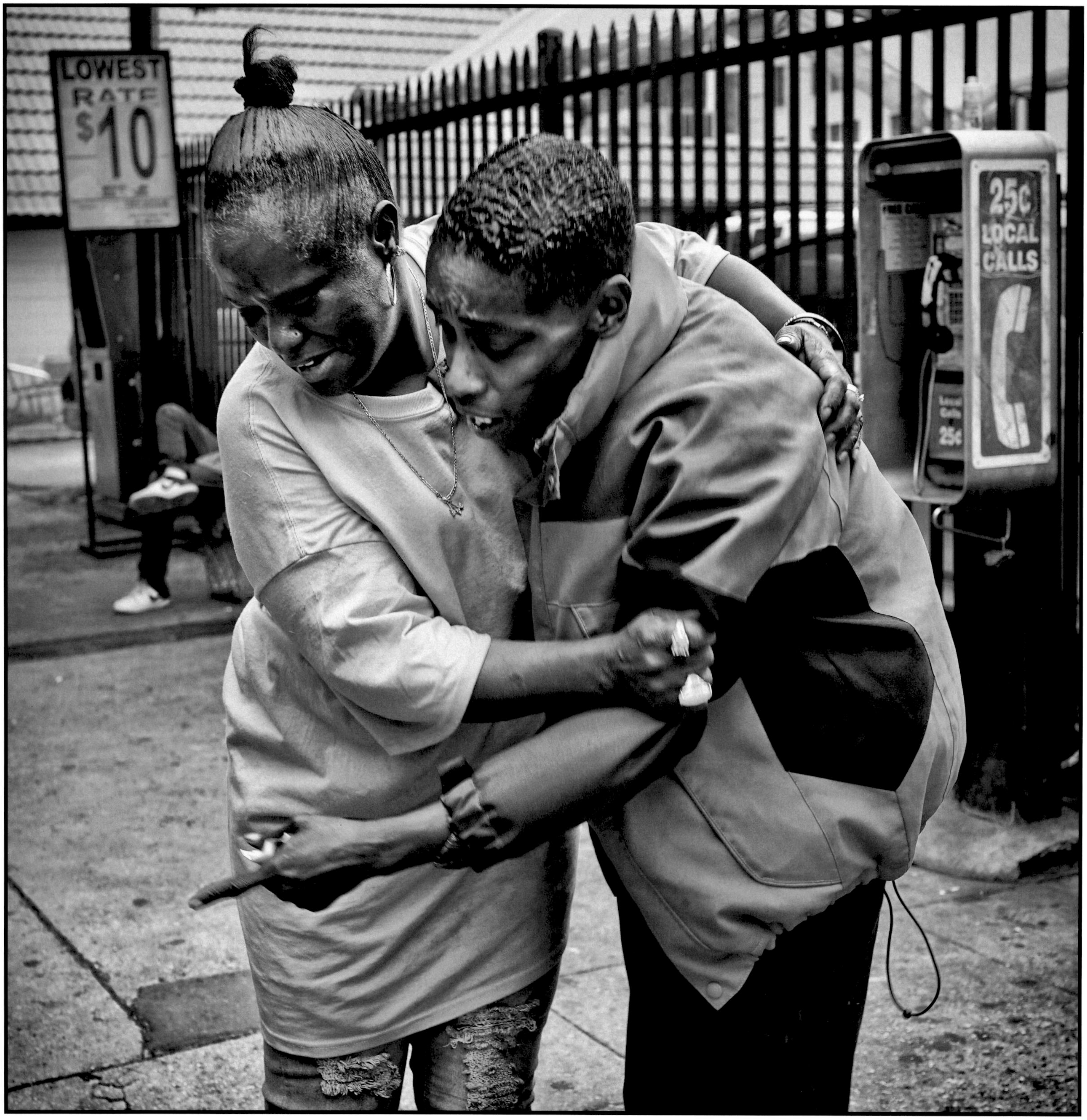
LOWEST
RATE
$10
25¢
LOCAL
CALLS

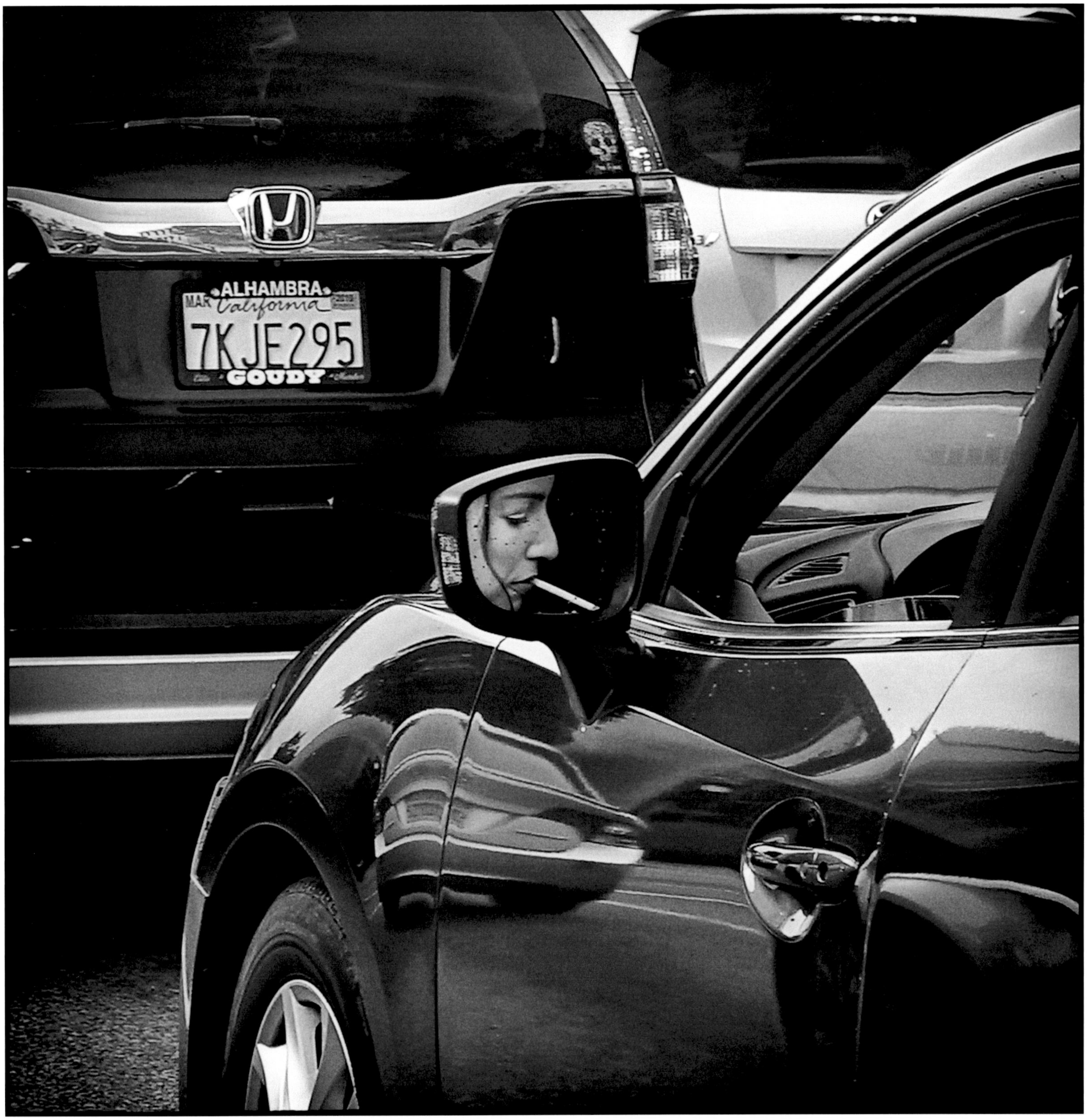
ALHAMBRA
California
7KJE295
GOUDY

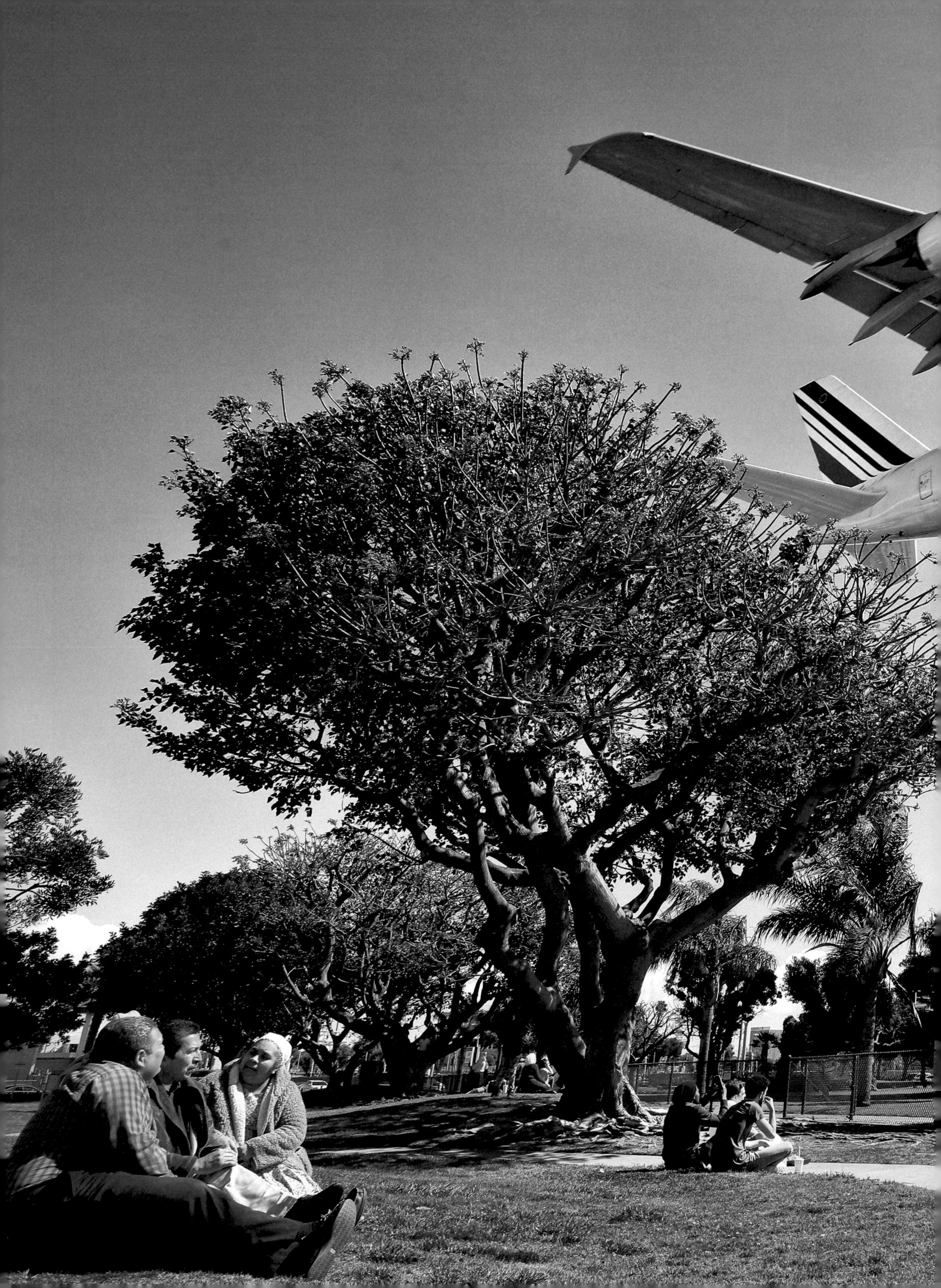

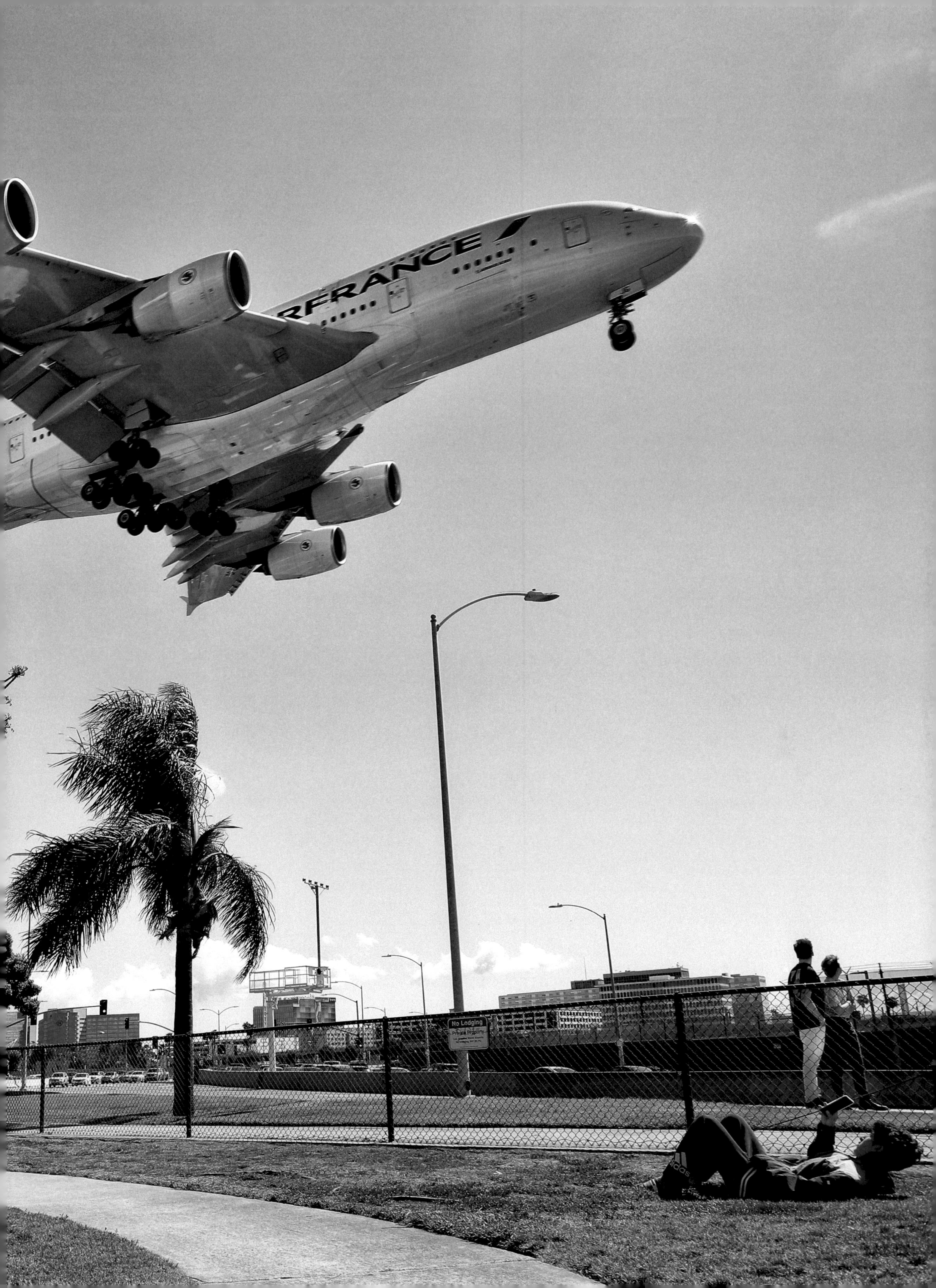
RFRANCE
No Lodging
Private Property

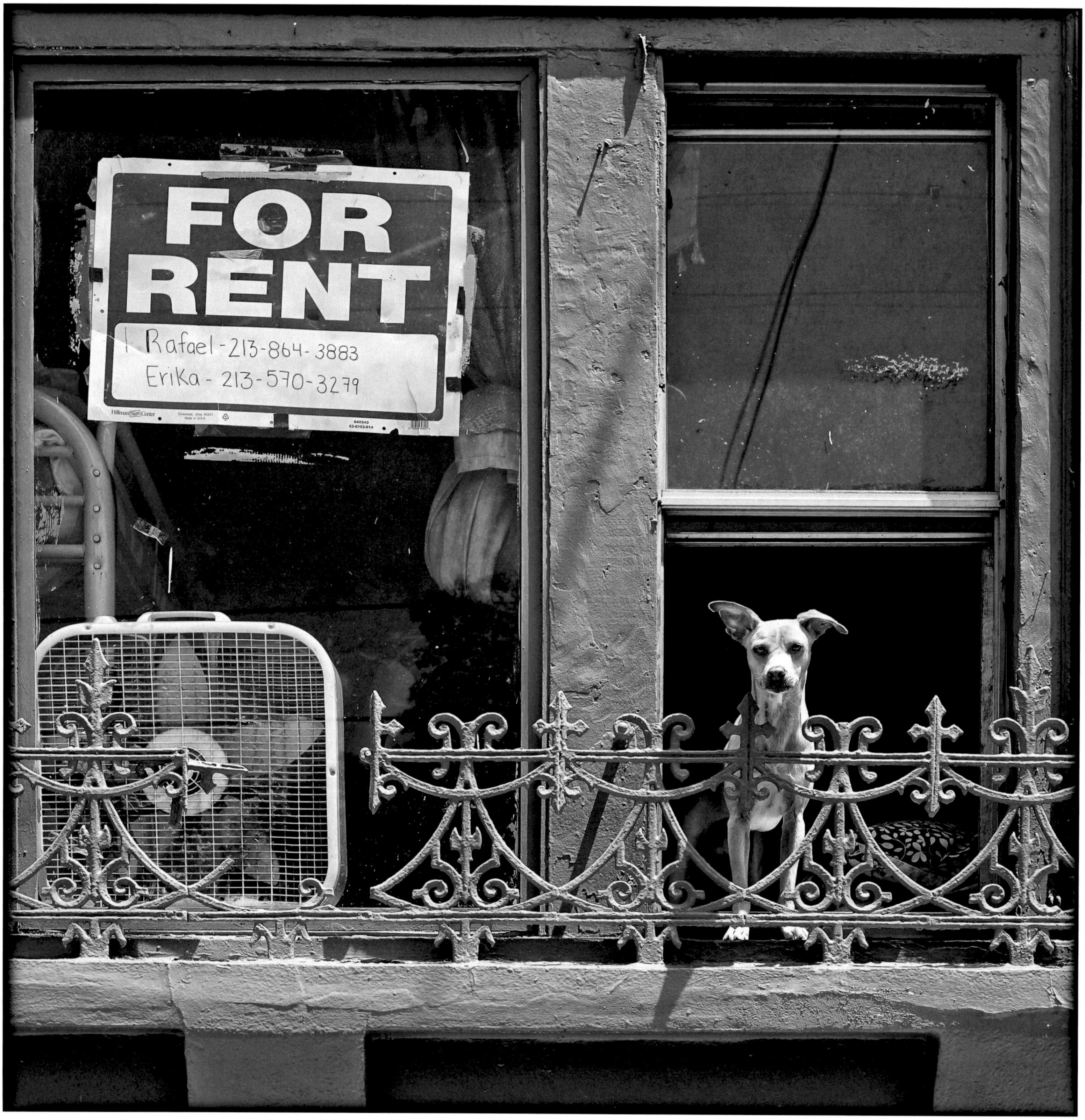
FOR
RENT
Rafael-213-864-3883
Erika - 213-570-3279

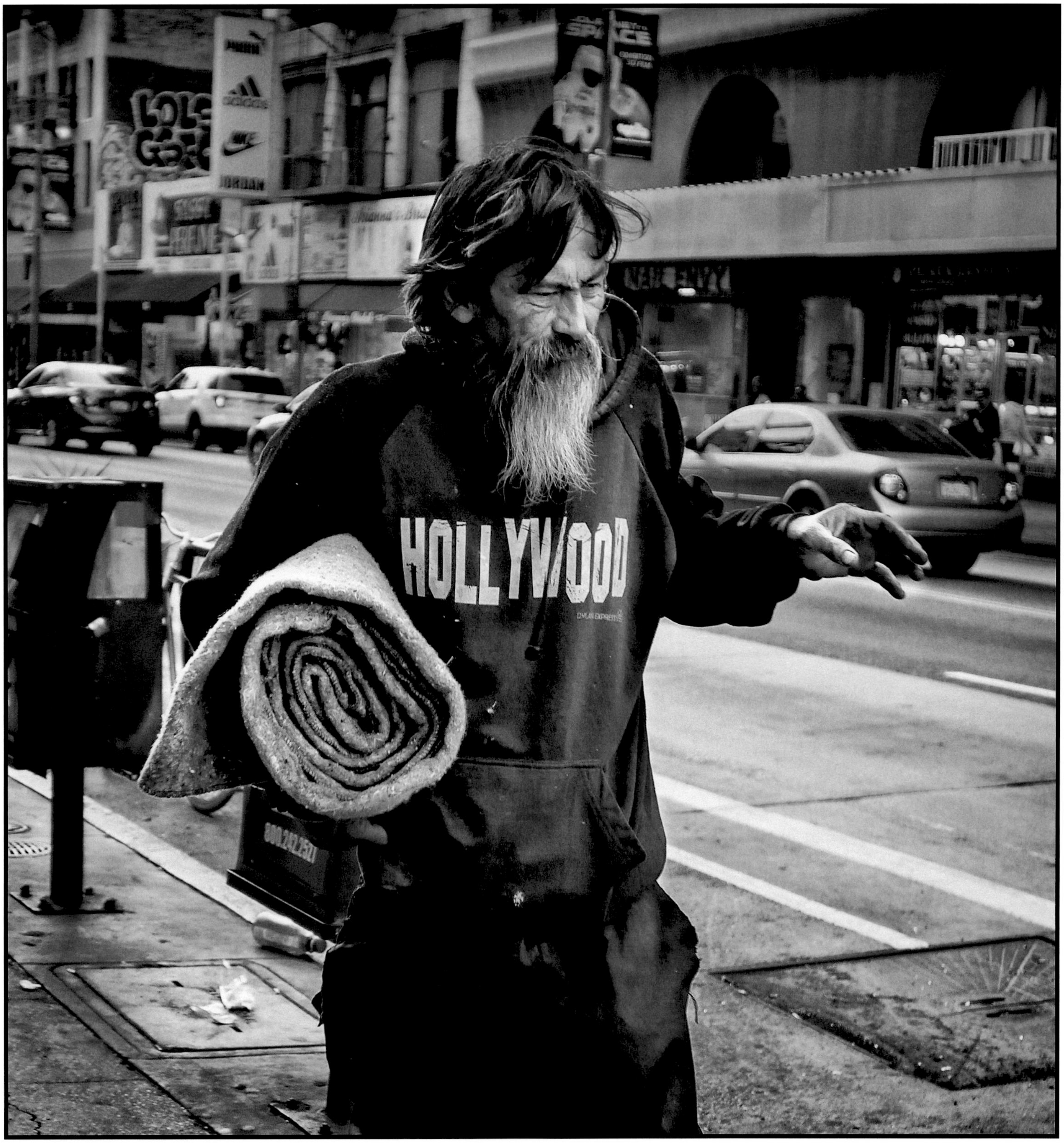
HOLLYWOOD

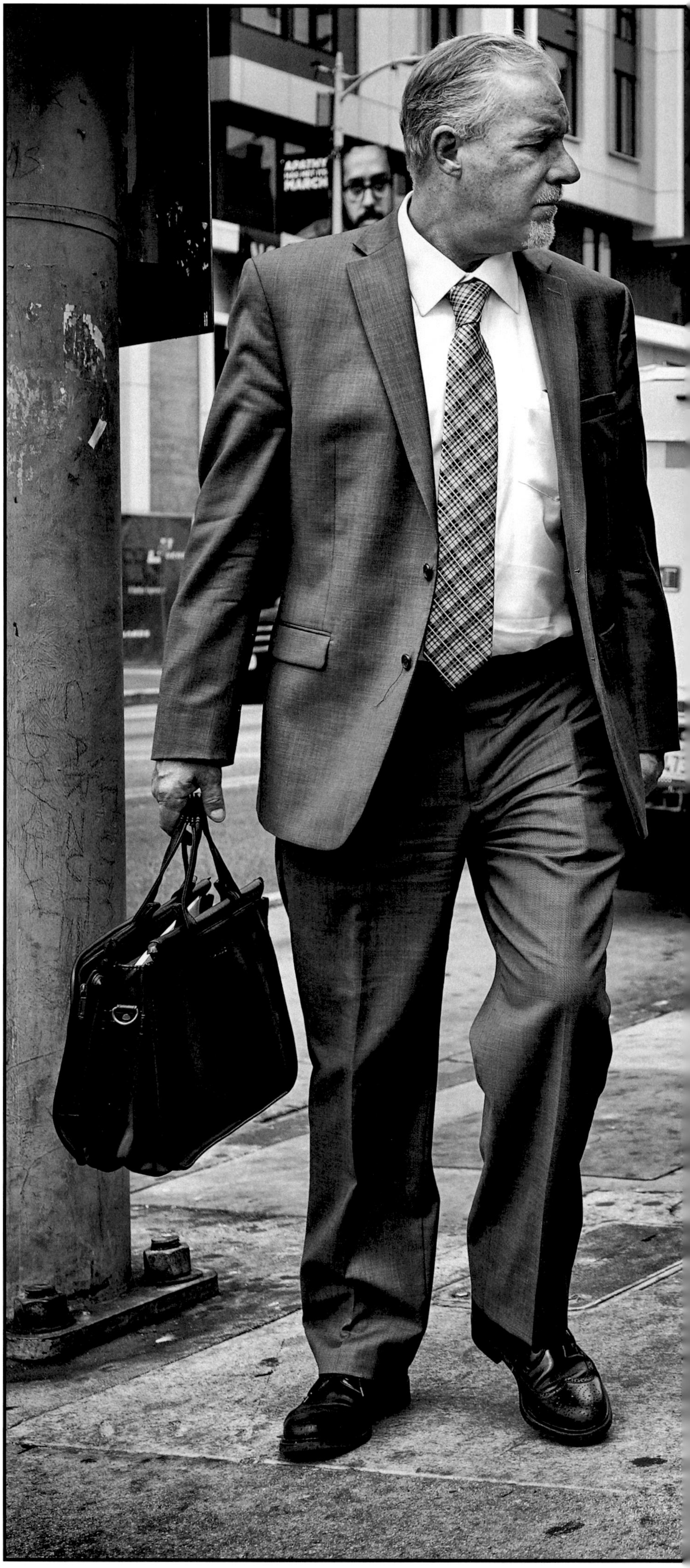
APATHY
MARCH

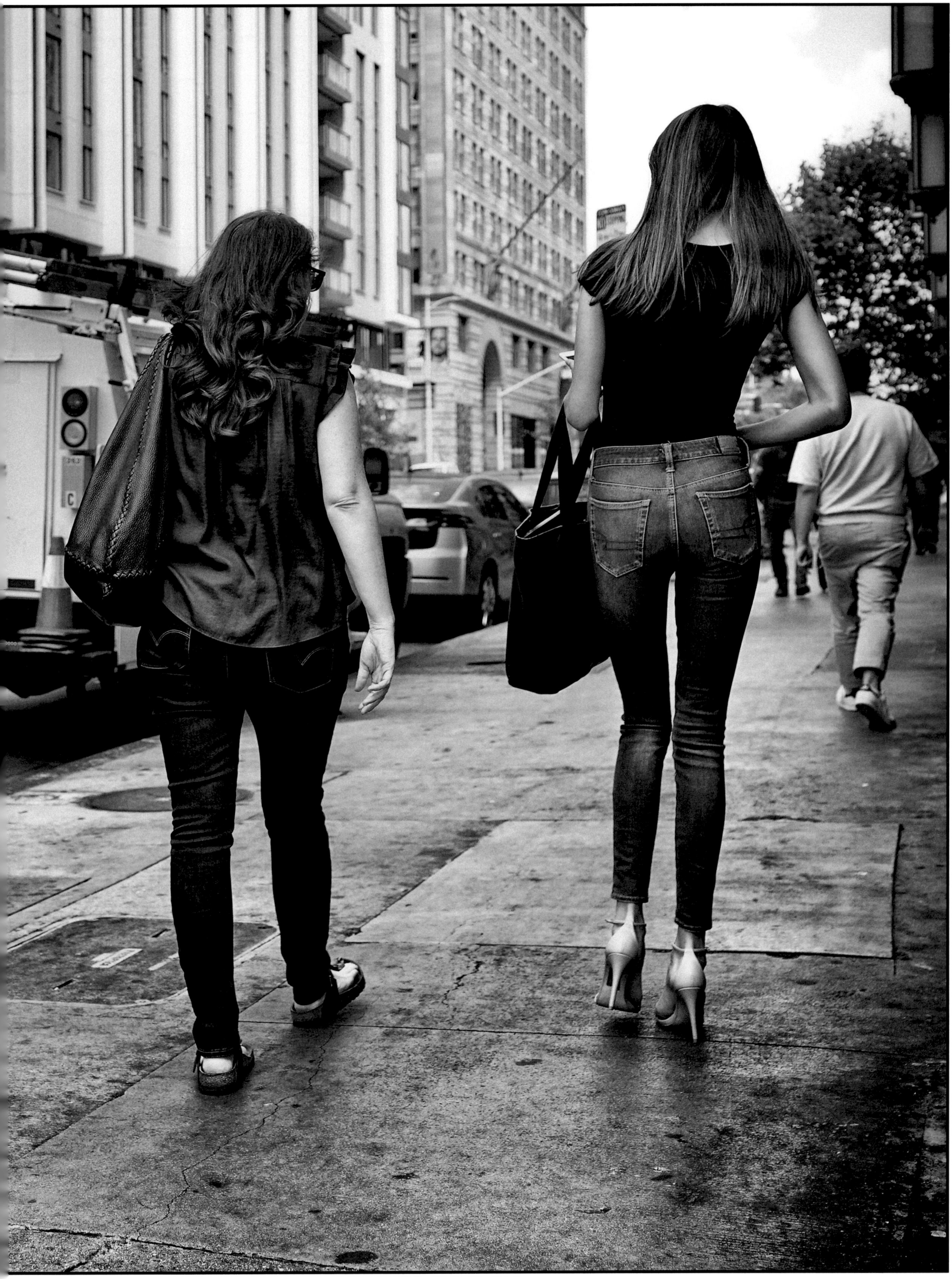

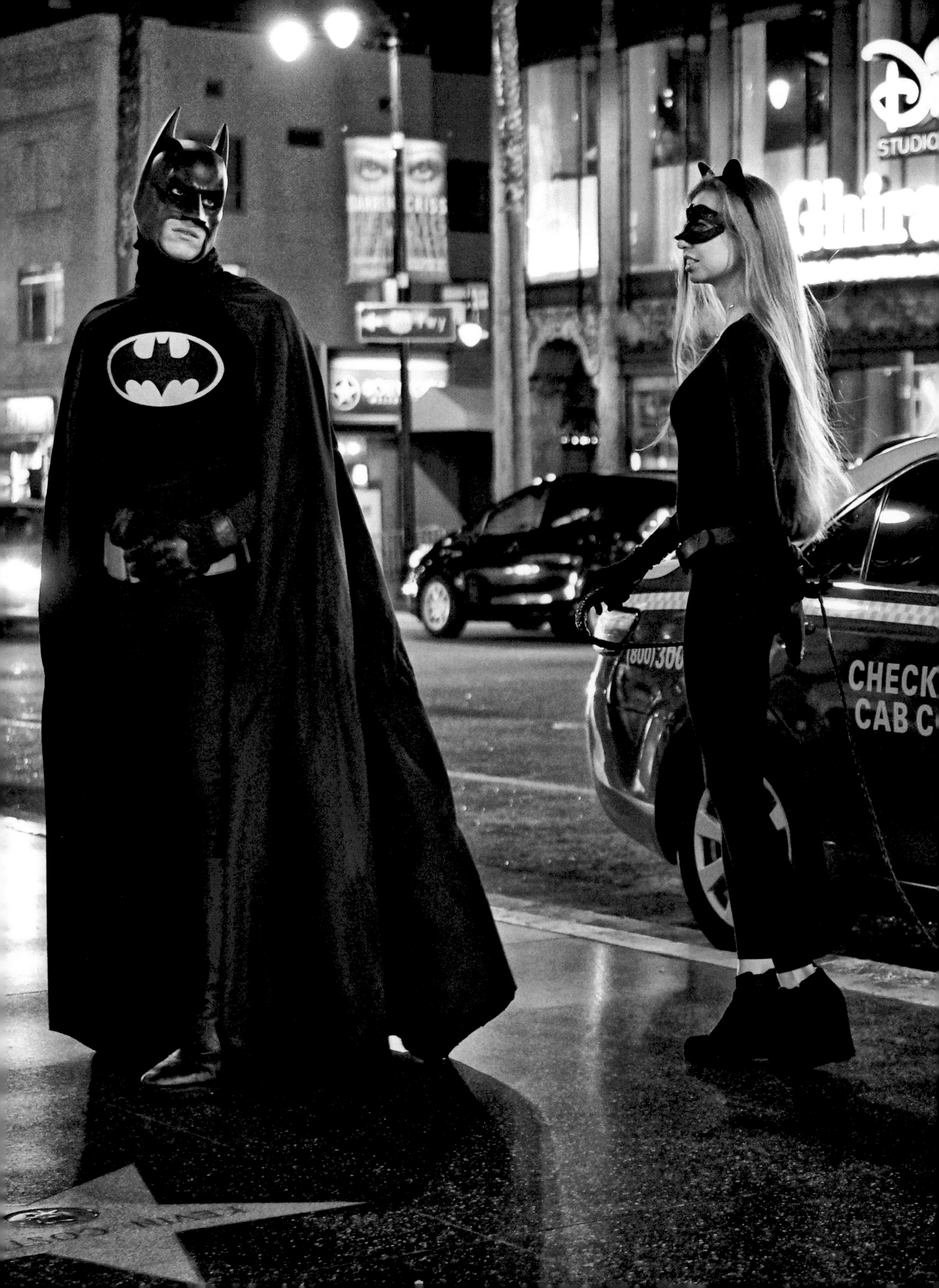
STUDIO
CHECK
CAB C

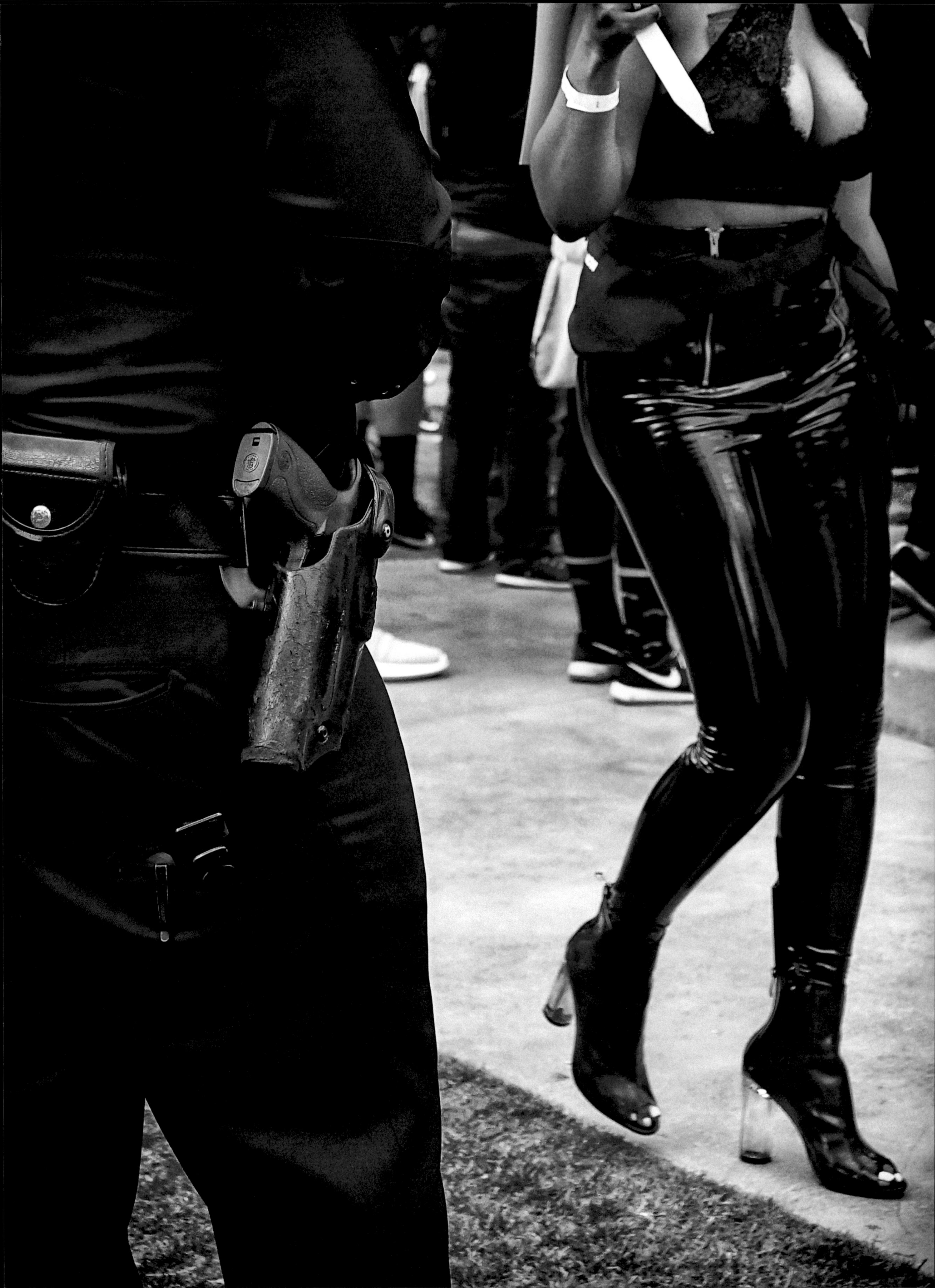

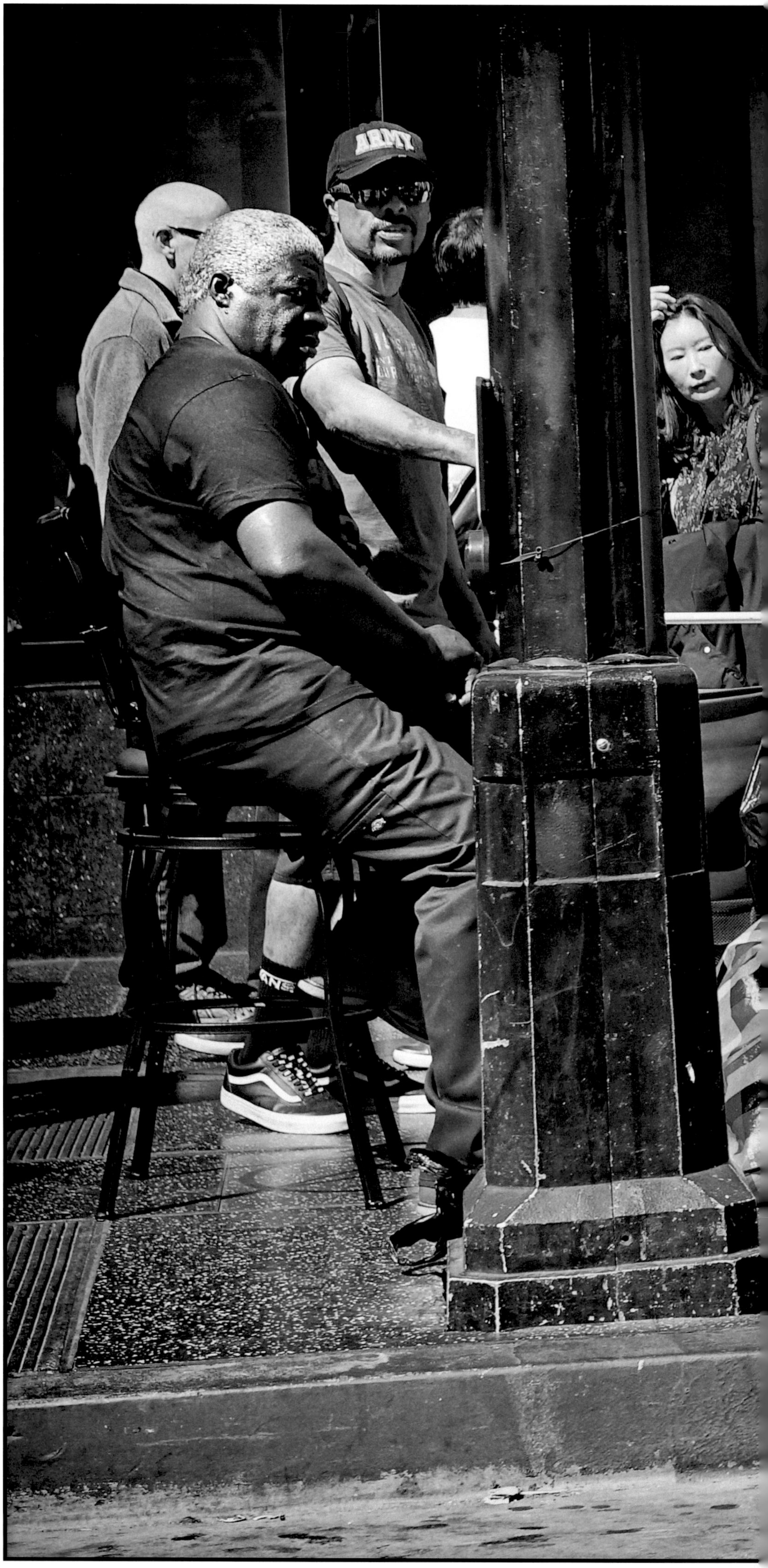
ARMY

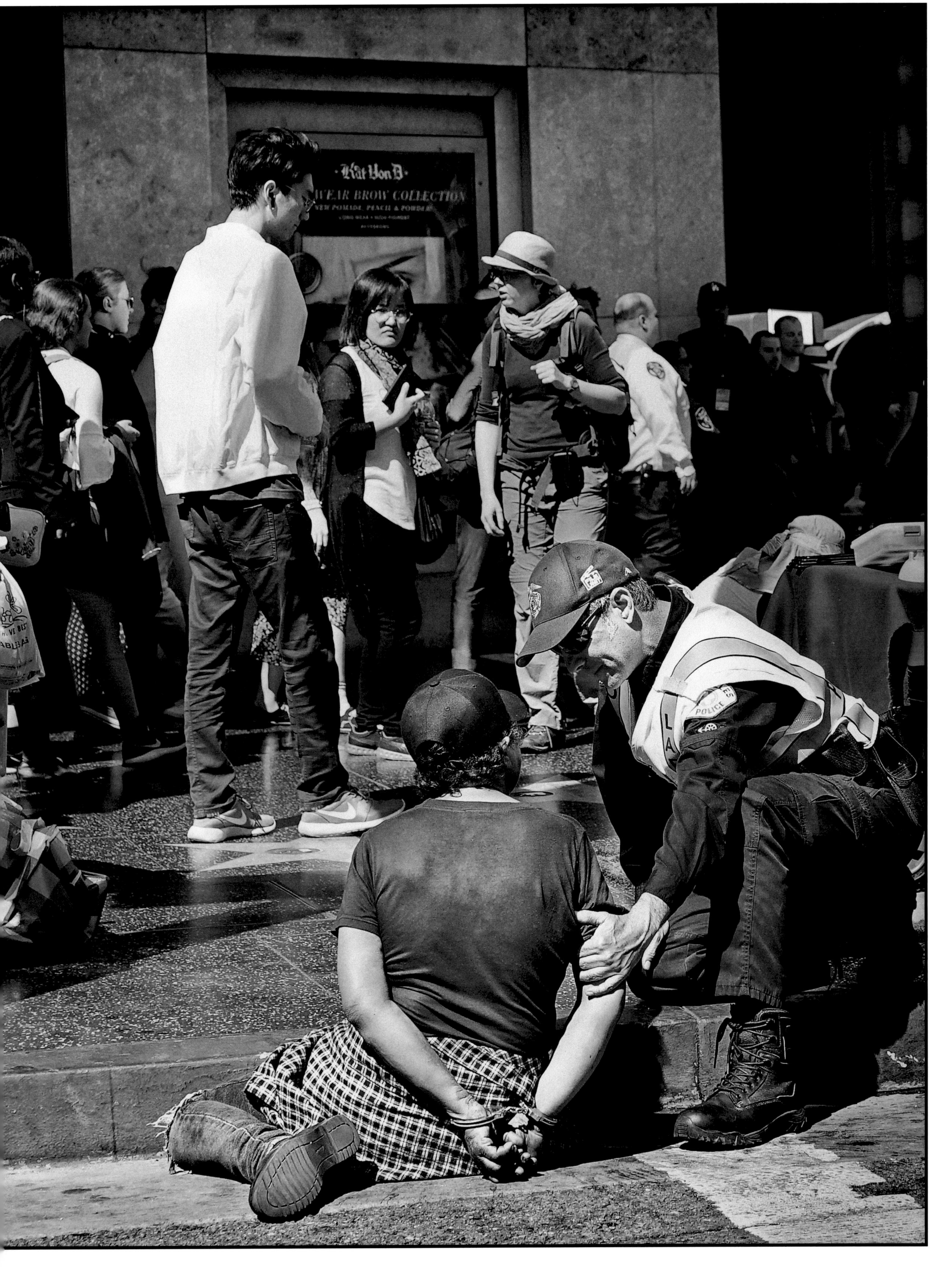
Kat Von D
WEAR BROW COLLECTION
NEW POMADE, PENCIL & POWDER
POLICE

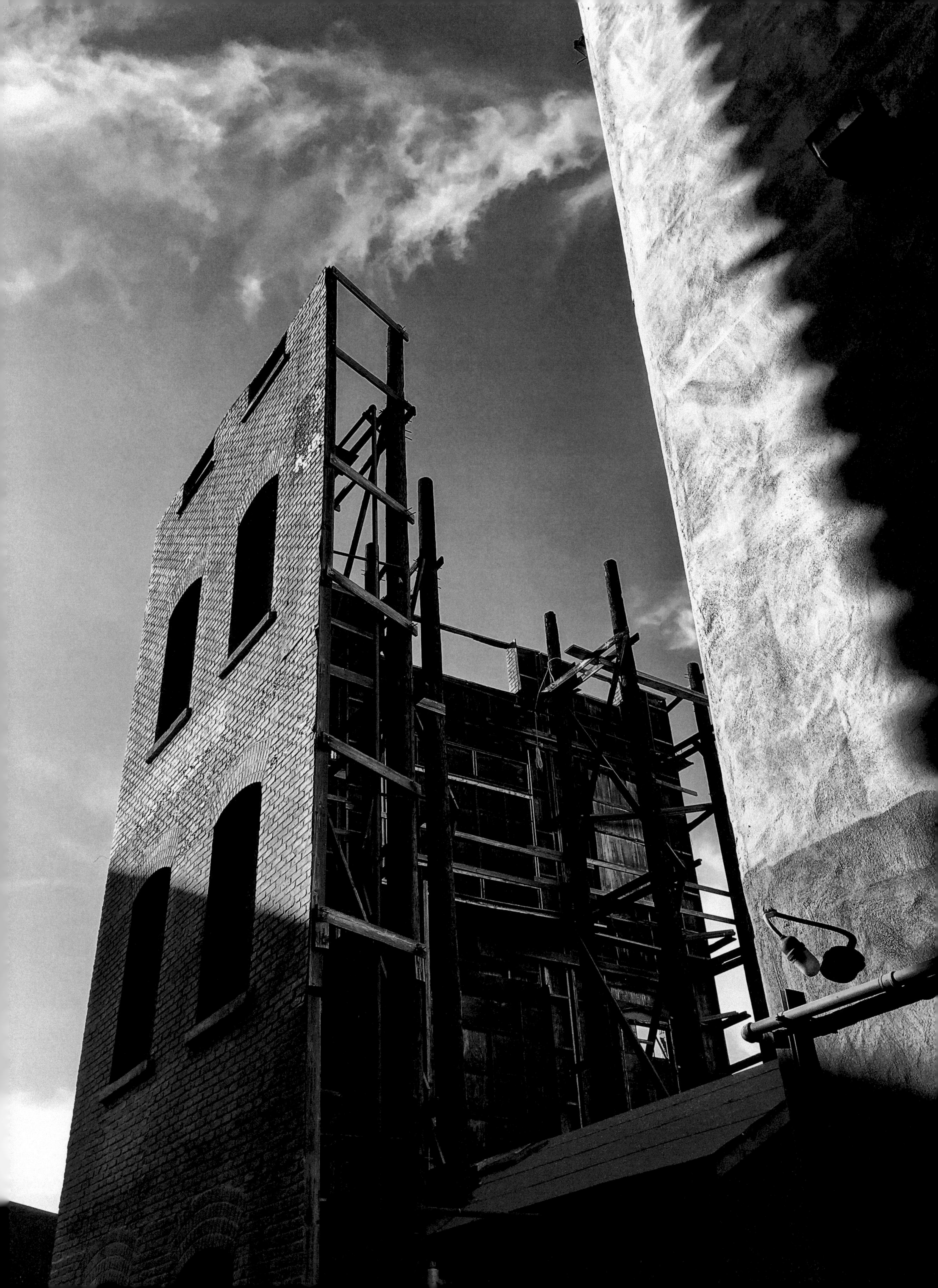

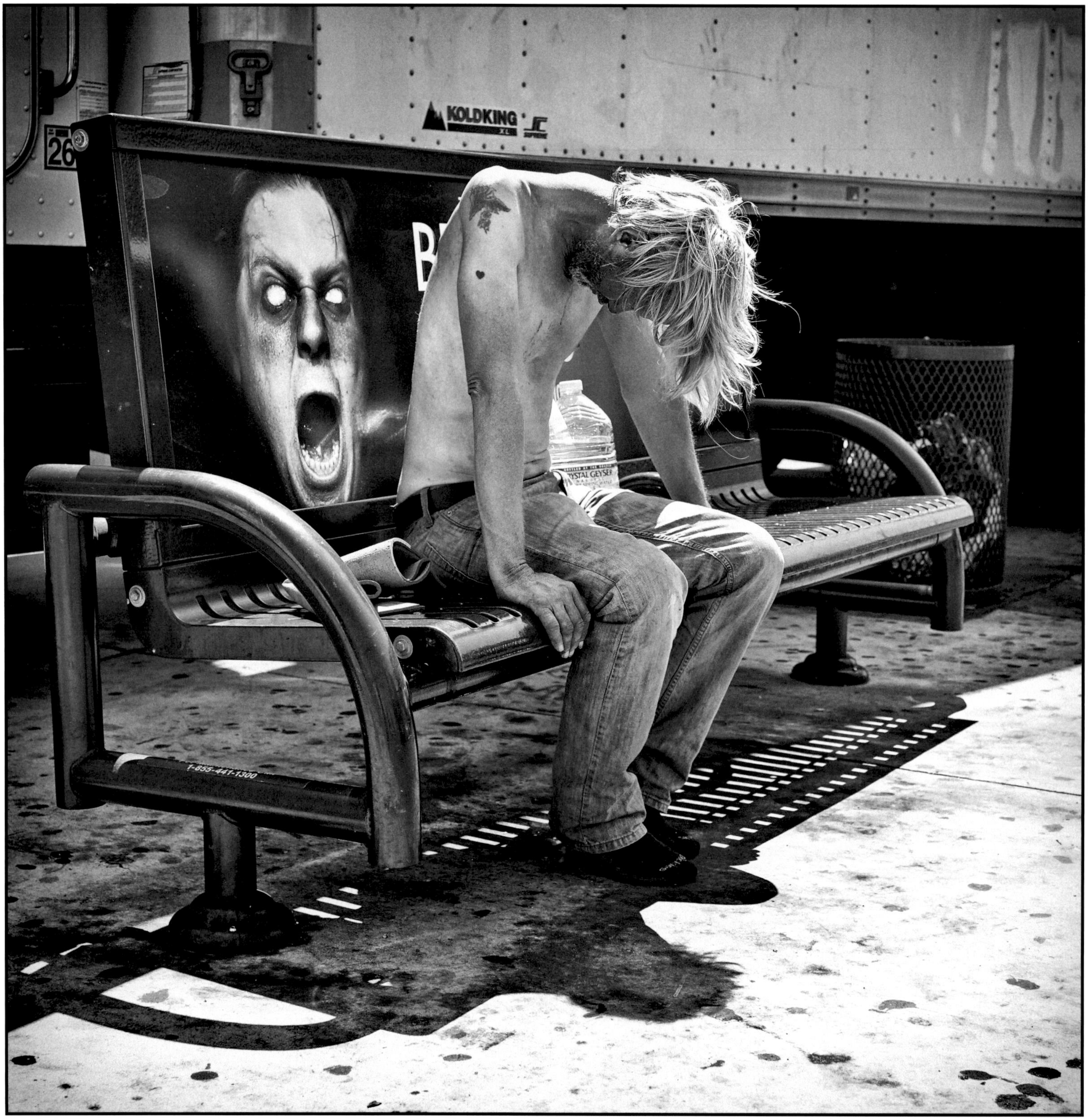
26
KOLDKING
XL
1-855-441-1300

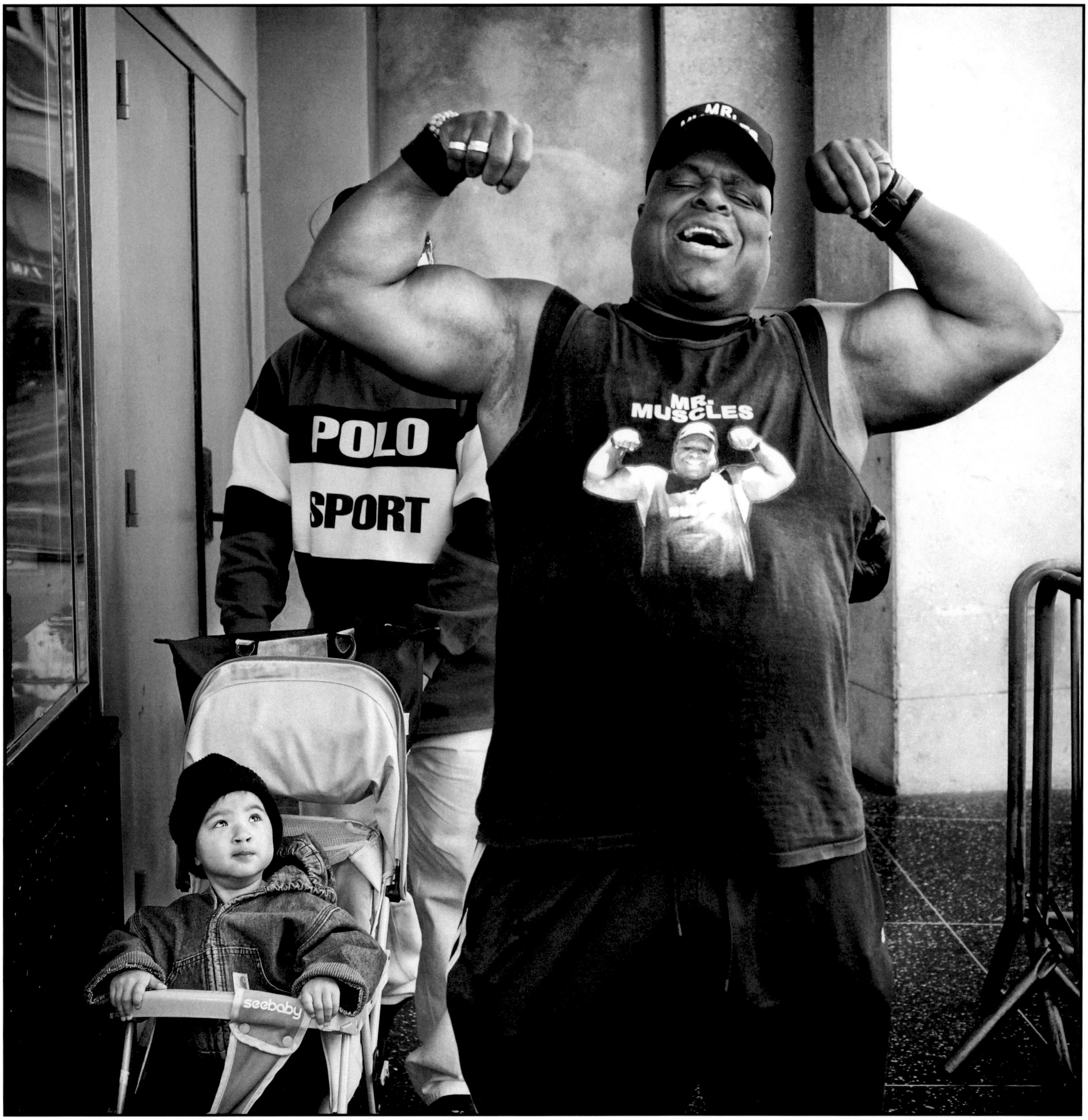
POLO
SPORT
MR.
MUSCLES
seebaby

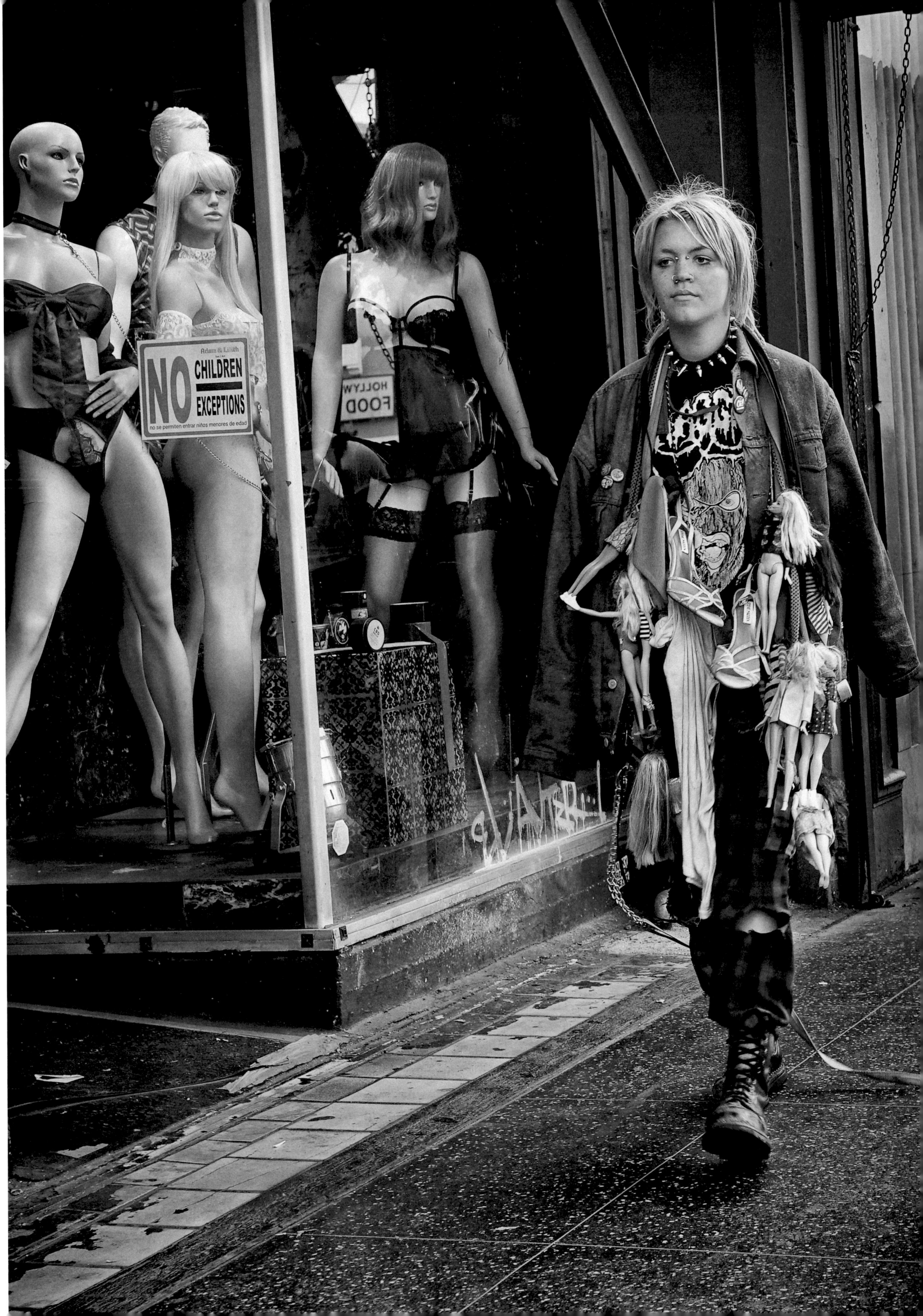
Adam & Lilith
NO CHILDREN
EXCEPTIONS
no se permiten entrar niños menores de edad
HOLLYW
FOOD

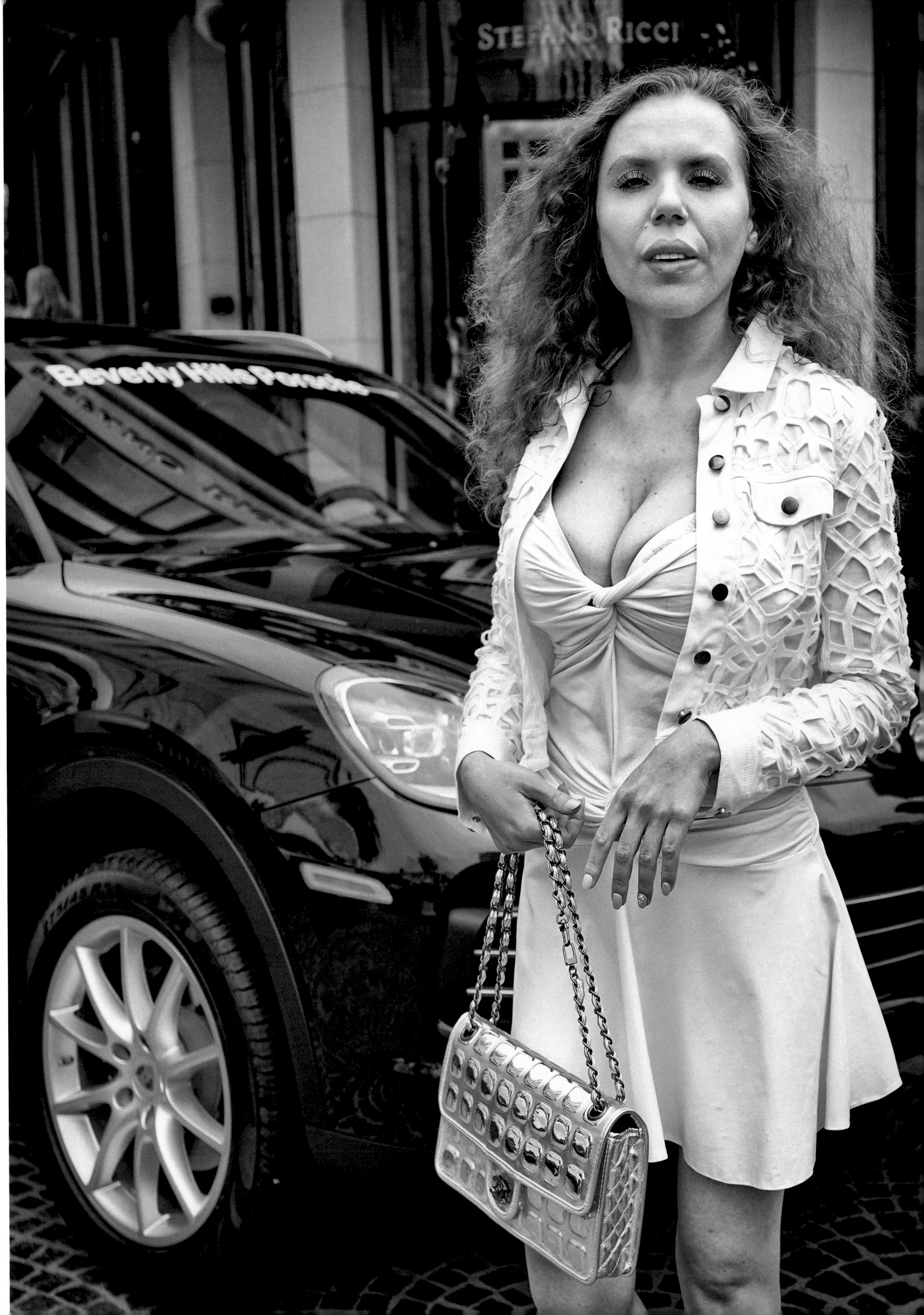
Beverly Hills Porsche

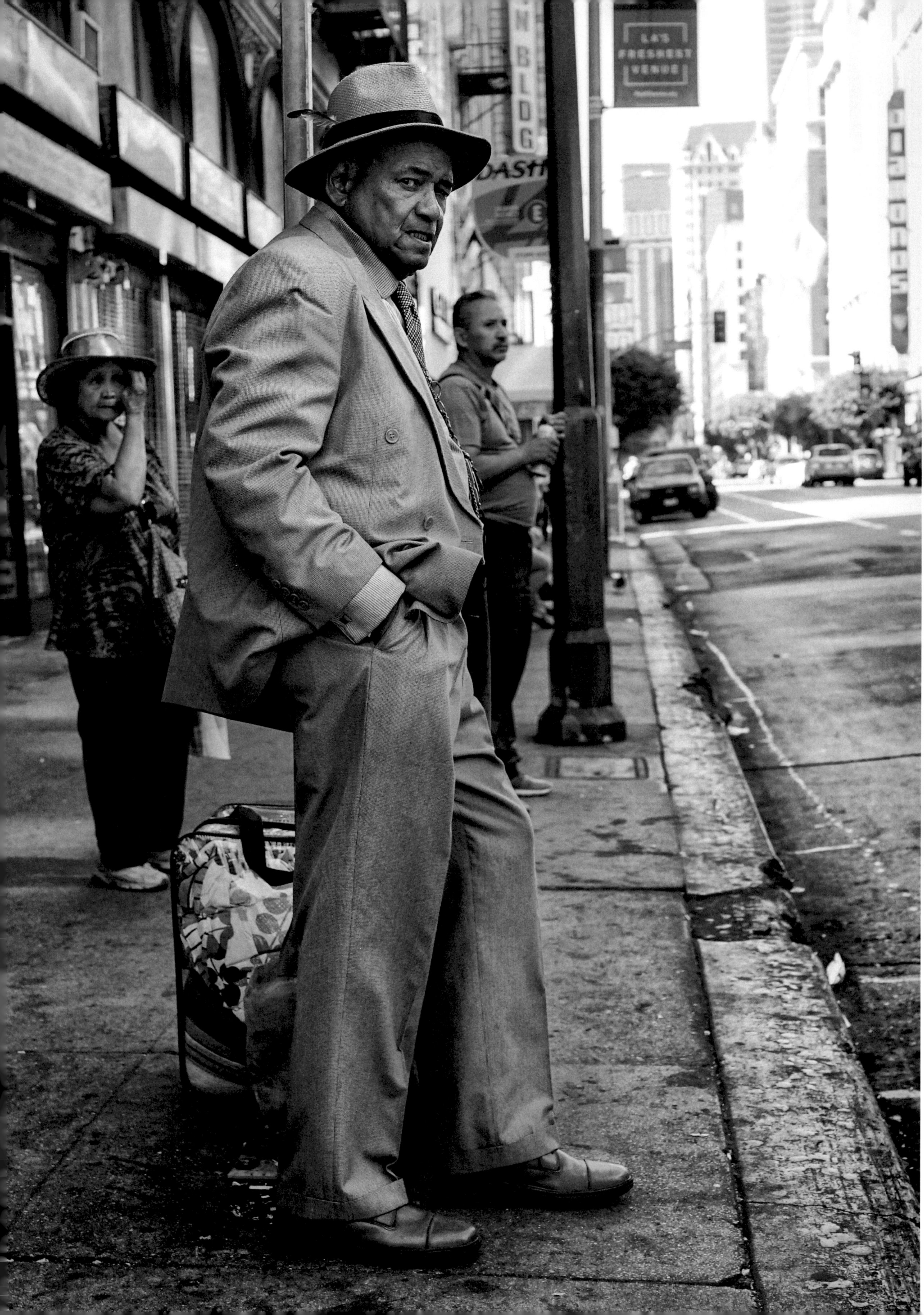
LA'S
FRESHEST
VENUE

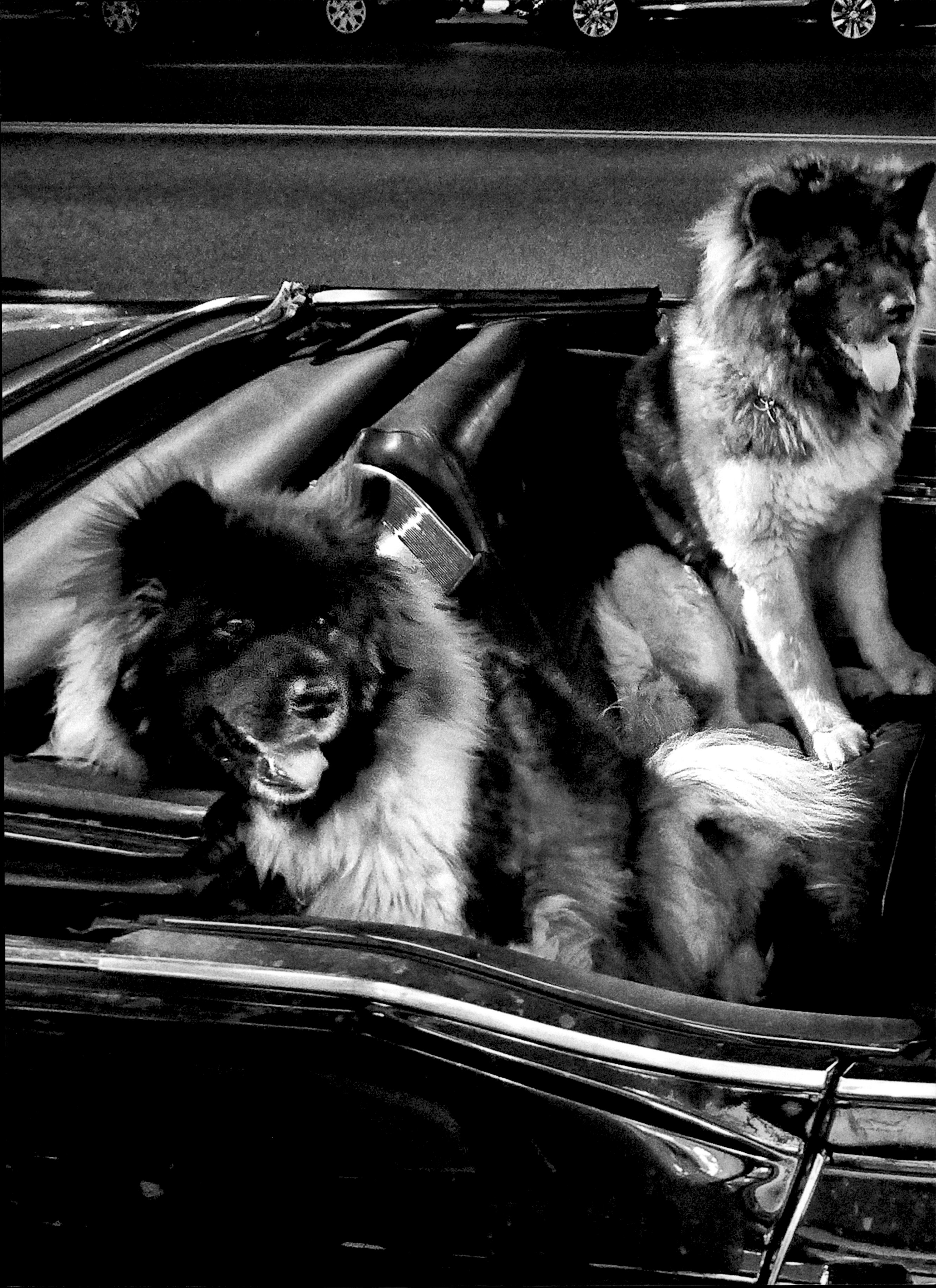

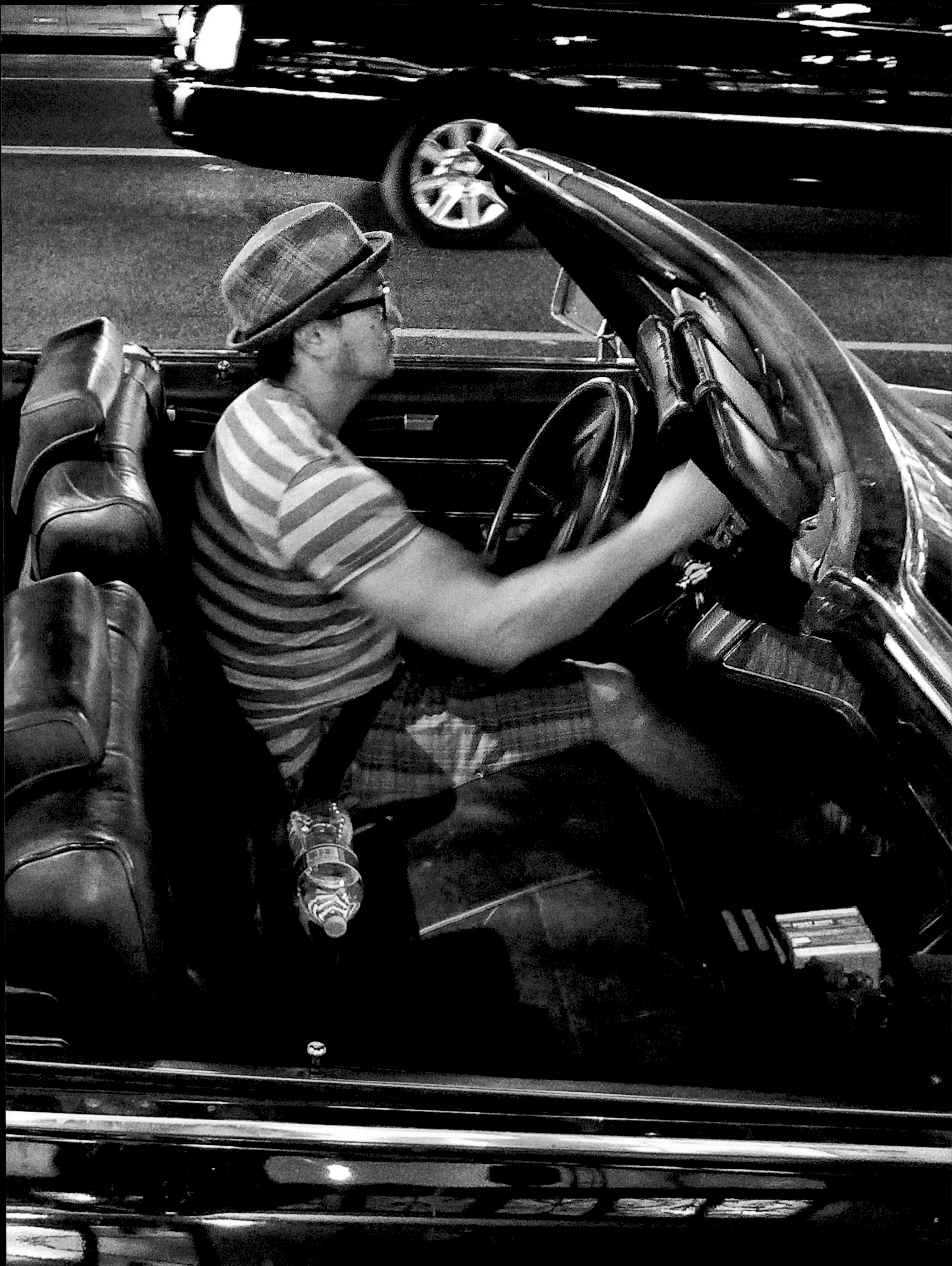

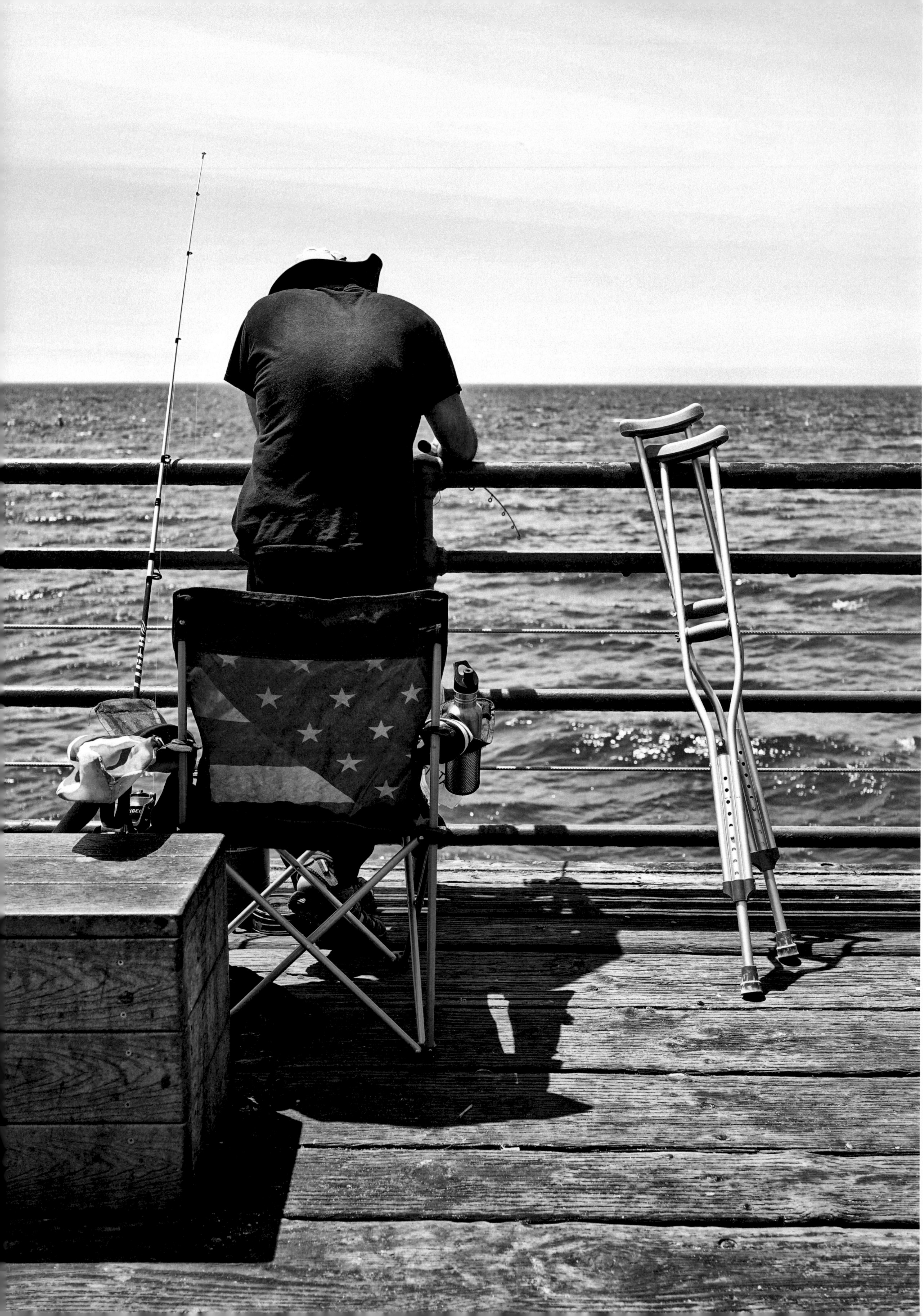

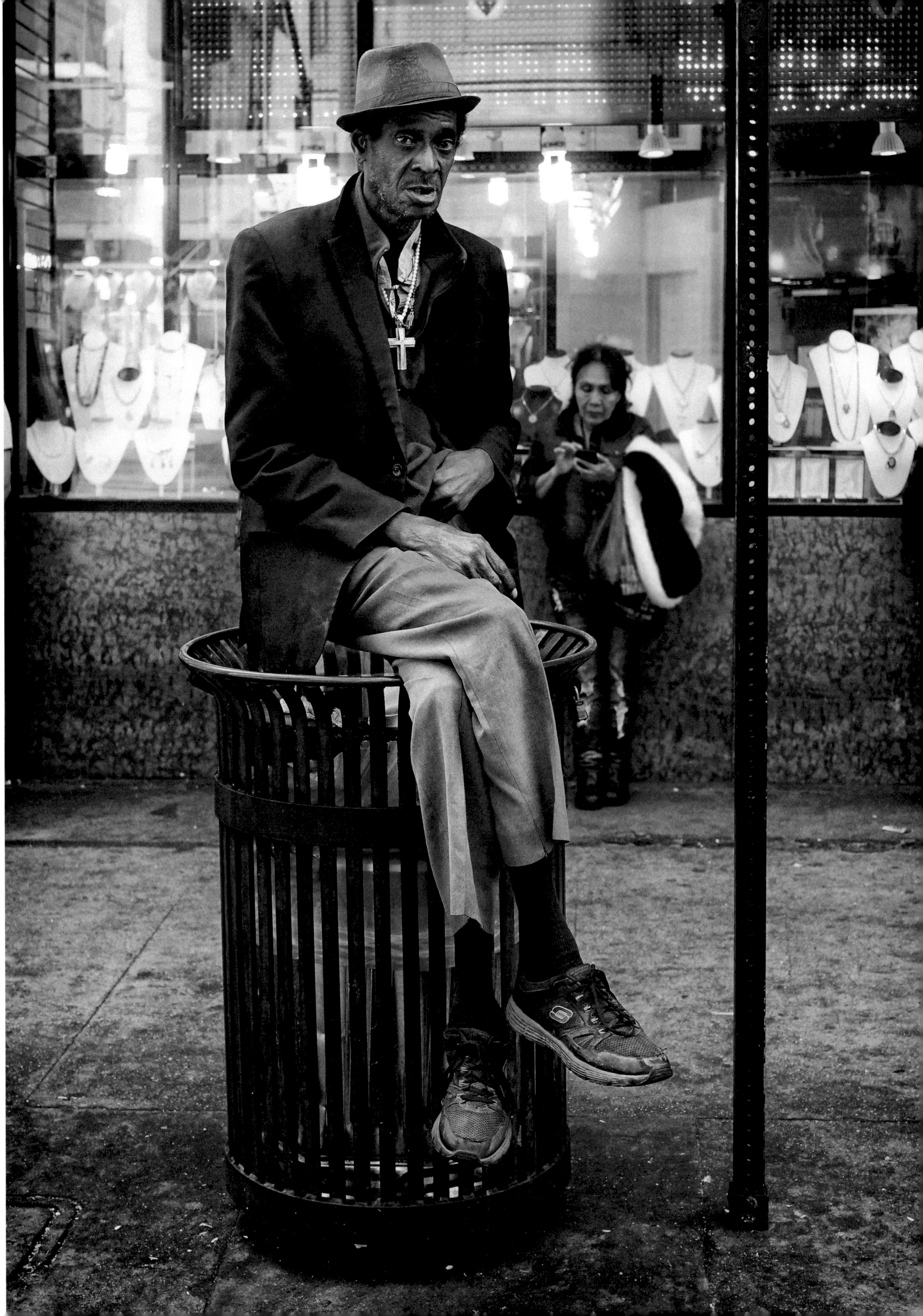

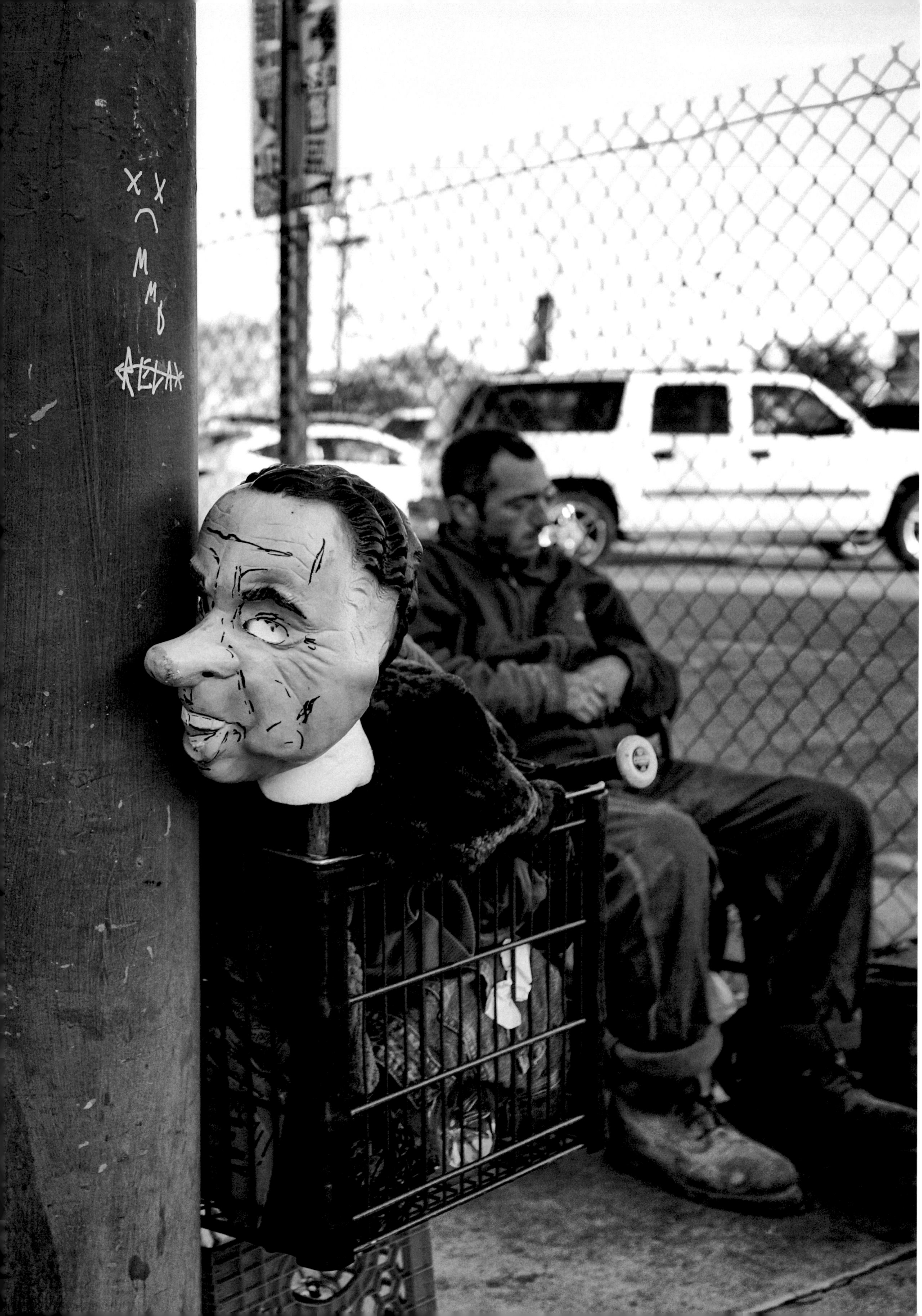

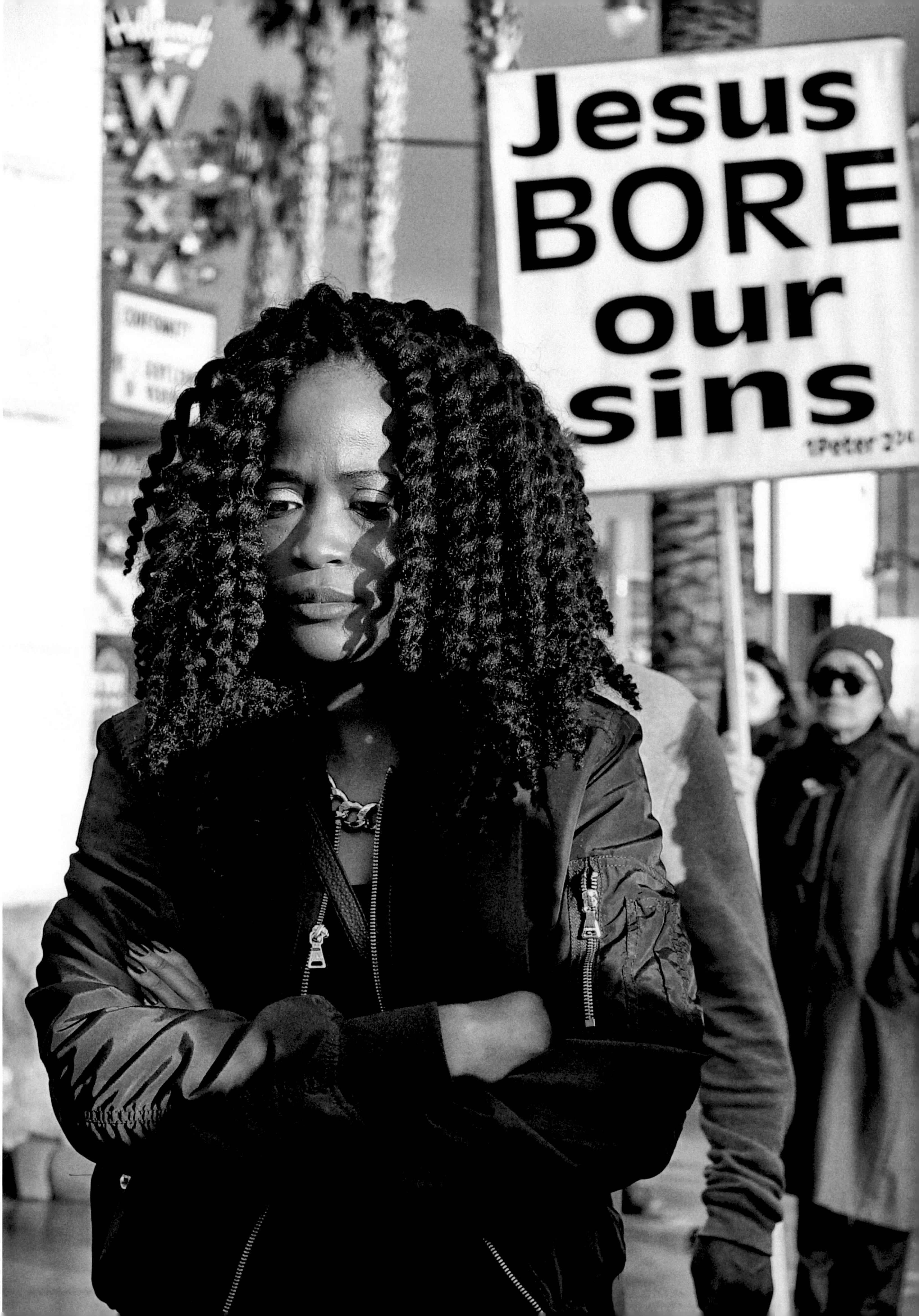
Jesus
BORE
our
sins

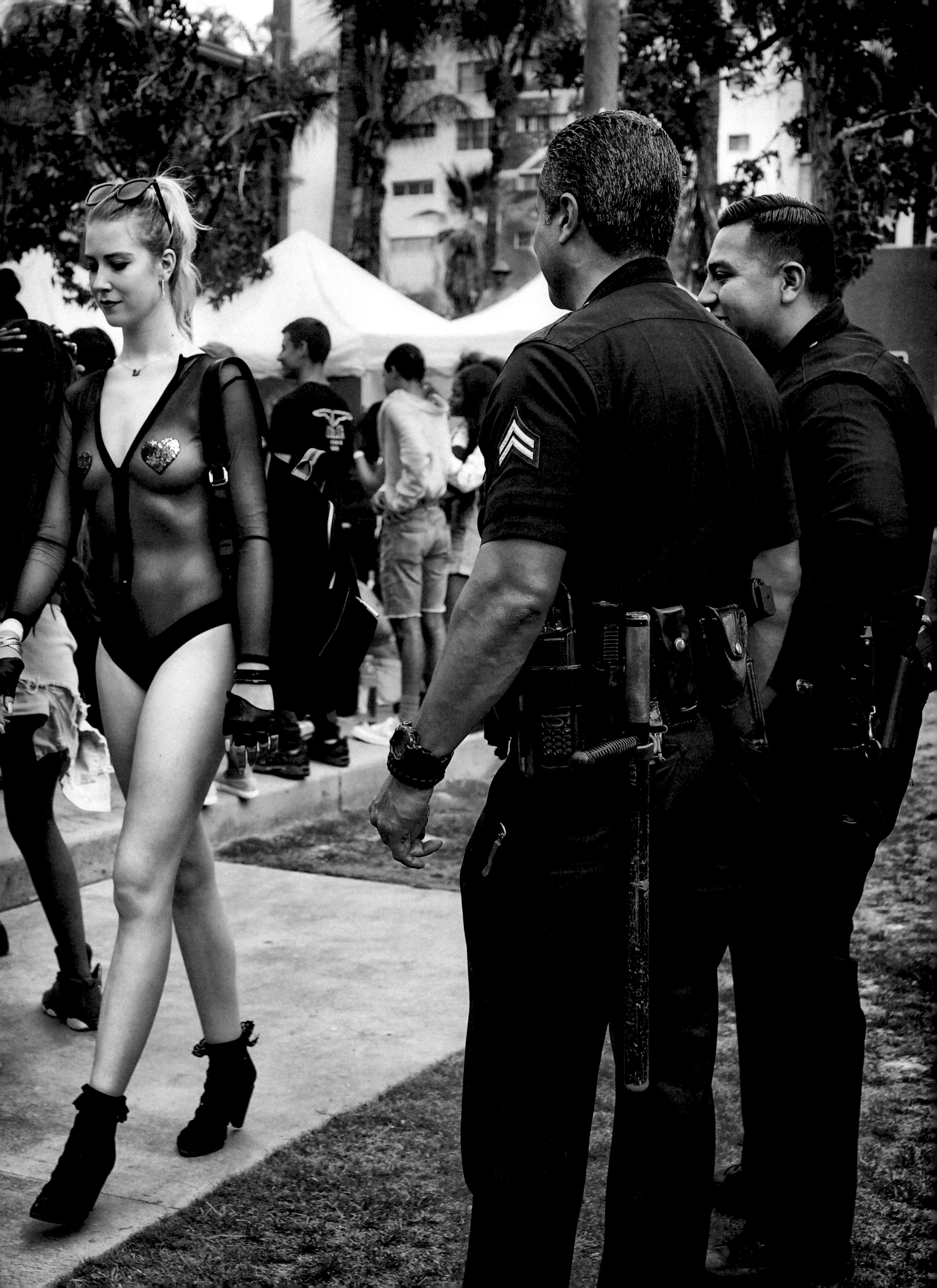

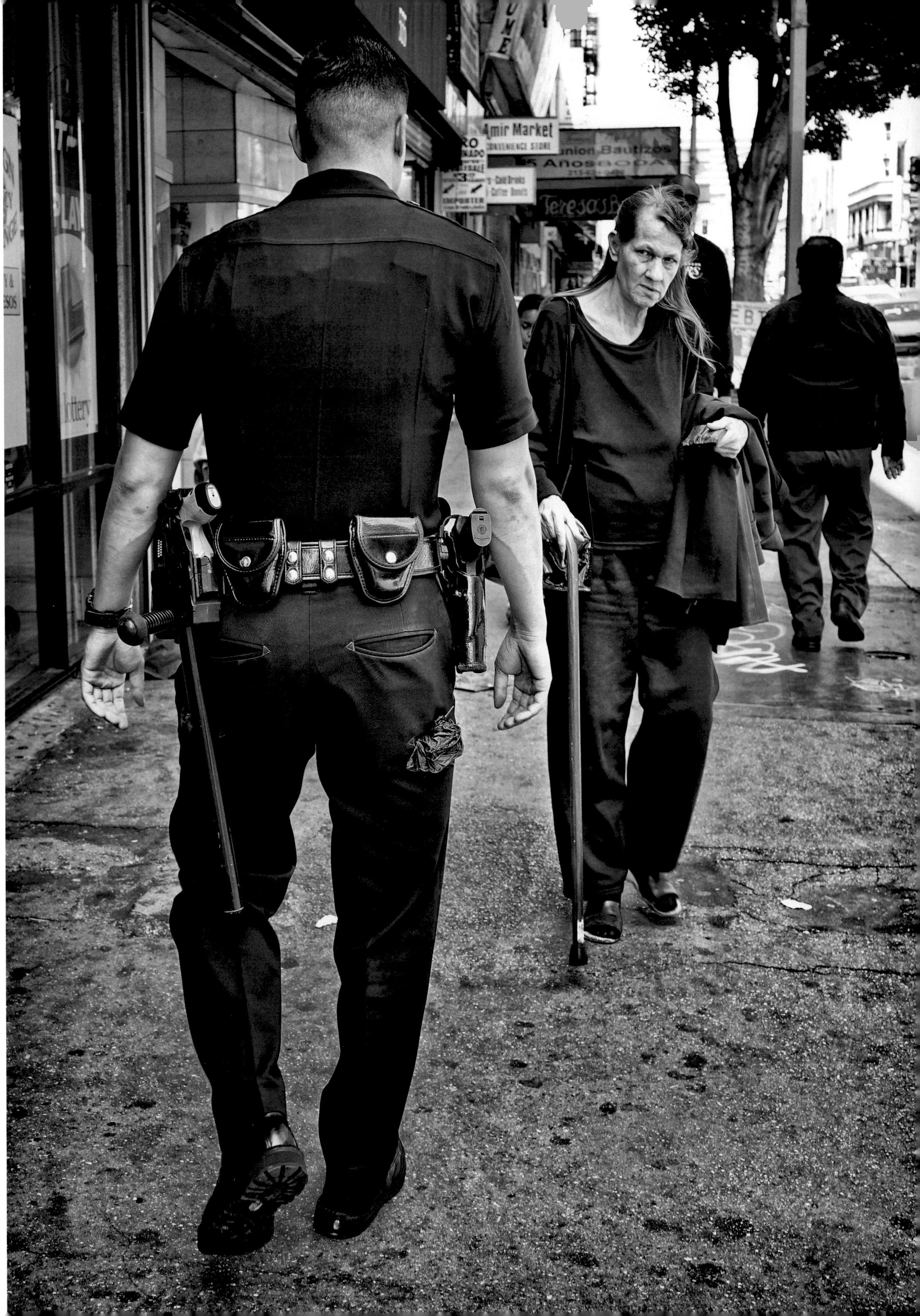
Amir Market
CONVENIENCE STORE
Lottery

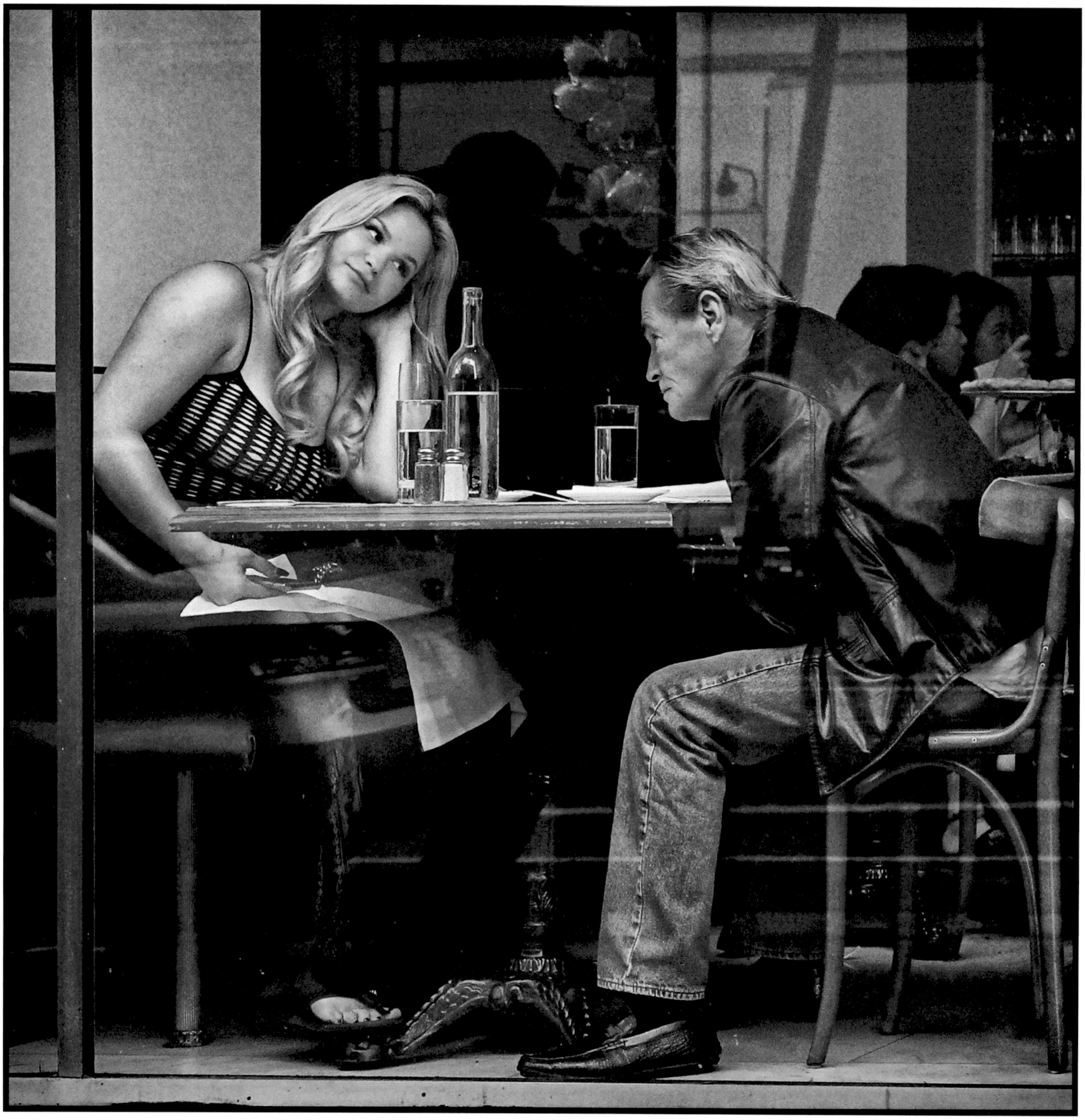

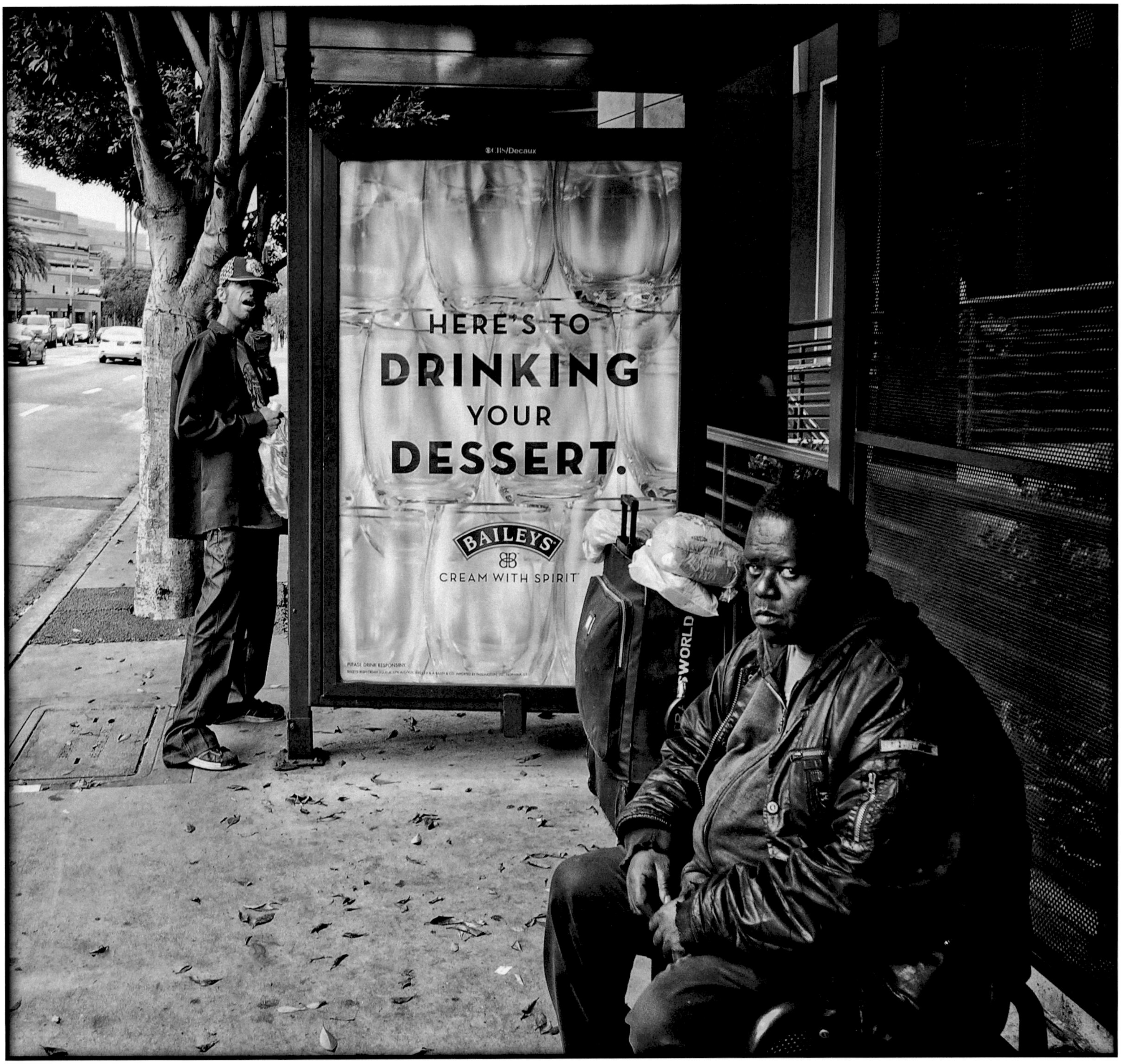
HERE'S TO
DRINKING
YOUR
DESSERT.
BAILEYS
CREAM WITH SPIRIT

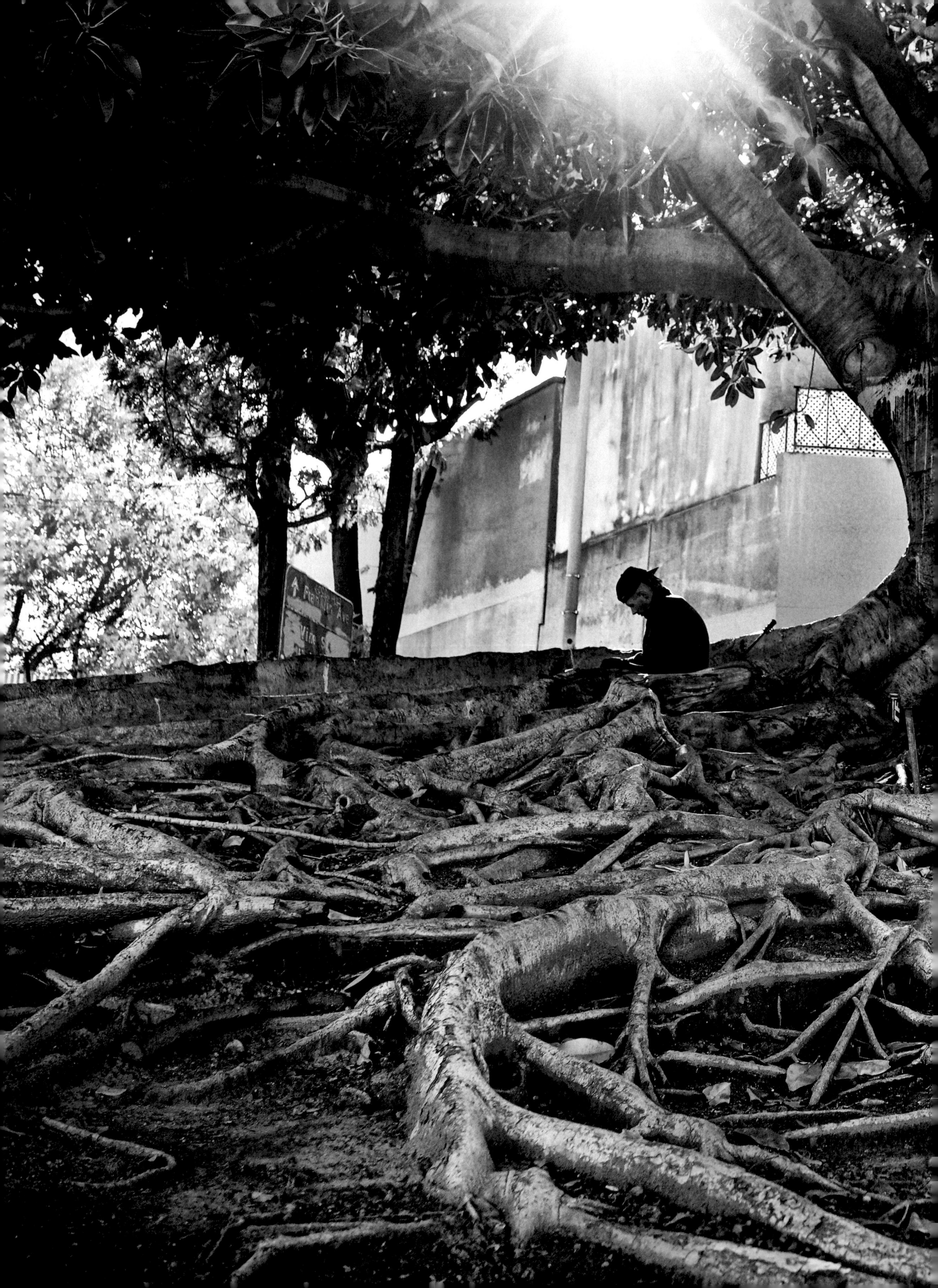

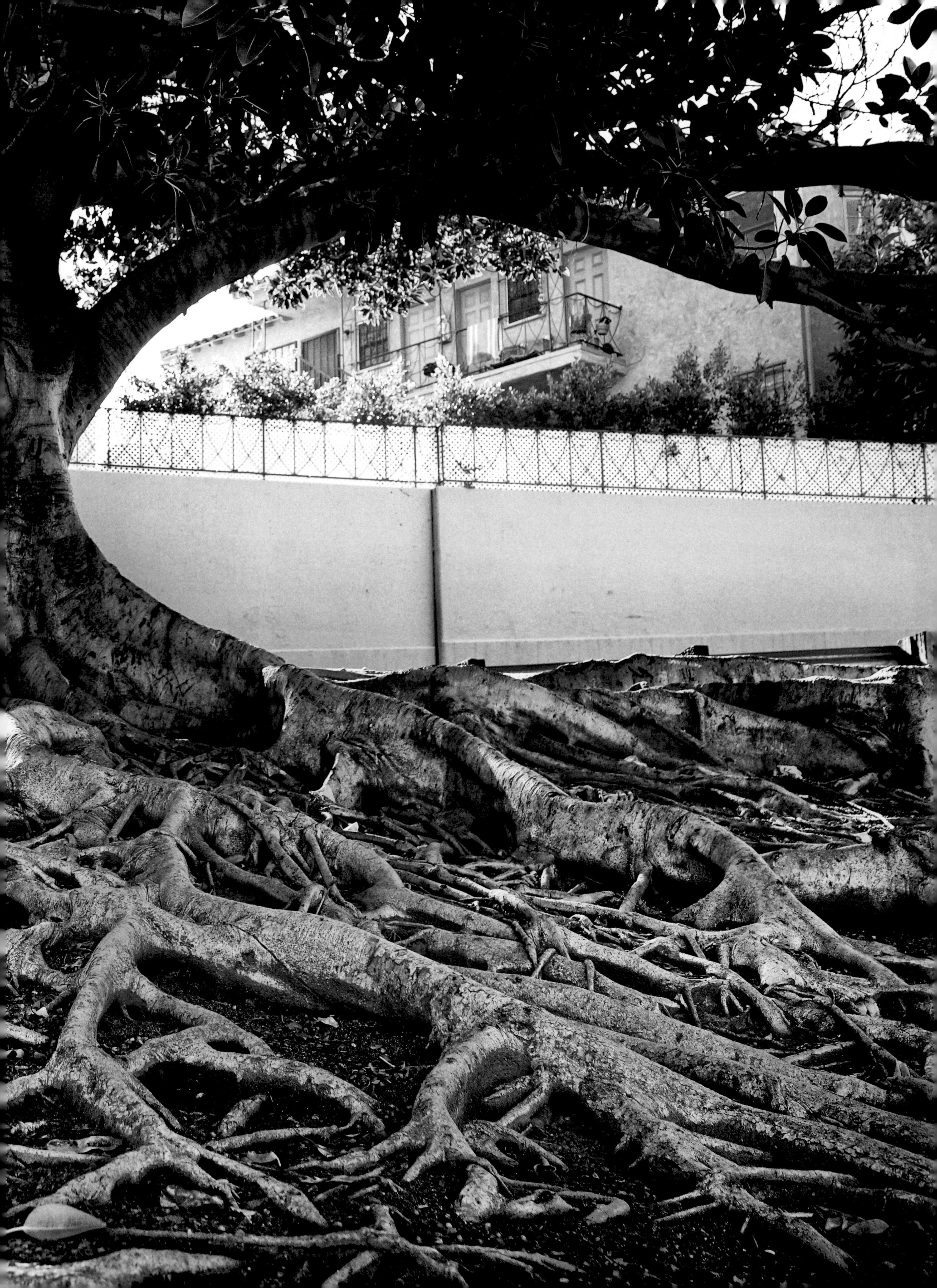

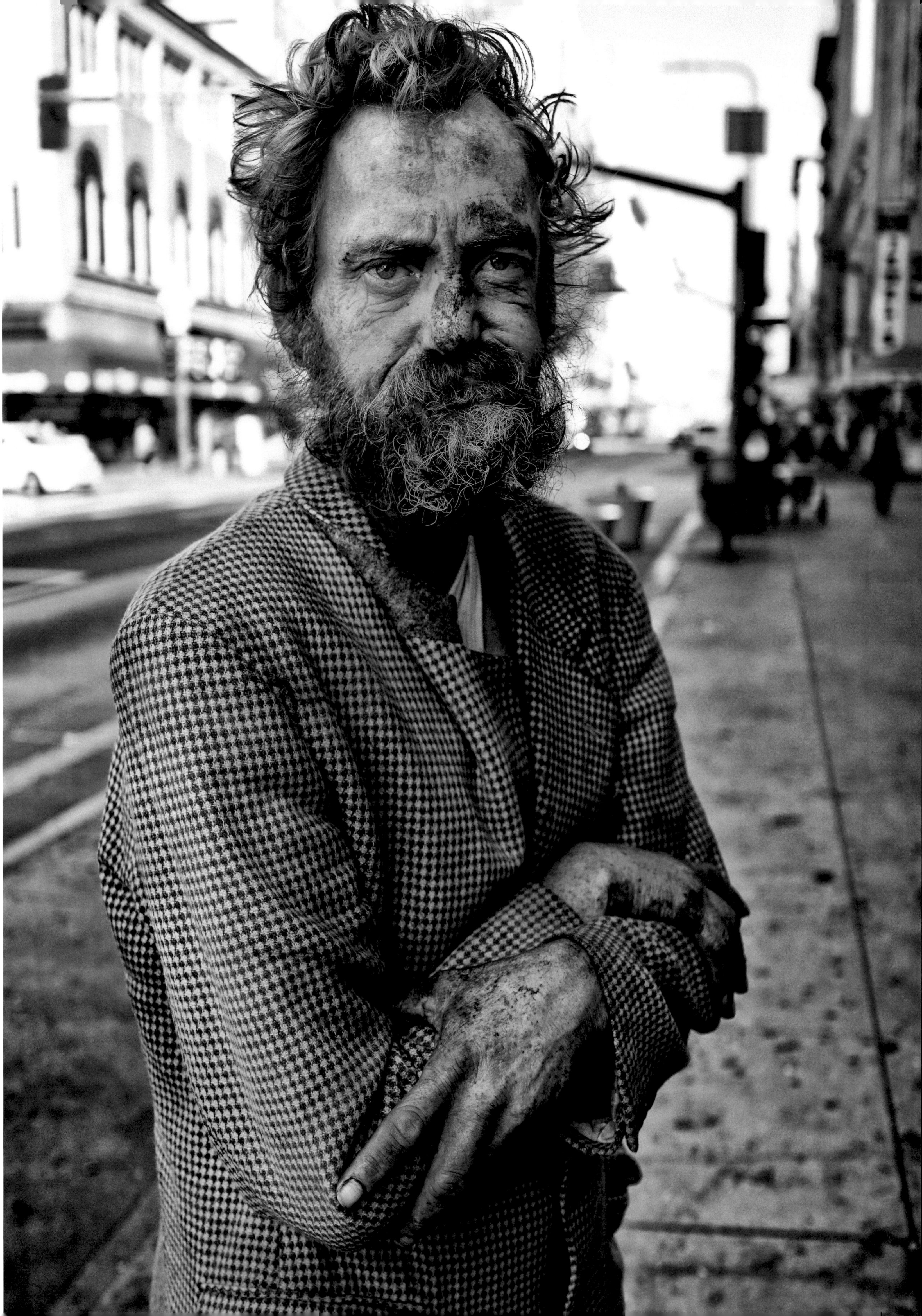

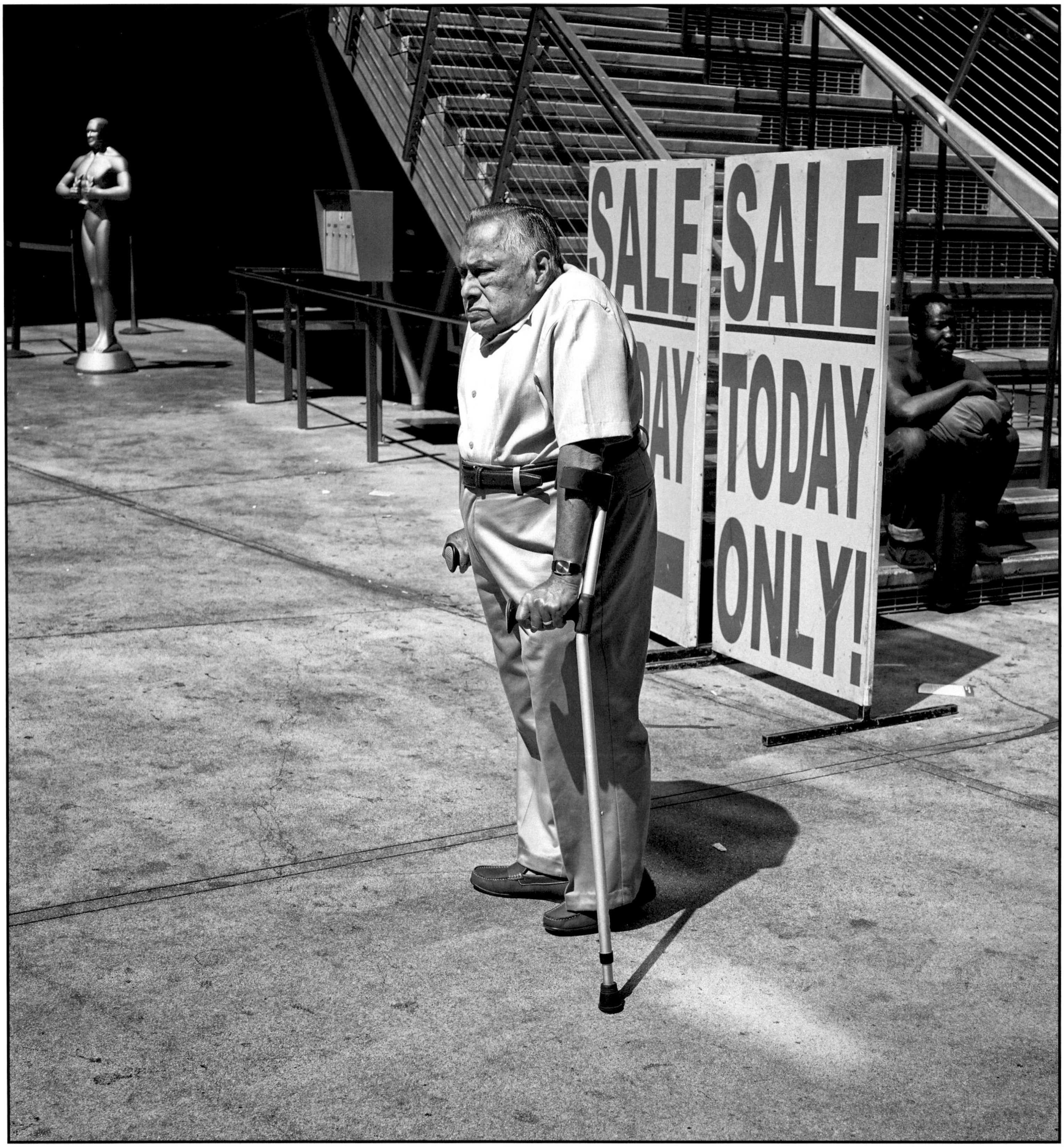
SALE
SALE
TODAY
ONLY!

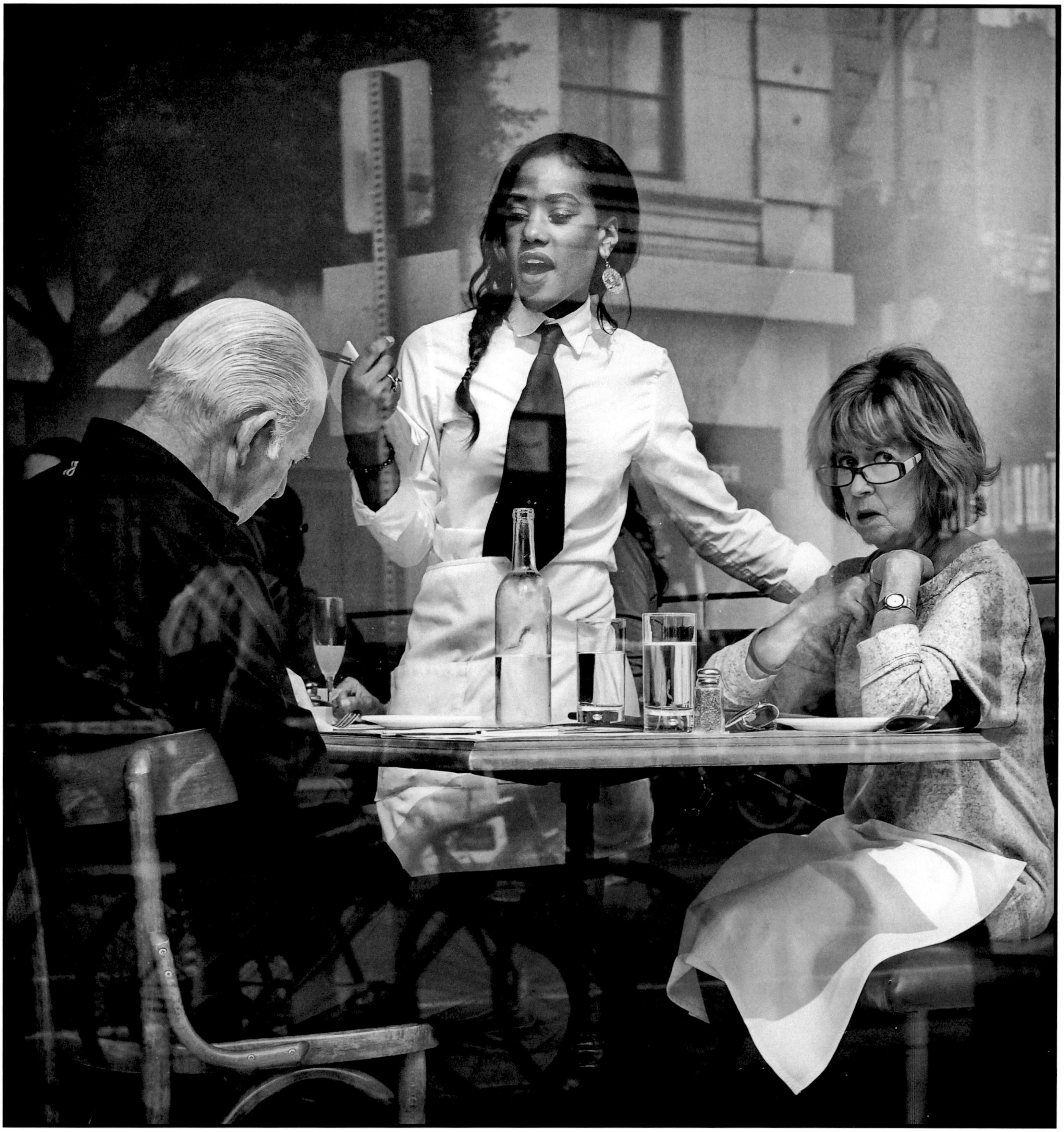

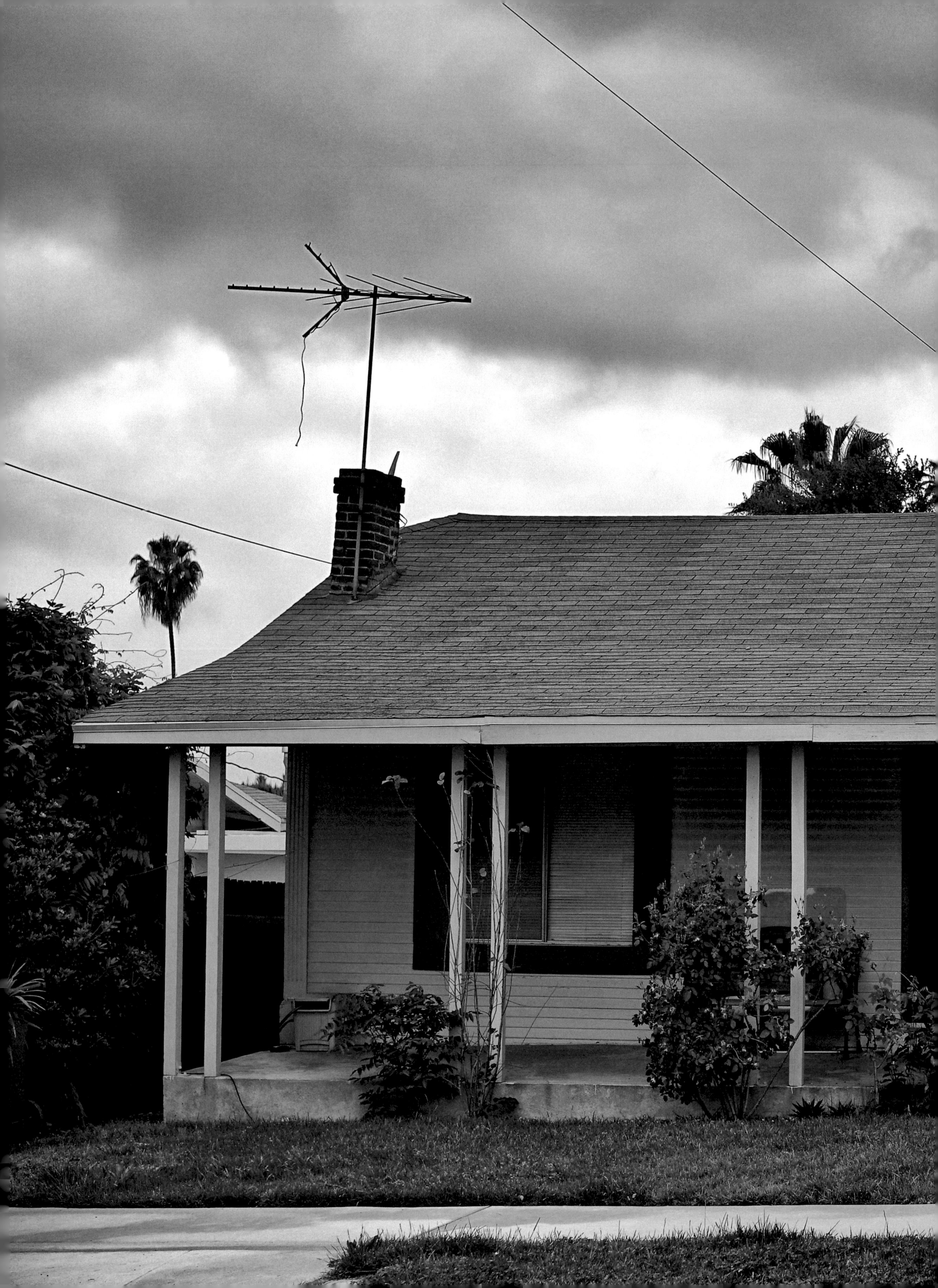

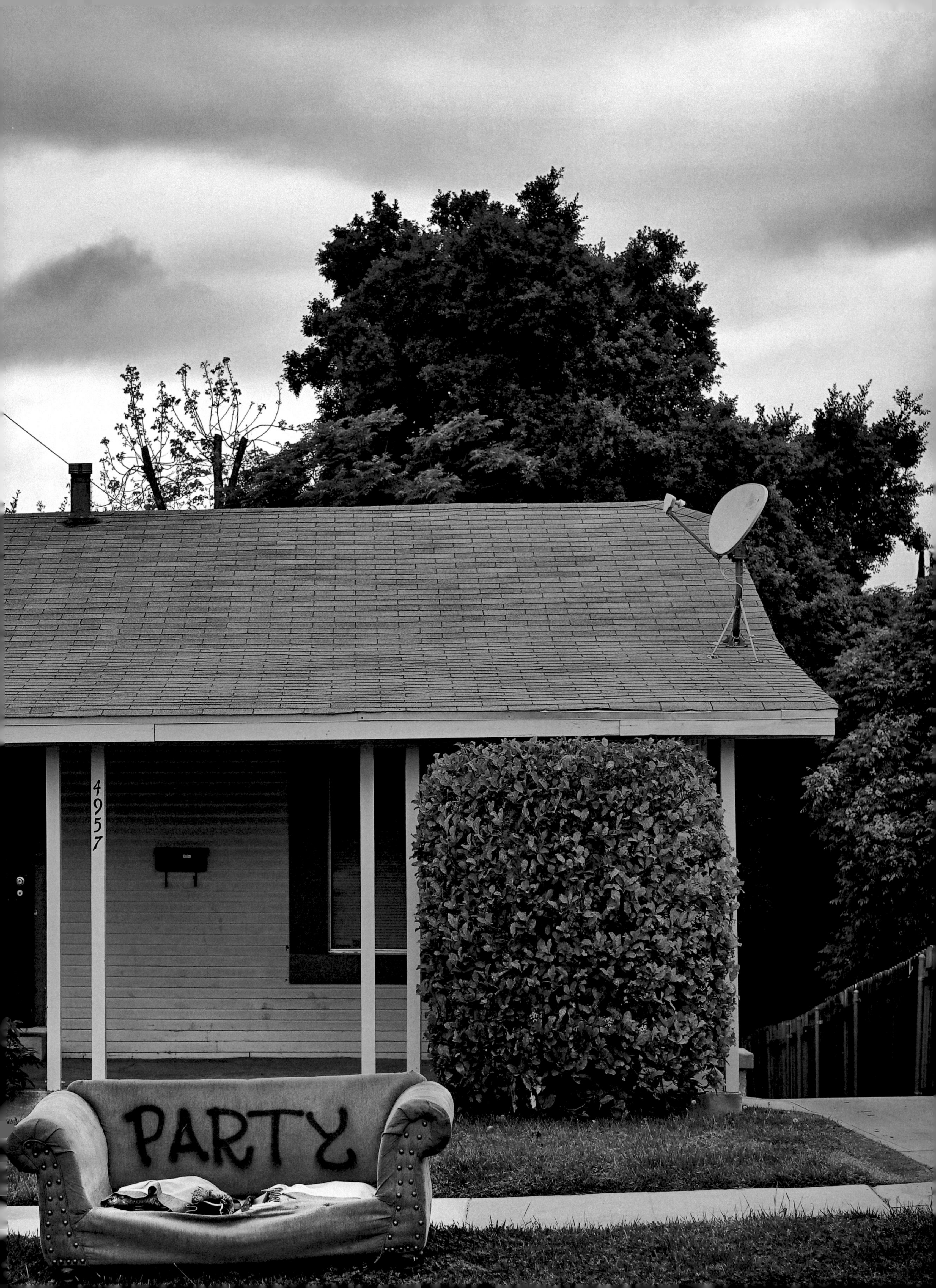
4957
PARTY

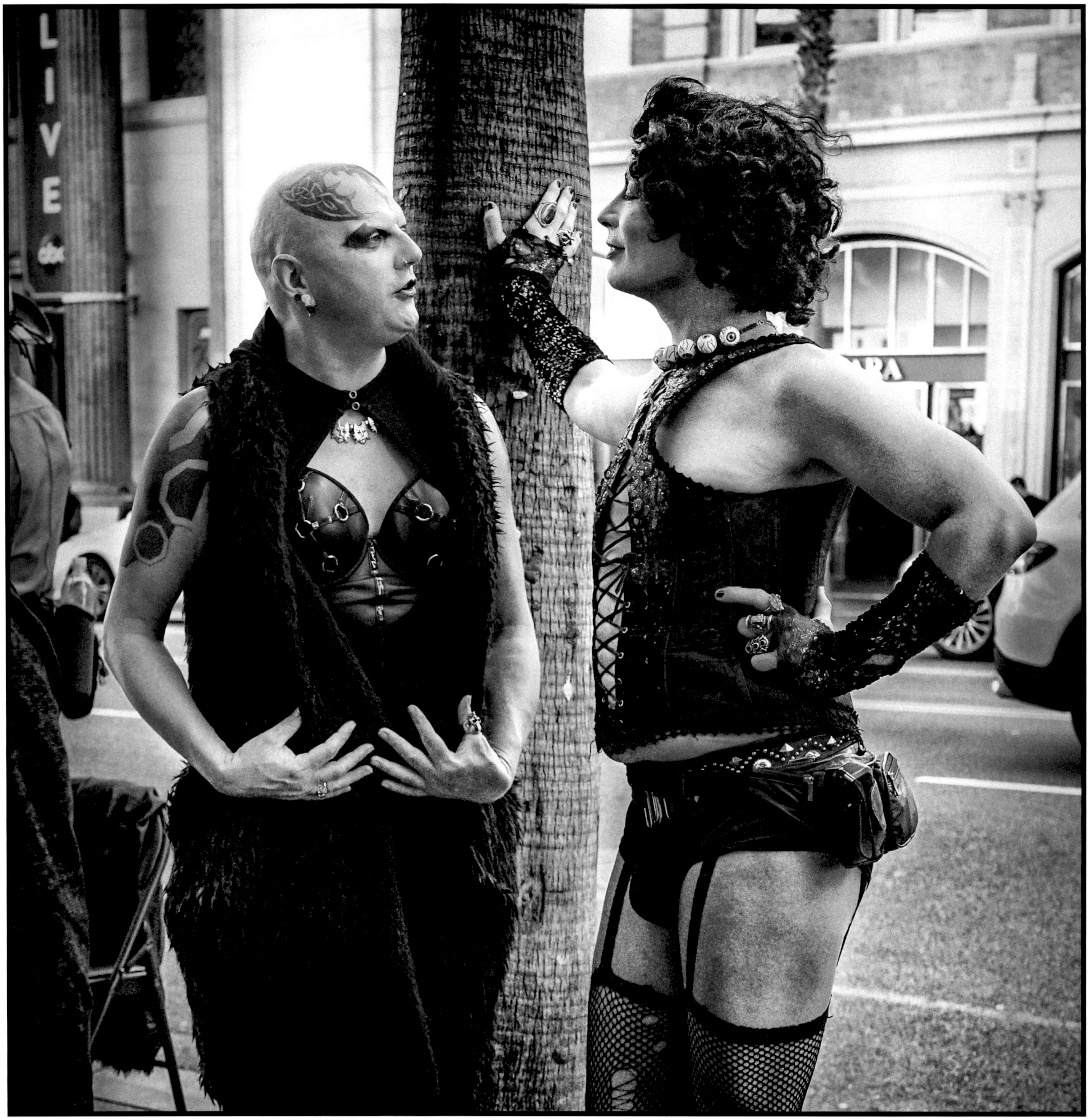
LIVE

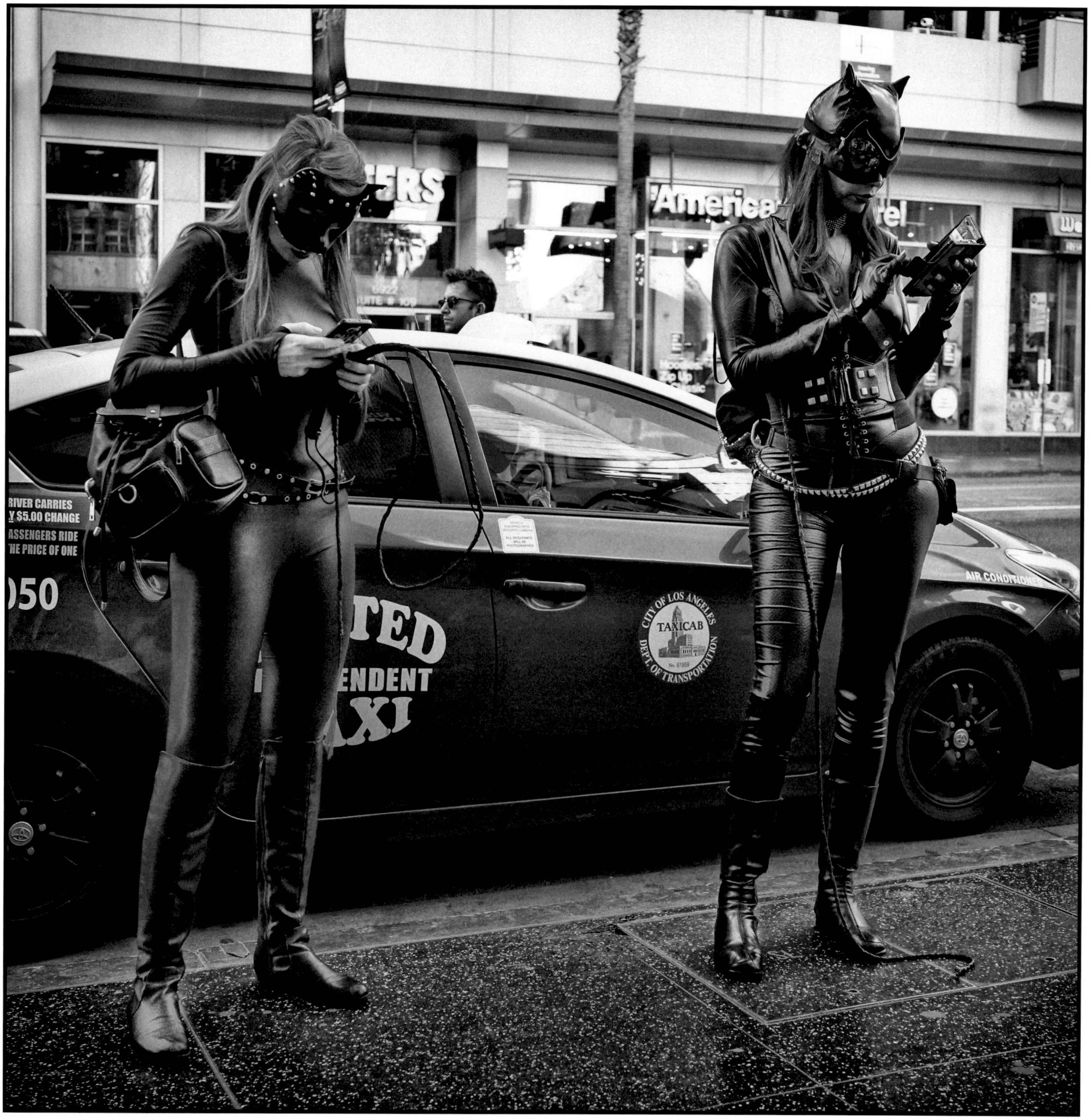
RIVER CARRIES
Y $5.00 CHANGE
ASSENGERS RIDE
THE PRICE OF ONE
050
TED
ENDENT
AXI
CITY OF LOS ANGELES
TAXICAB
DEPT. OF TRANSPORTATION
AIR CONDITIONED
America

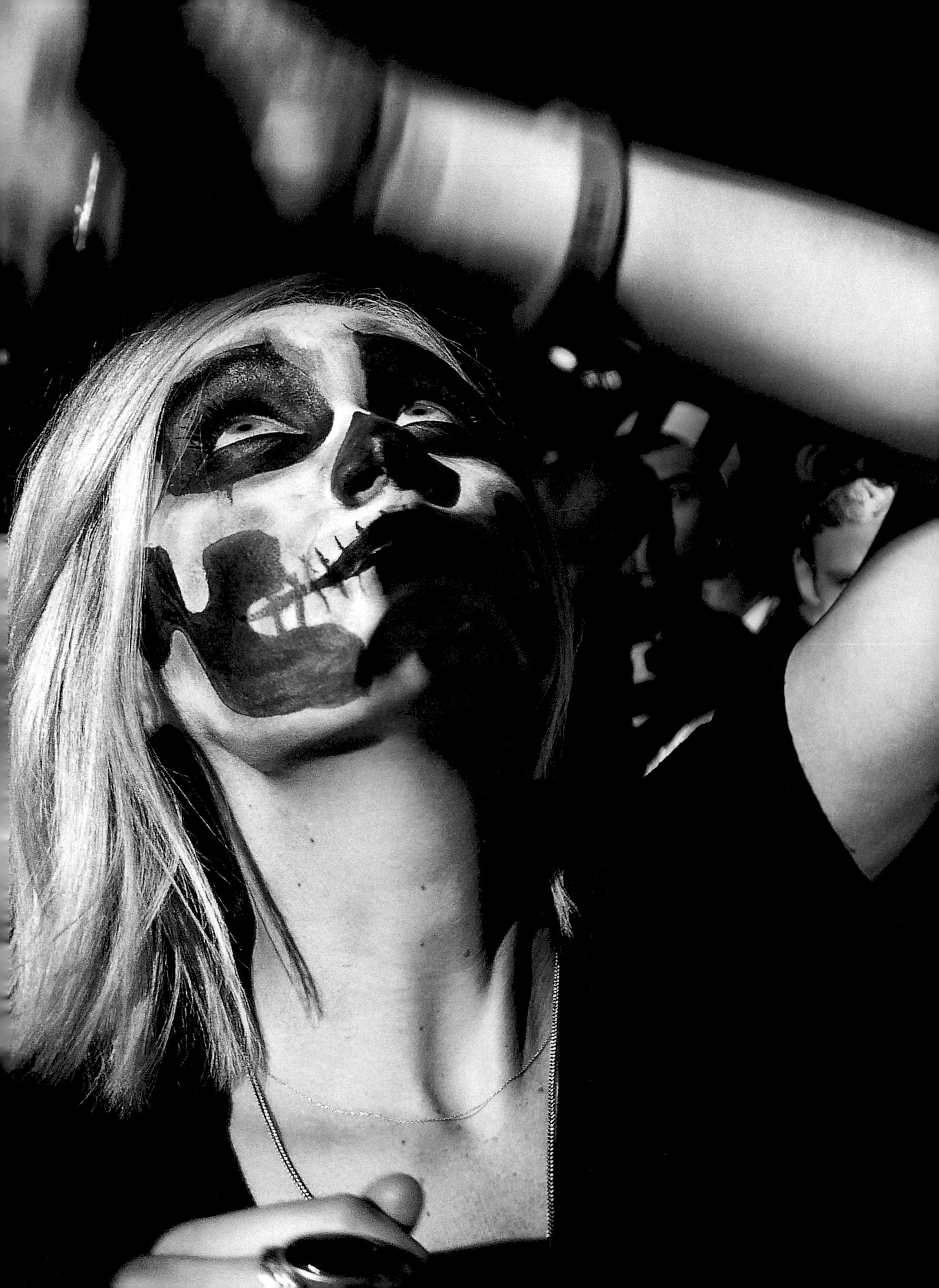

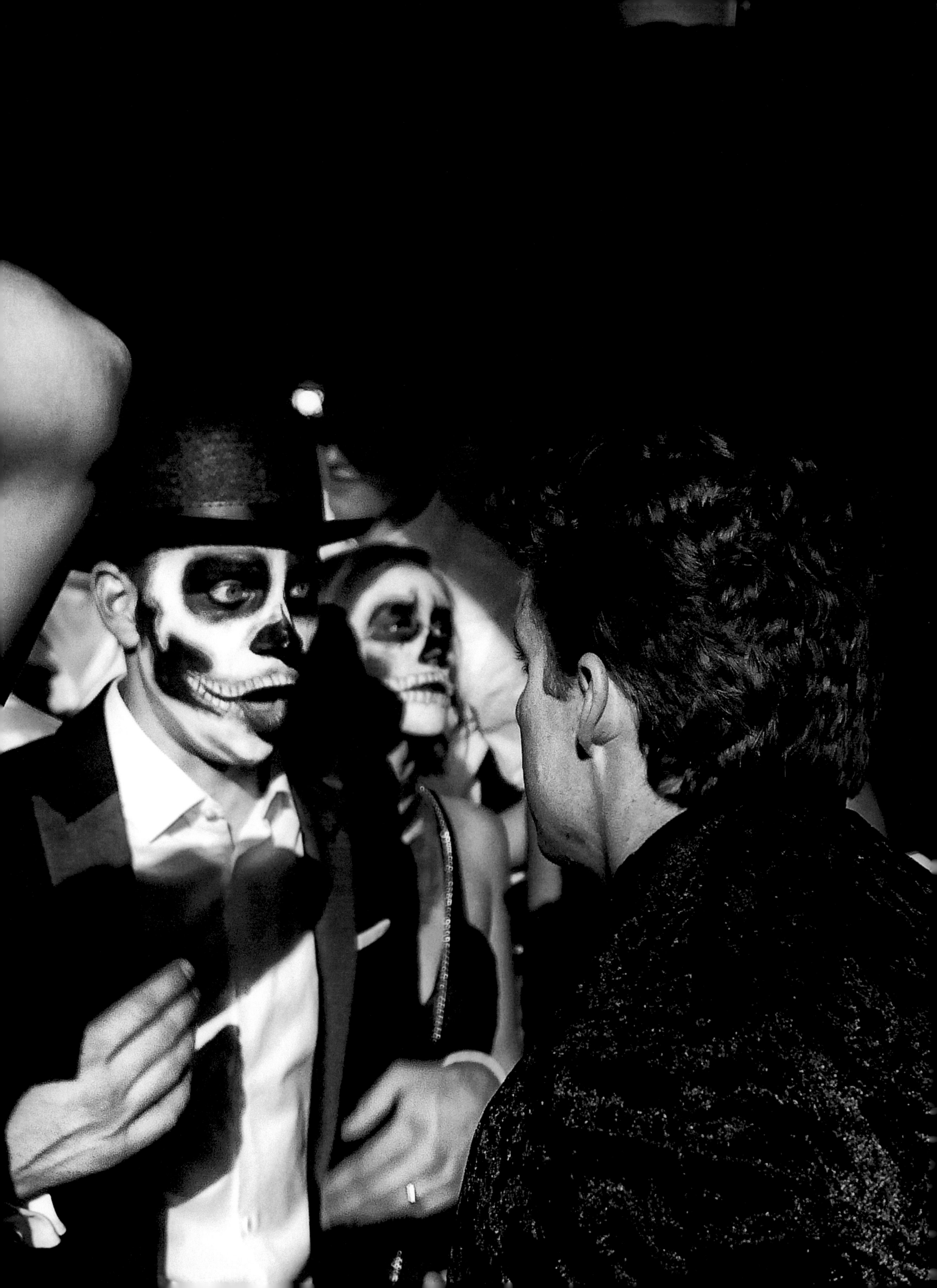

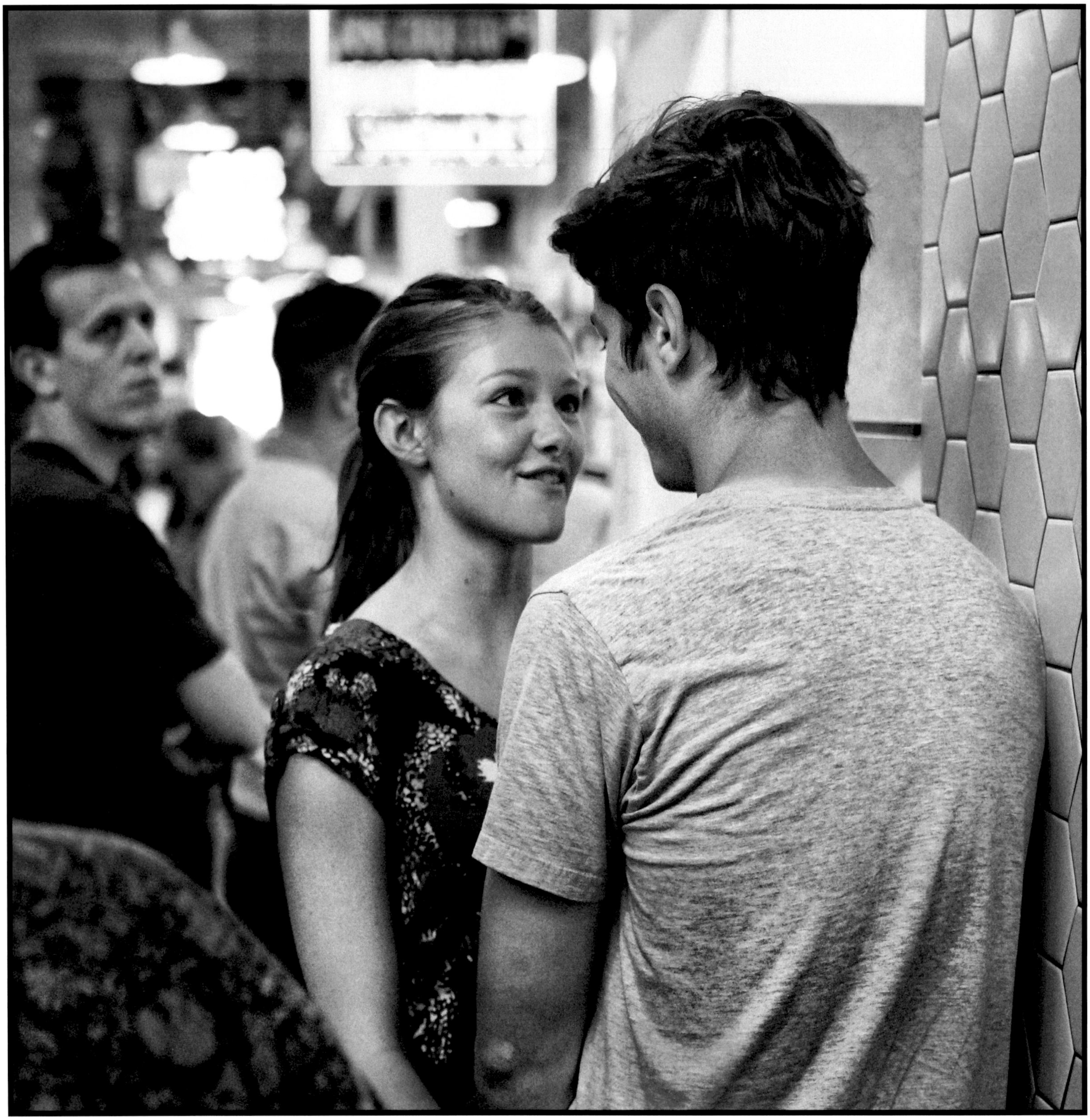

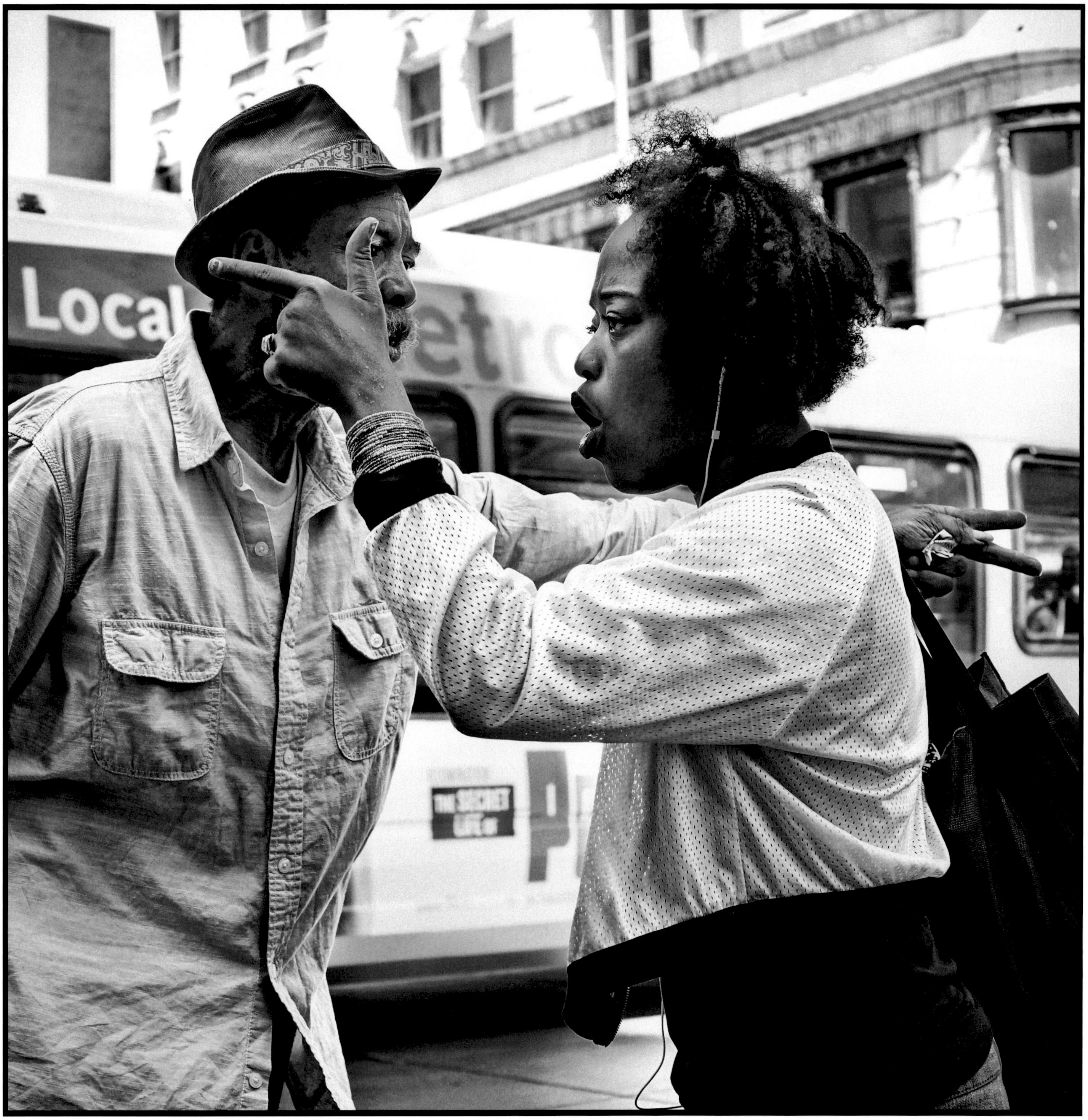
Local
THE SECRET

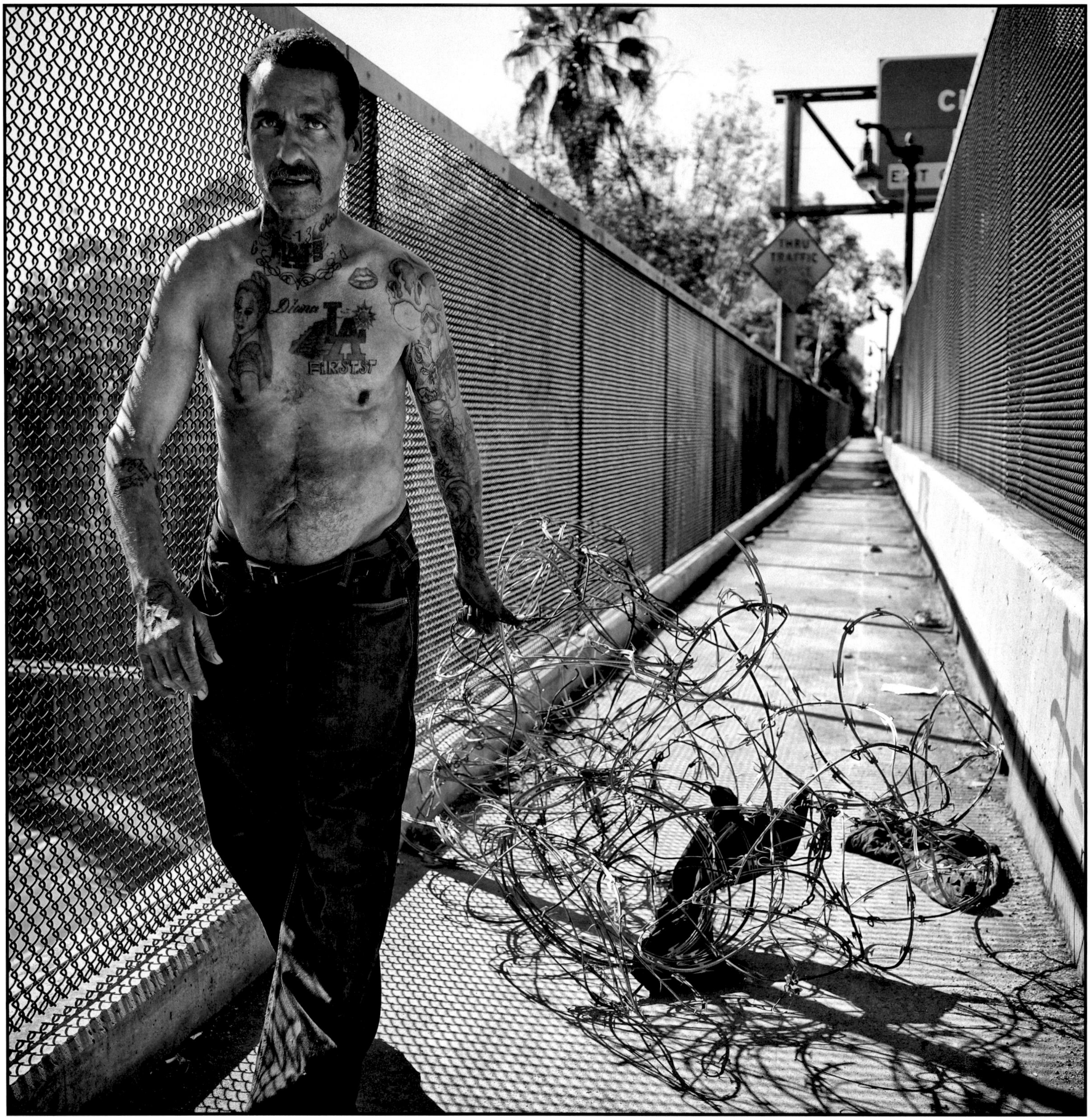
THRU TRAFFIC

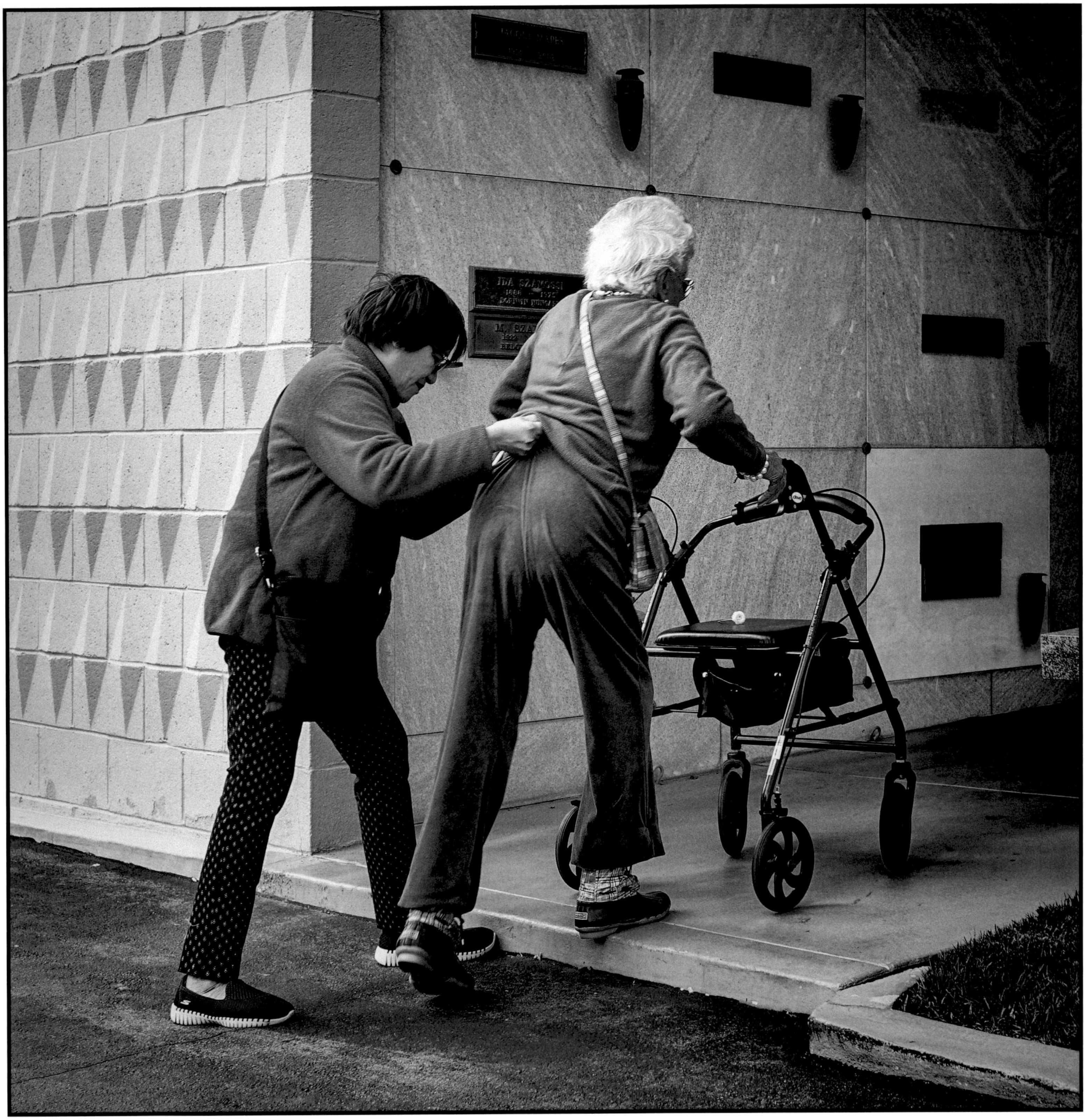

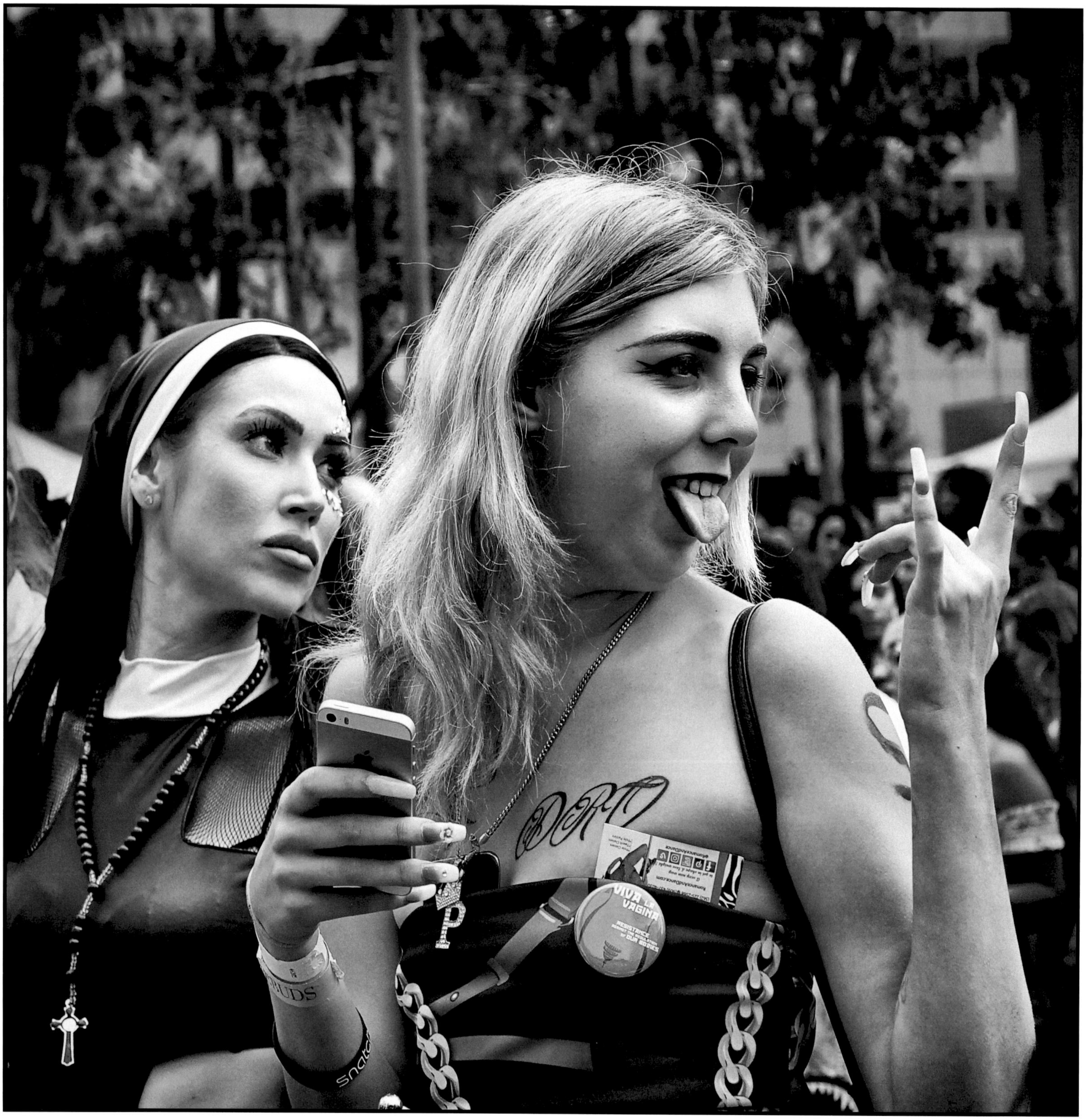
VIVA LA VAGINA
RESISTANCE

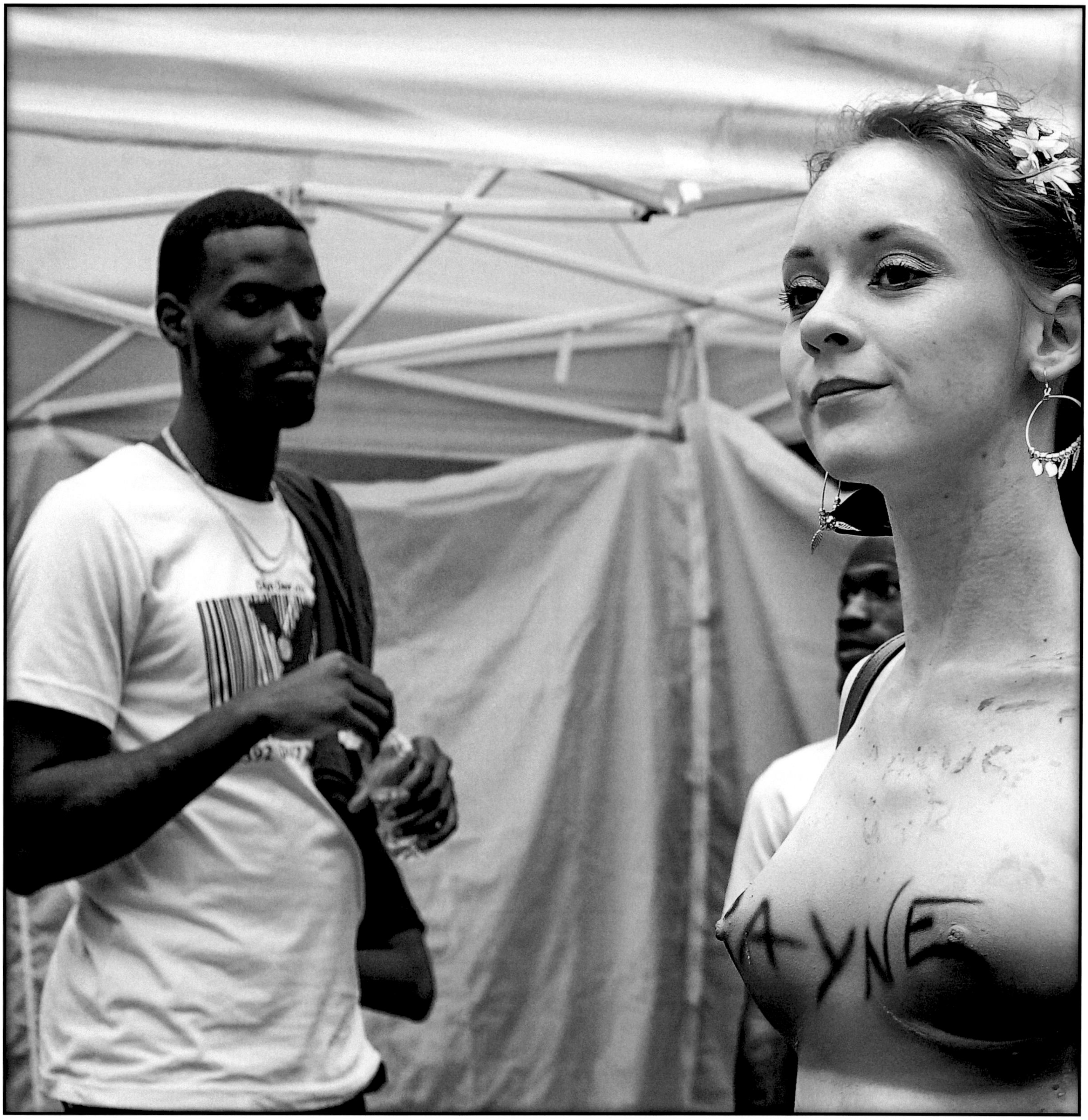
AYNE

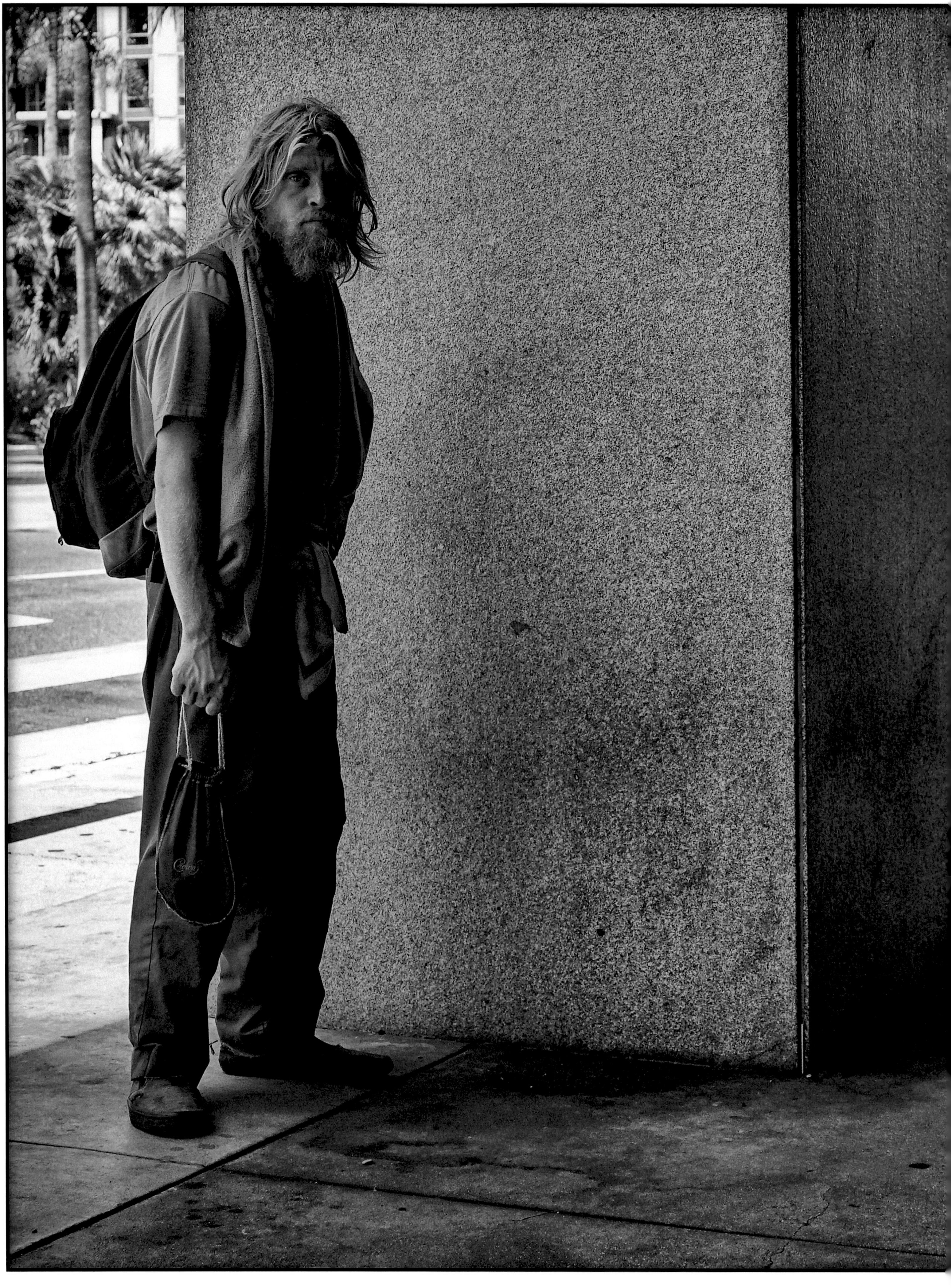

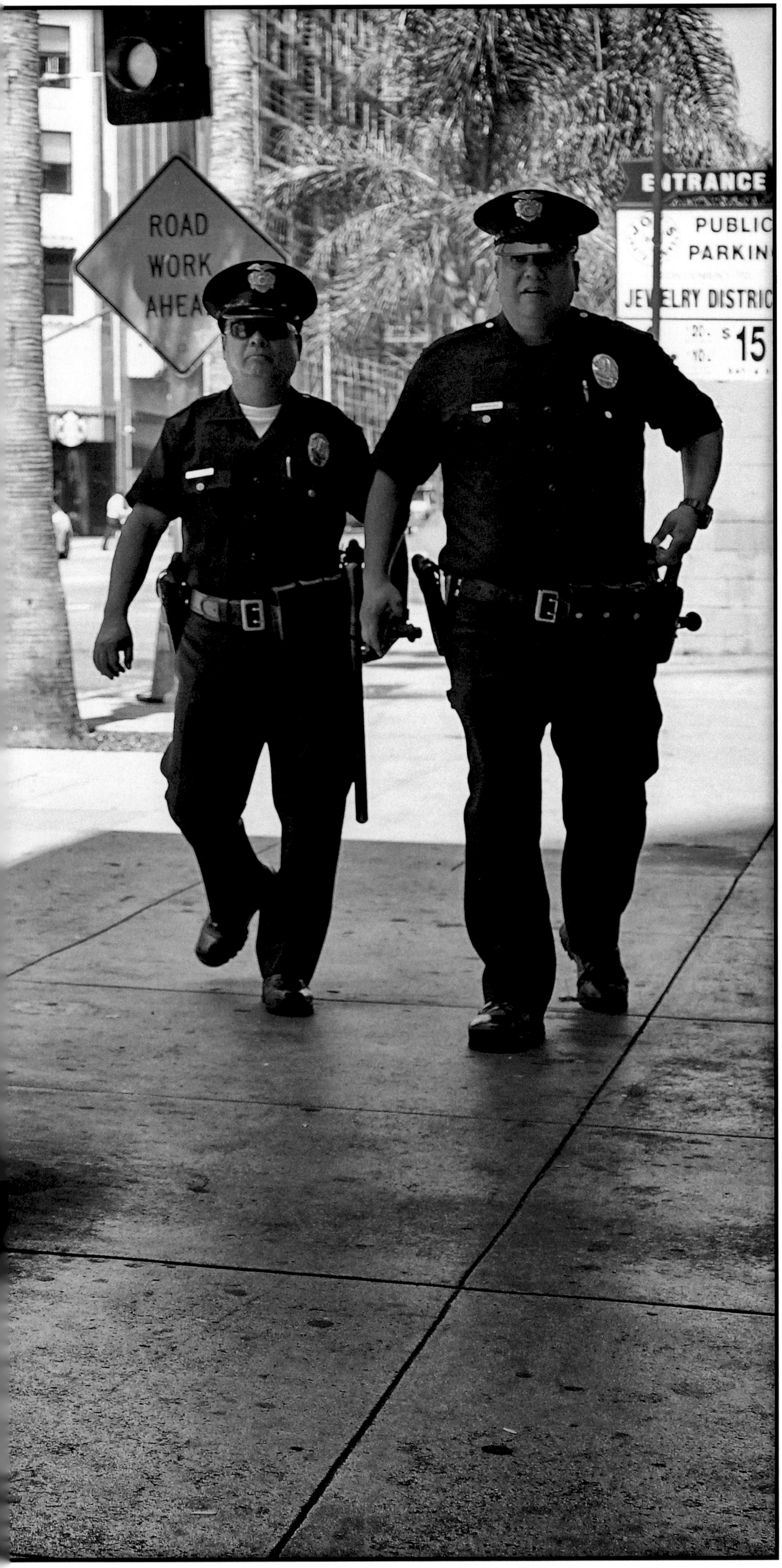
ROAD
WORK

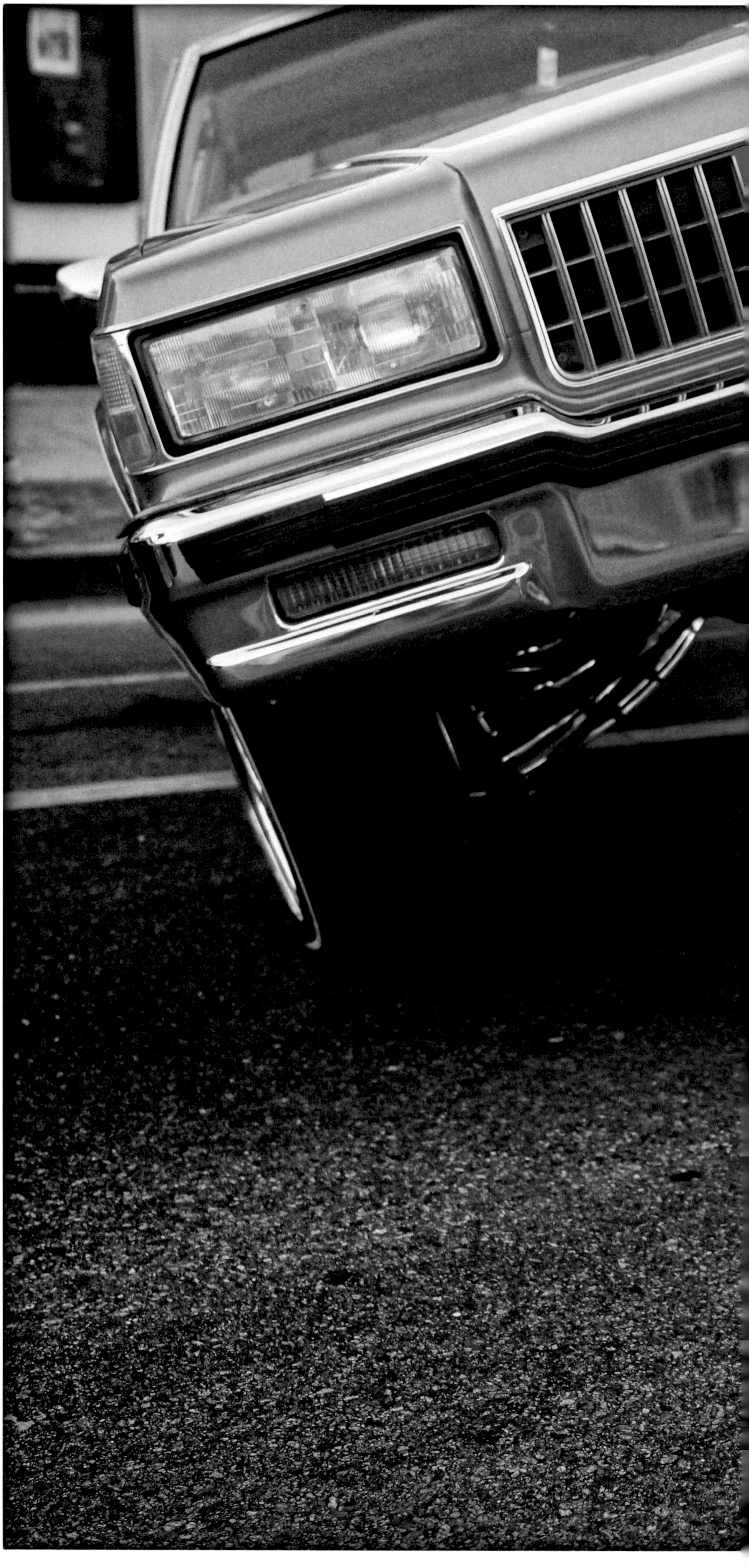

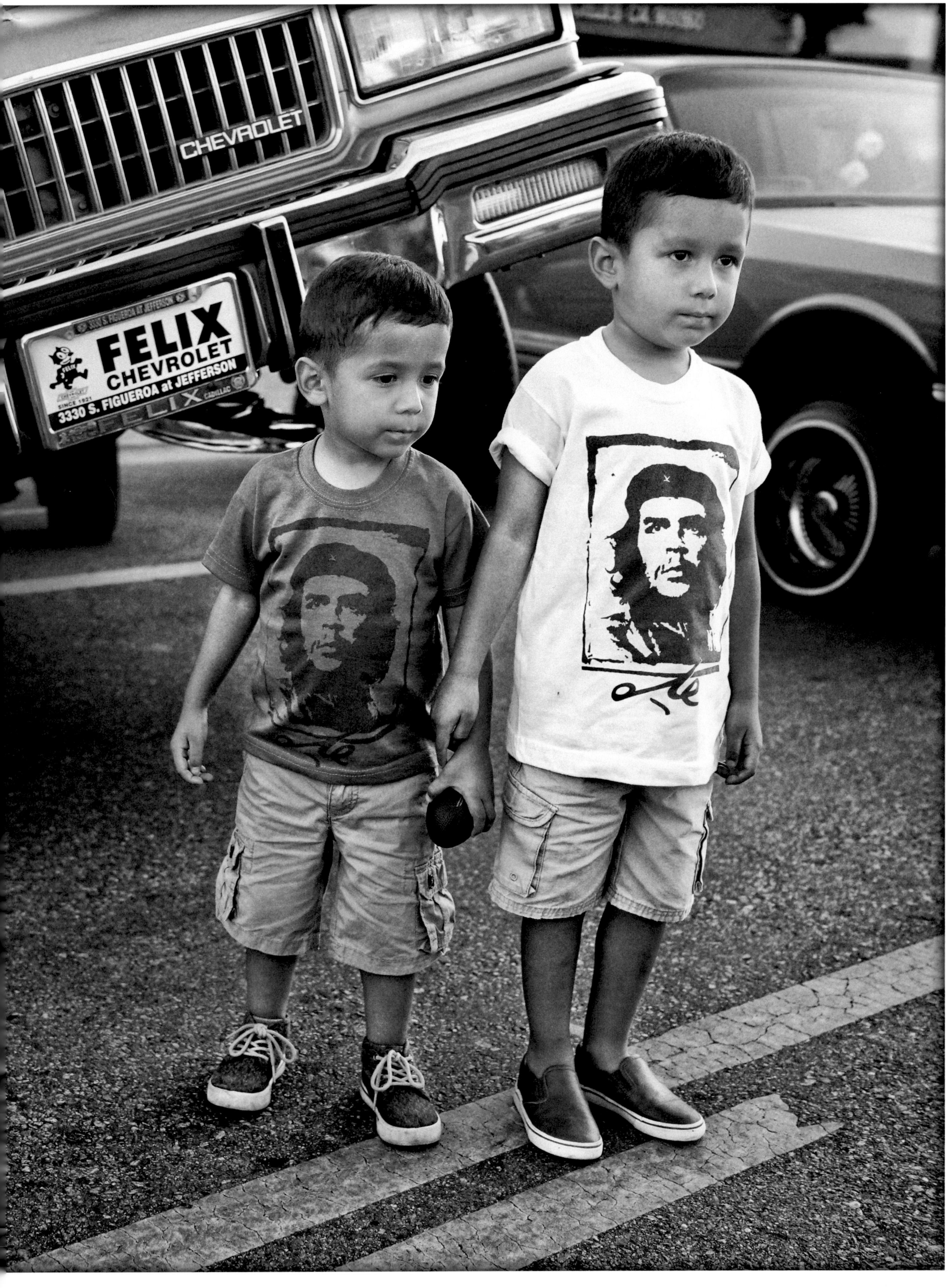
CHEVROLET
FELIX
CHEVROLET
FIGUEROA at JEFFERSON
3330 S. FIGUEROA at JEFFERSON

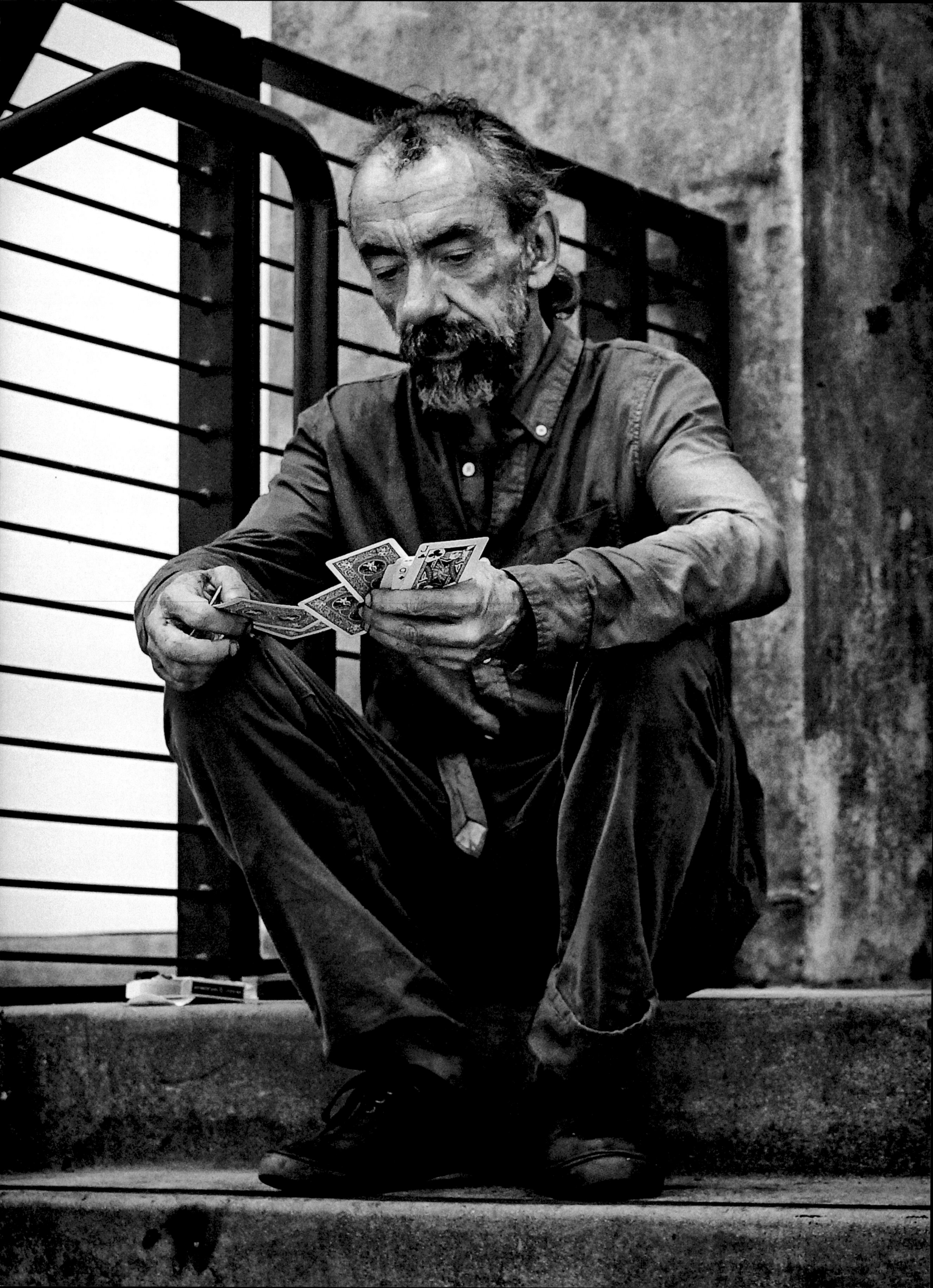

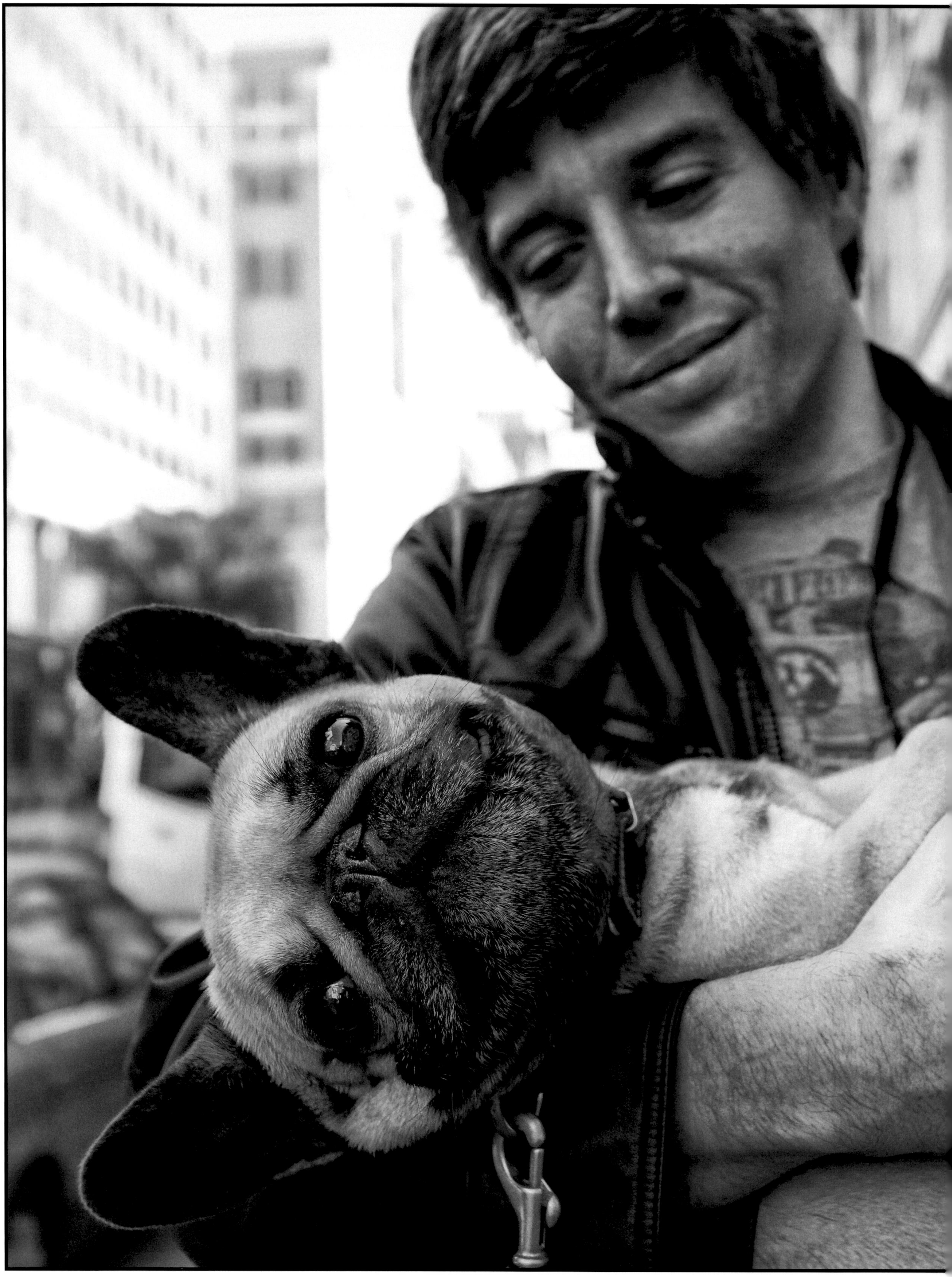

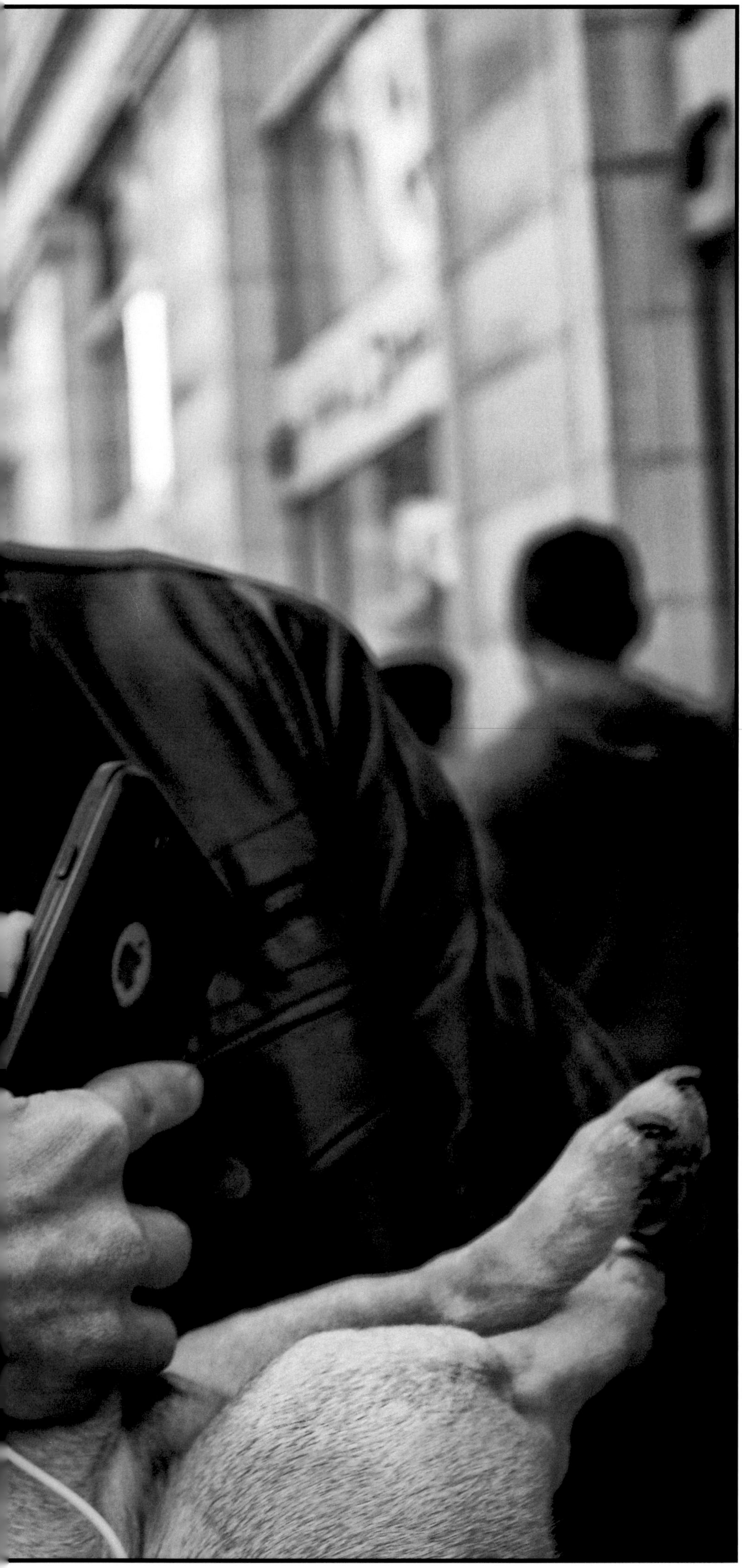

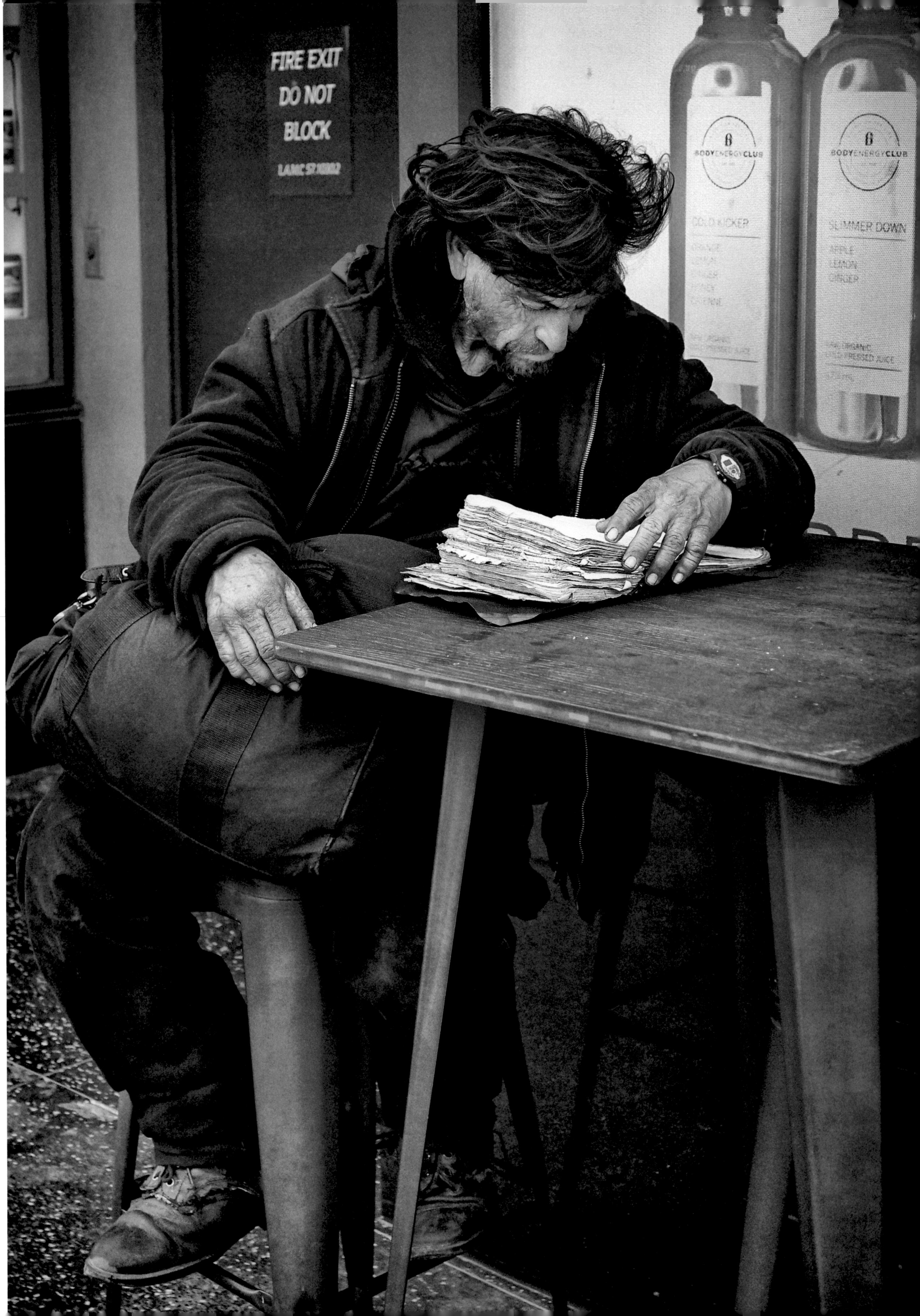
FIRE EXIT
DO NOT
BLOCK
BODYENERGYCLUB
COLD KICKER
BODYENERGYCLUB
SLIMMER DOWN
APPLE
LEMON
GINGER

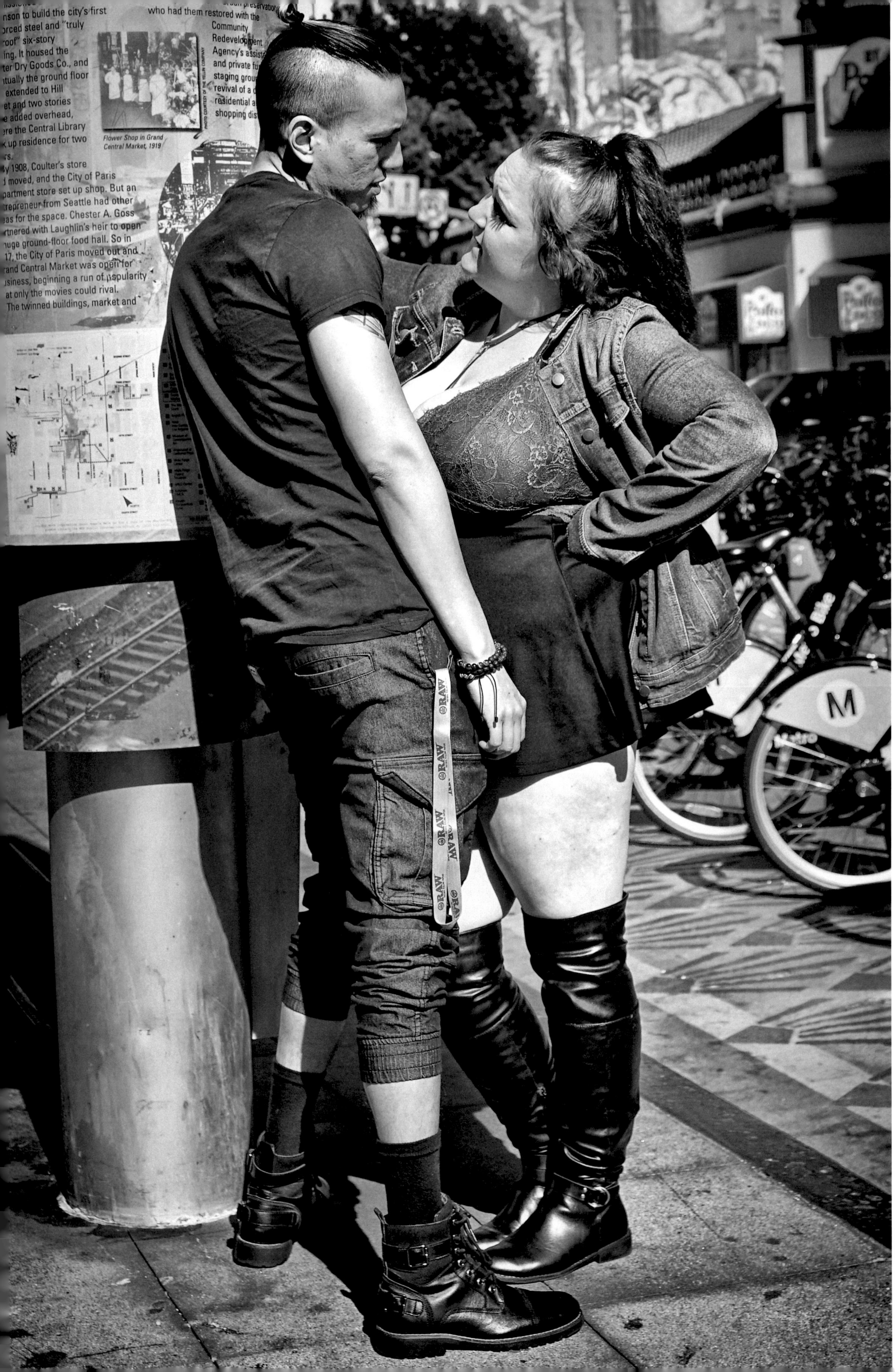

who had them restored with the
Community
Redevelopment
Flower Shop in Grand
Central Market, 1919
nson to build the city's first
orced steel and "truly
ing. It housed the
er Dry Goods Co., and
ntually the ground floor
extended to Hill
et and two stories
e added overhead,
ere the Central Library
k up residence for two
y 1908, Coulter's store
d moved, and the City of Paris
partment store set up shop. But an
trepreneur from Seattle had other
as for the space. Chester A. Goss
rtnered with Laughlin's heir to open
huge ground-floor food hall. So in
17, the City of Paris moved out and
and Central Market was open for
usiness, beginning a run of popularity
at only the movies could rival.
The twinned buildings, market and
RAW
M

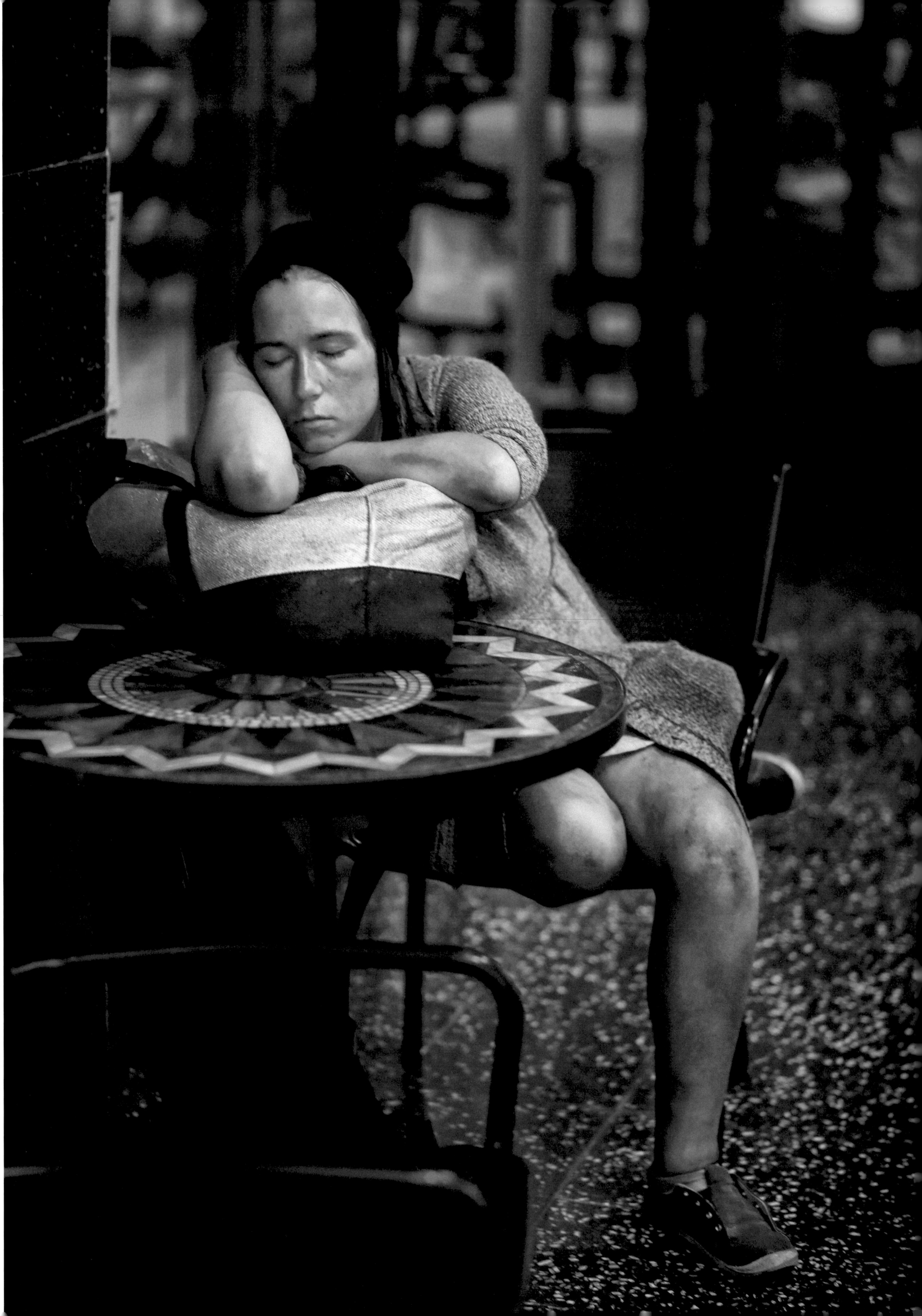

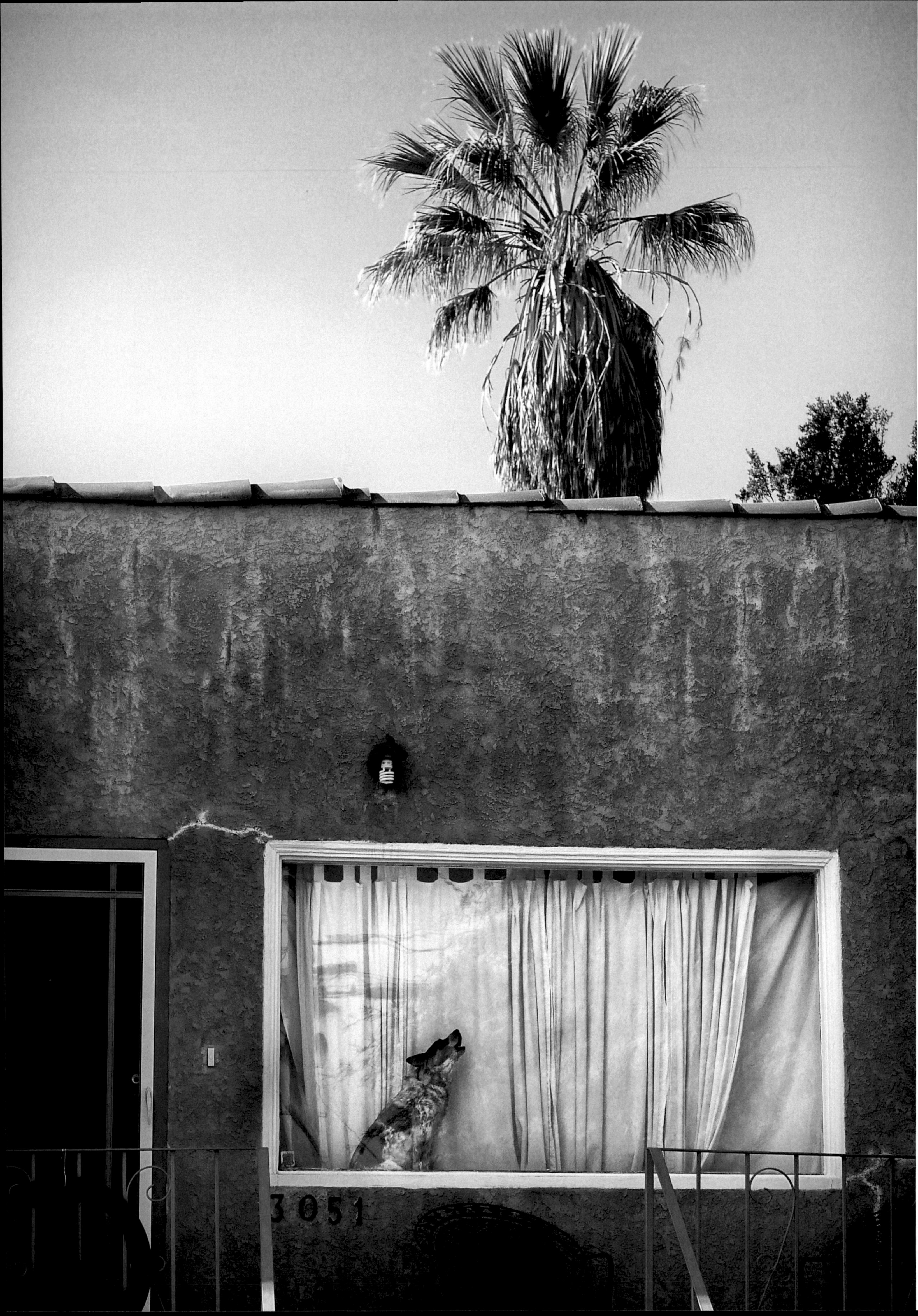
3051

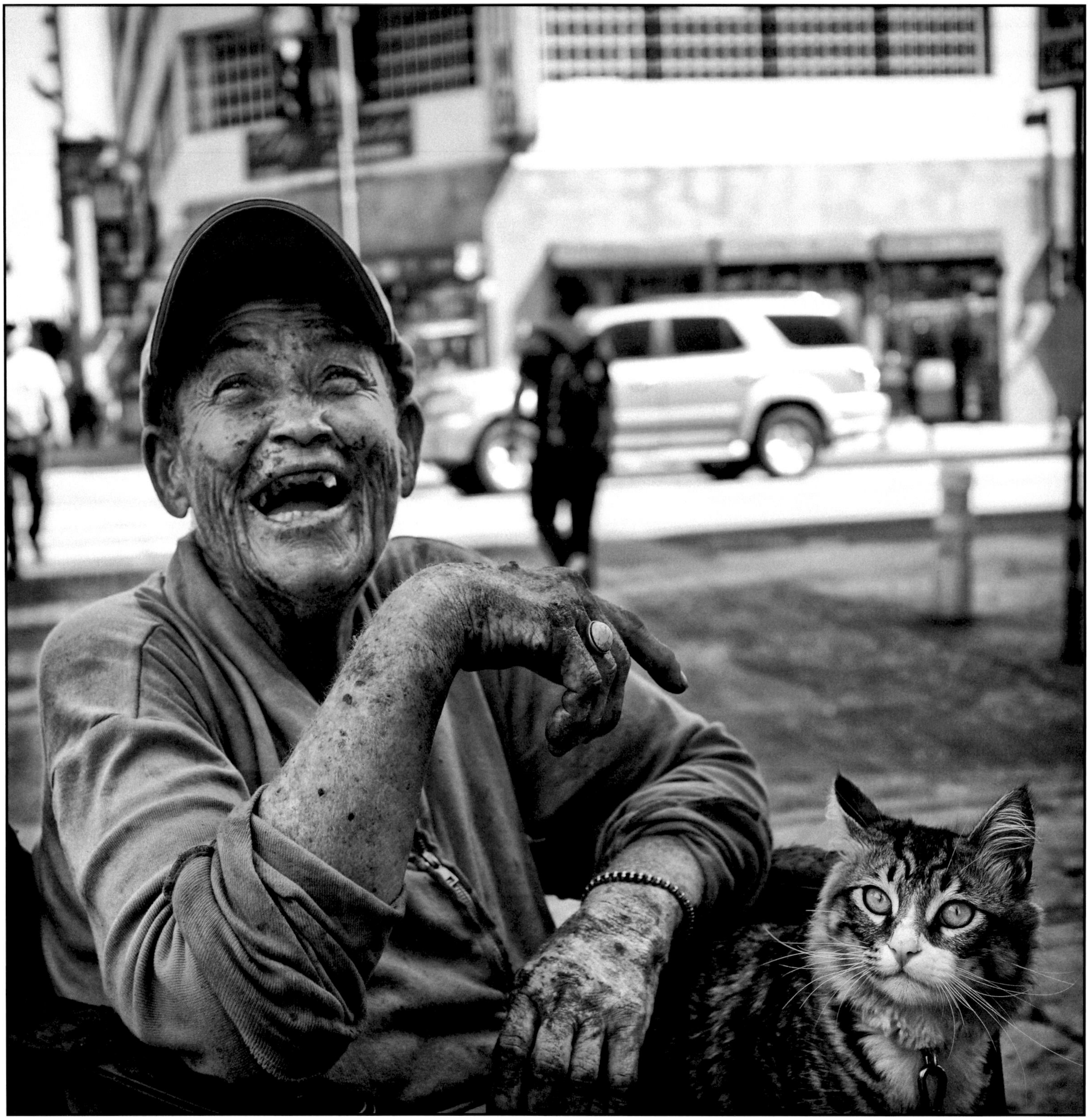

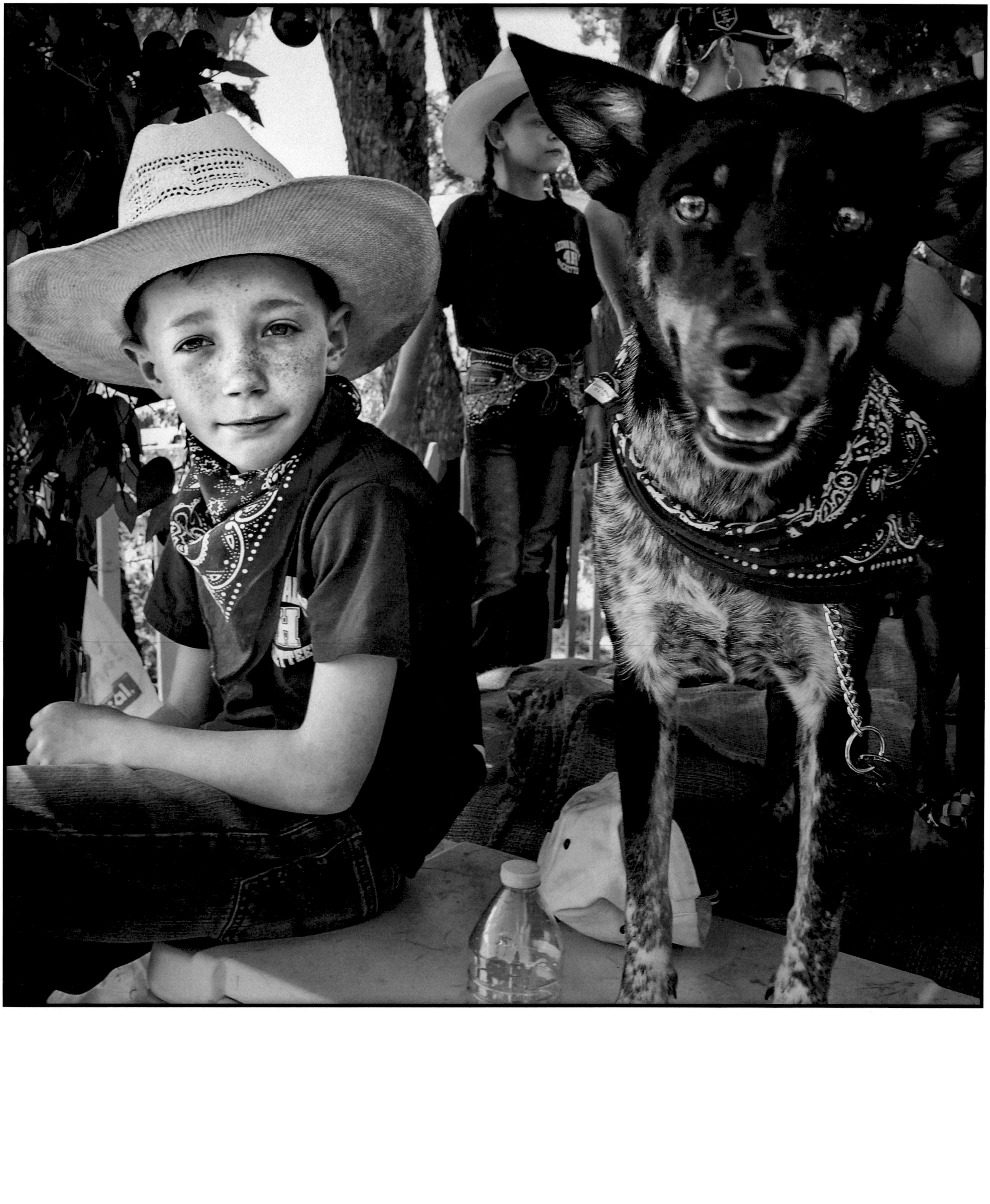

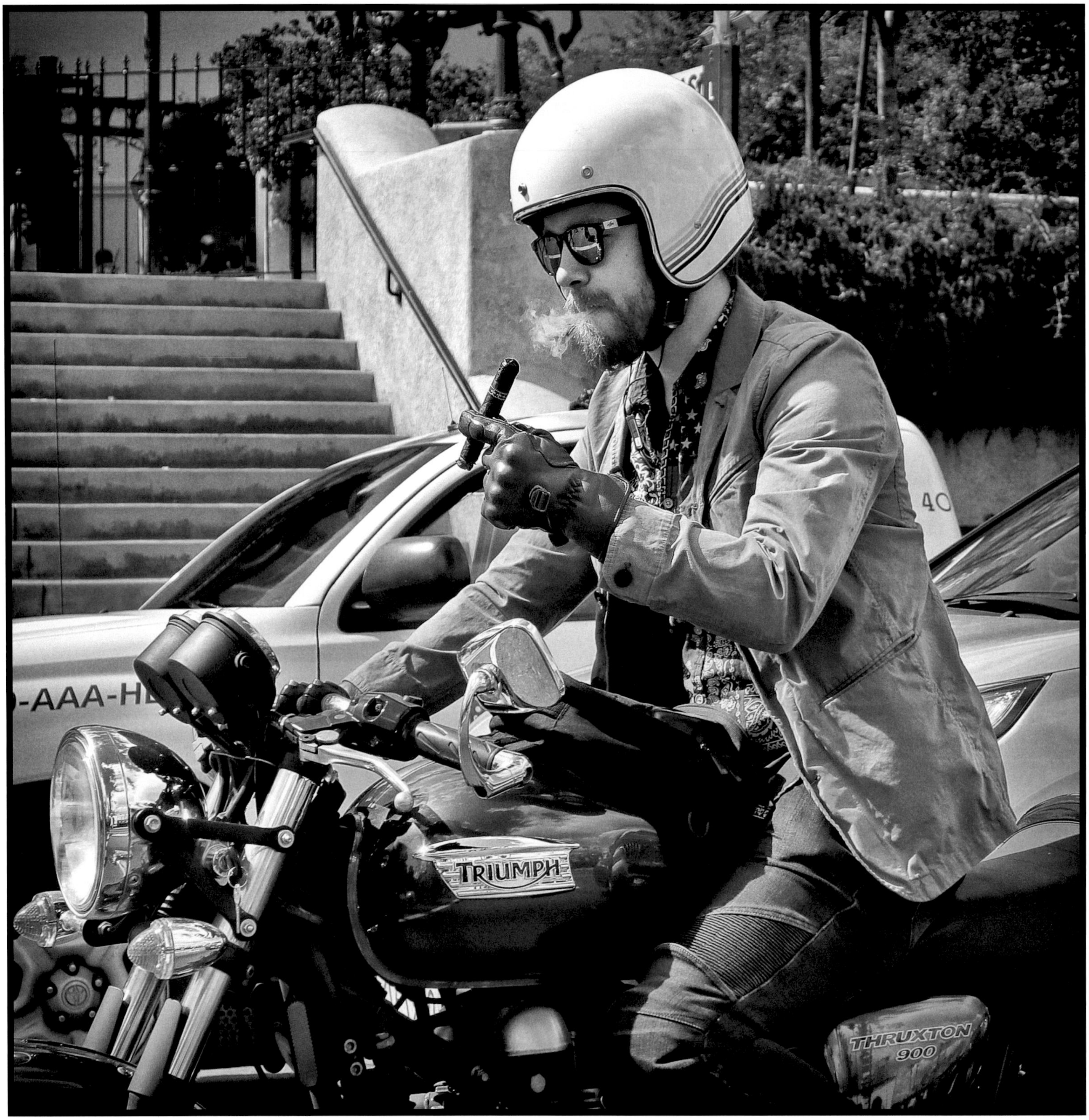
TRIUMPH
THRUXTON
900

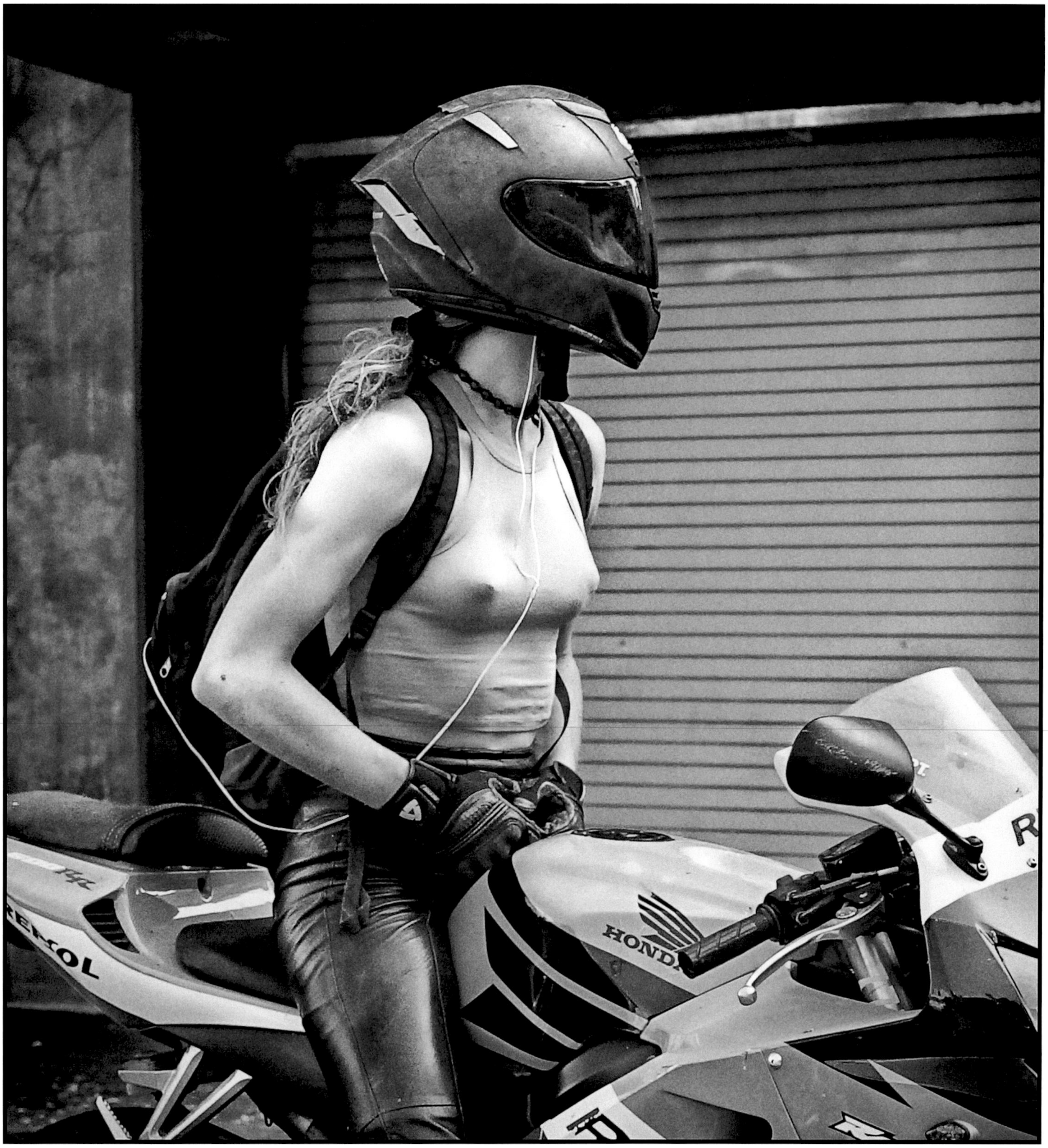

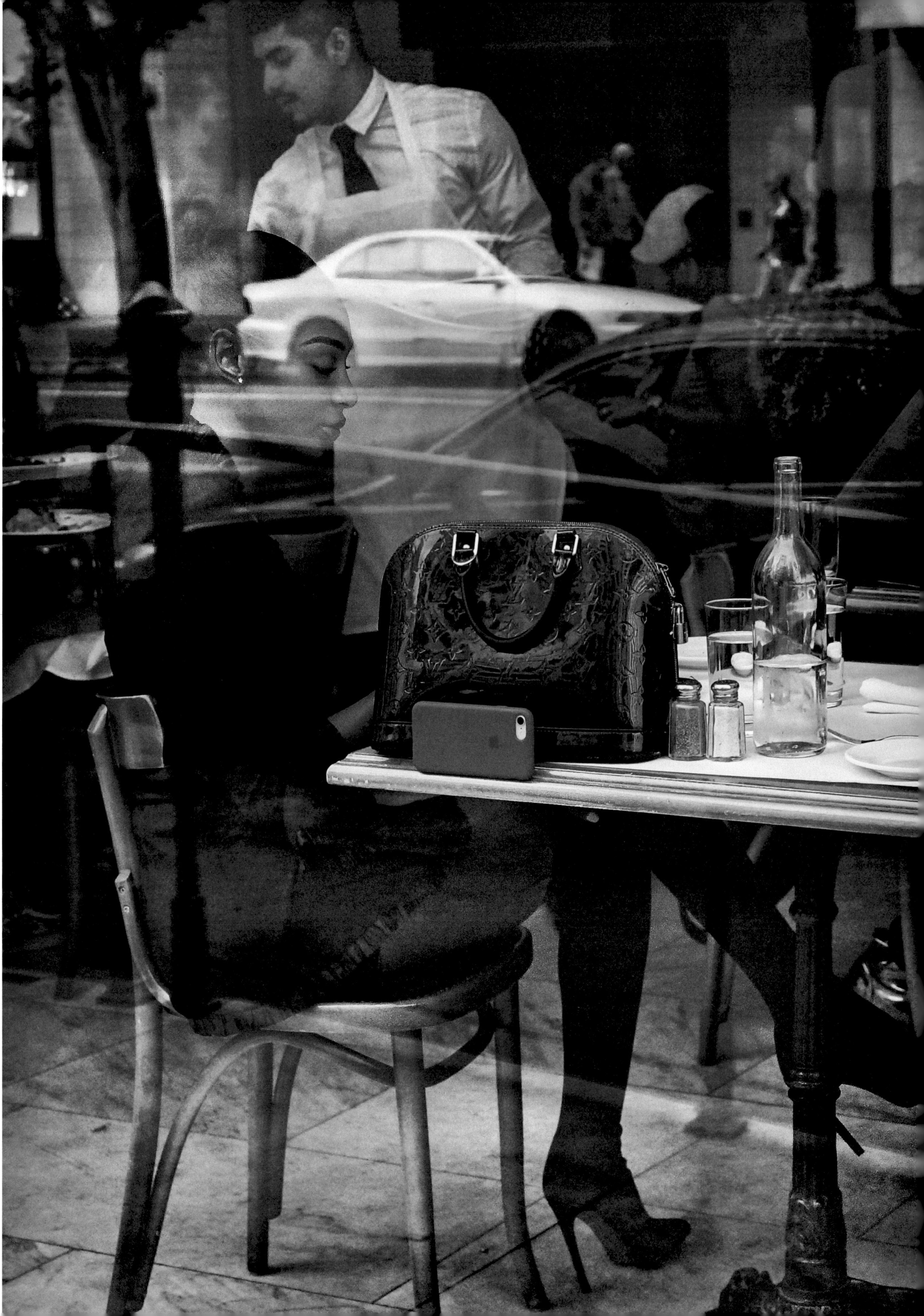

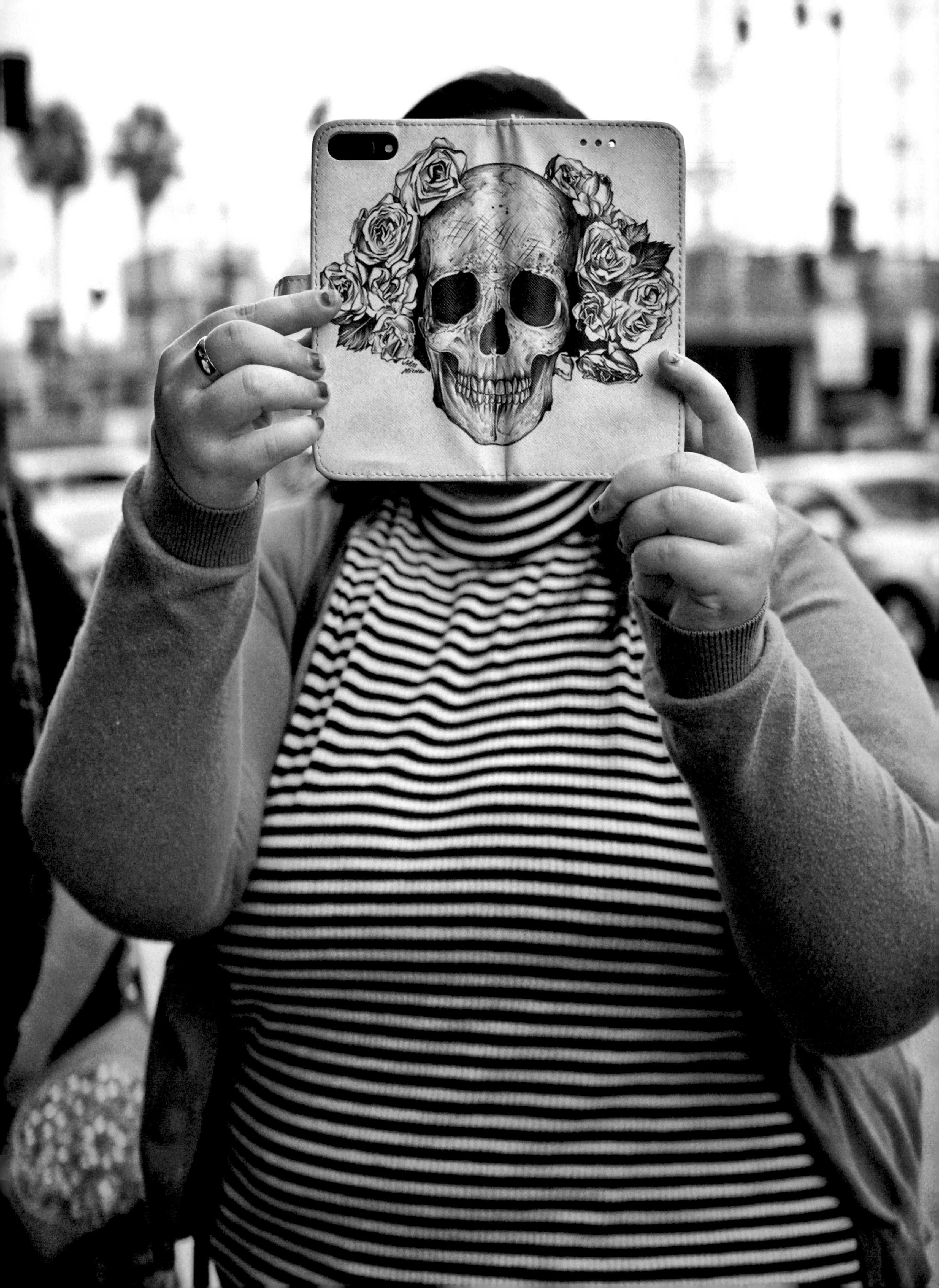

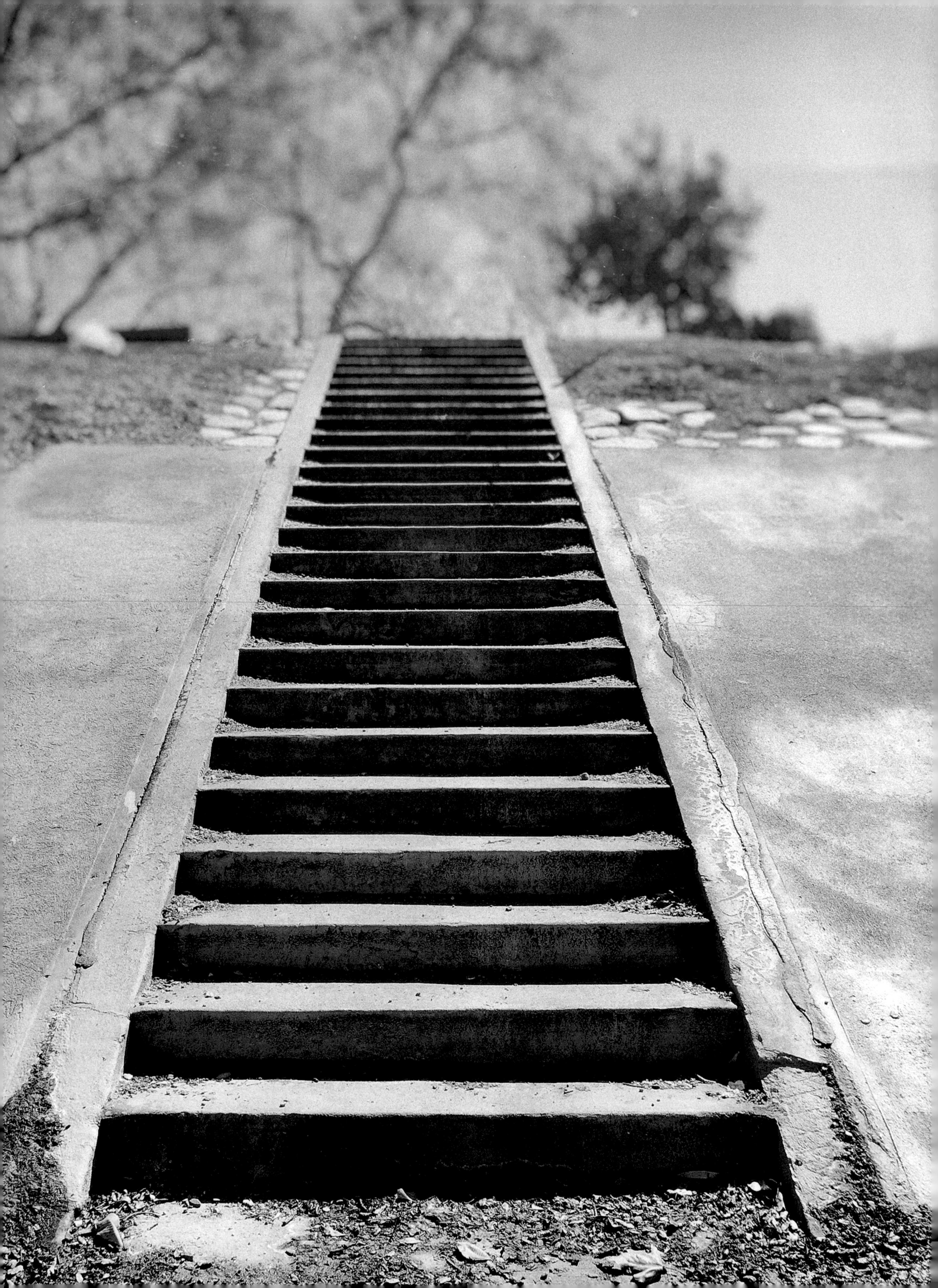

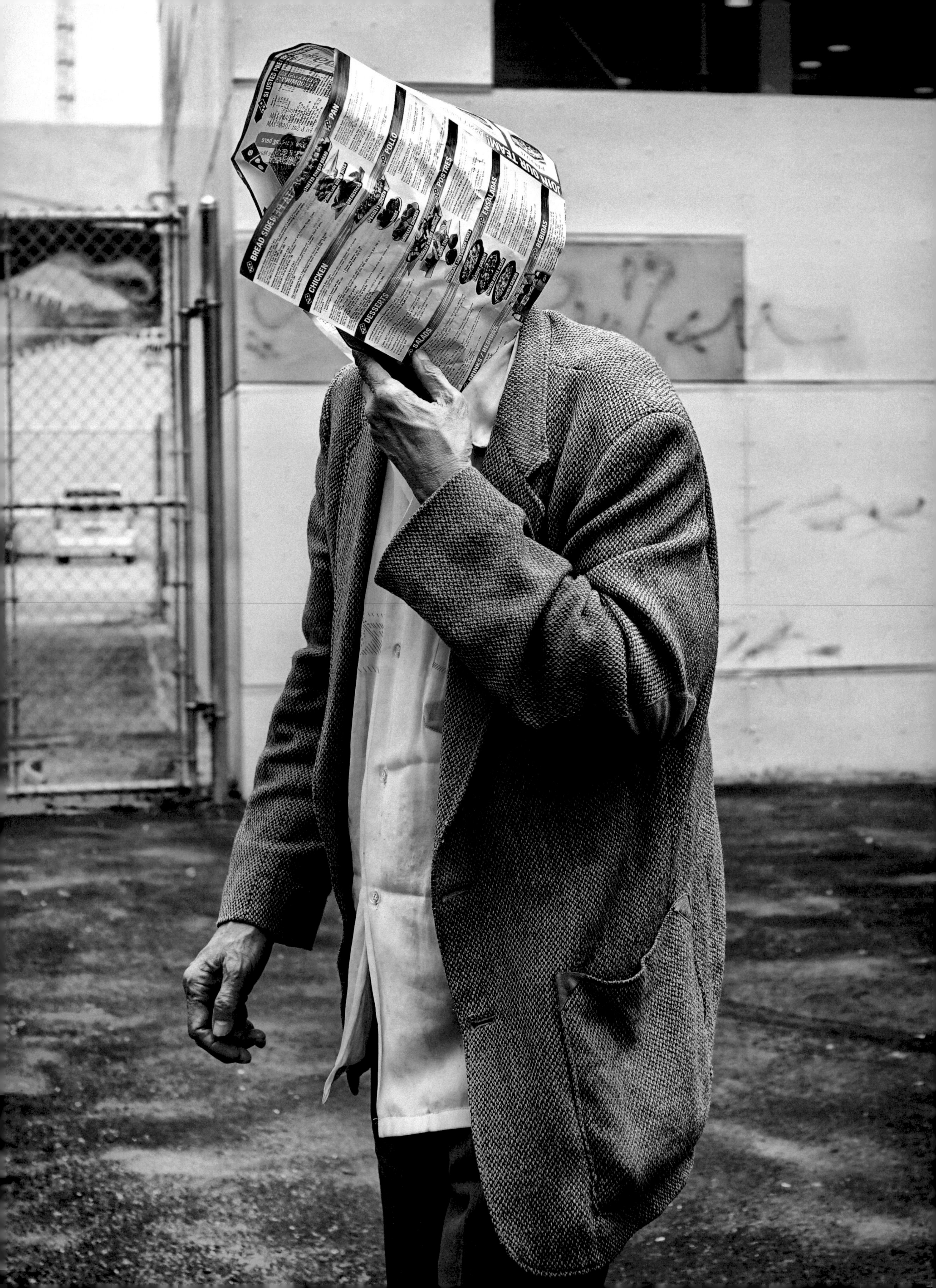
BREAD SIDES
PAN
CHICKEN
POLLO
DESSERTS
POSTRES
SALADS
ENSALADAS
BEBIDAS
DRINKS / BEBIDAS
JOIN OUR TEAM!

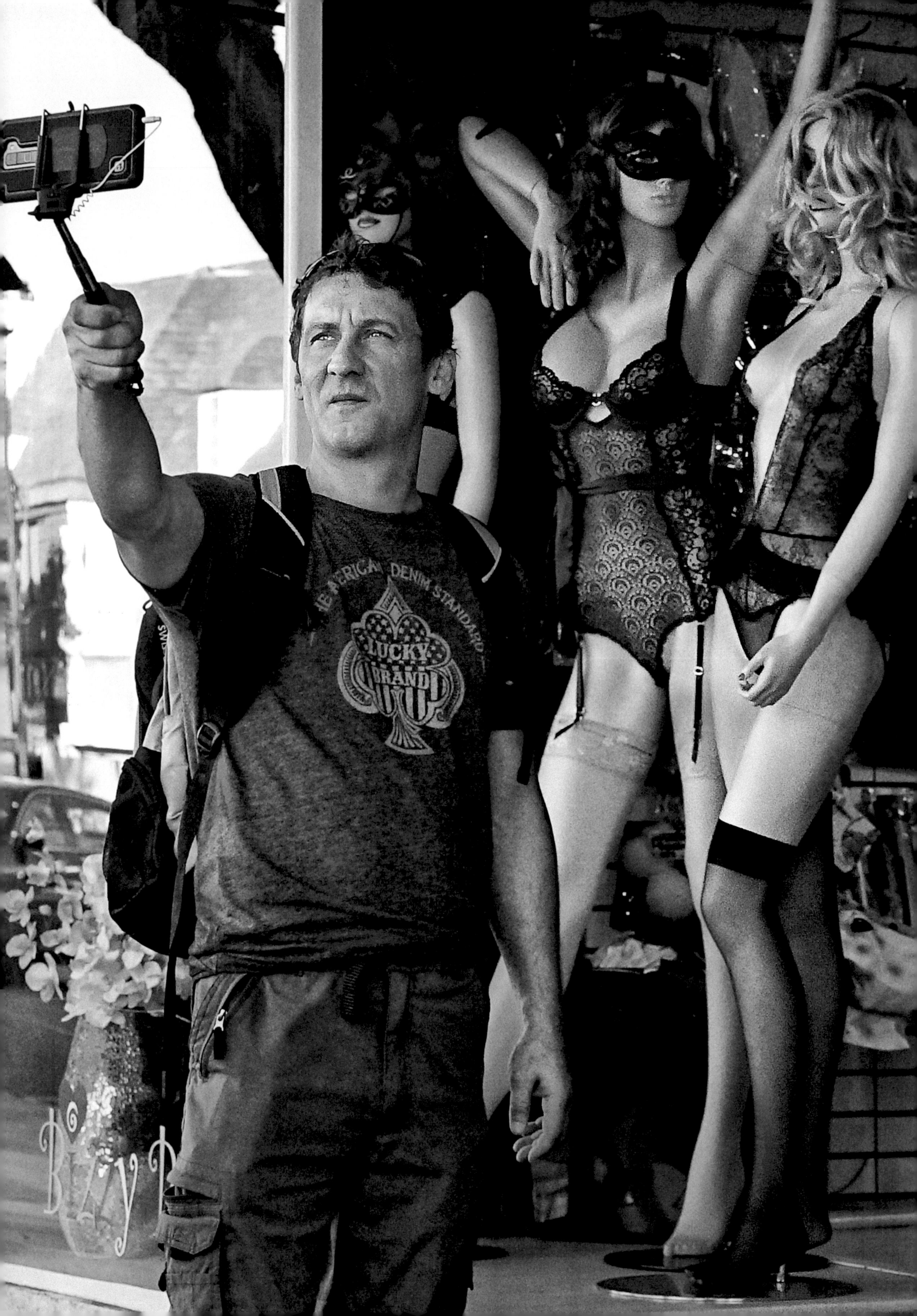
DENIM STANDARD
LUCKY
BRAND

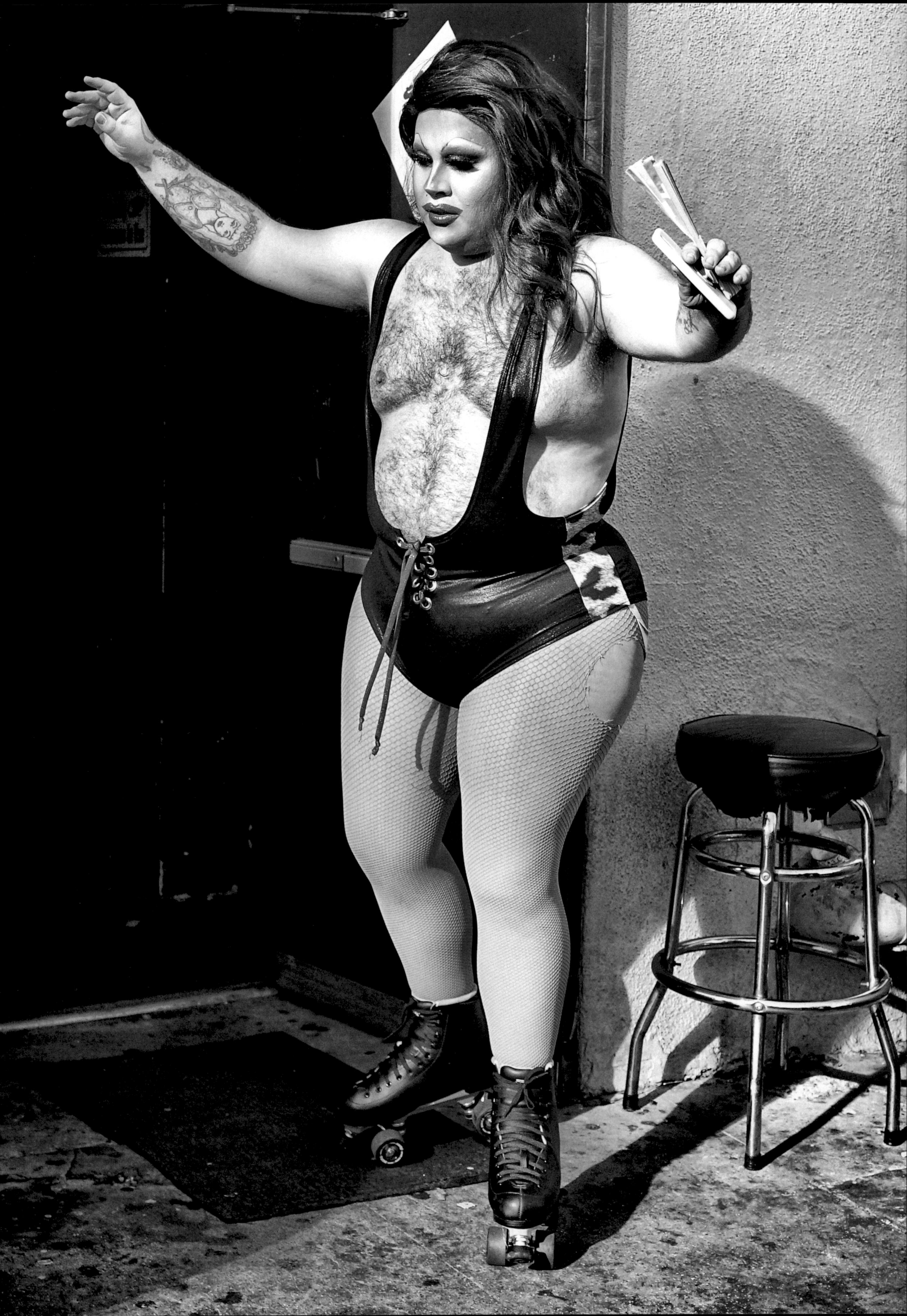

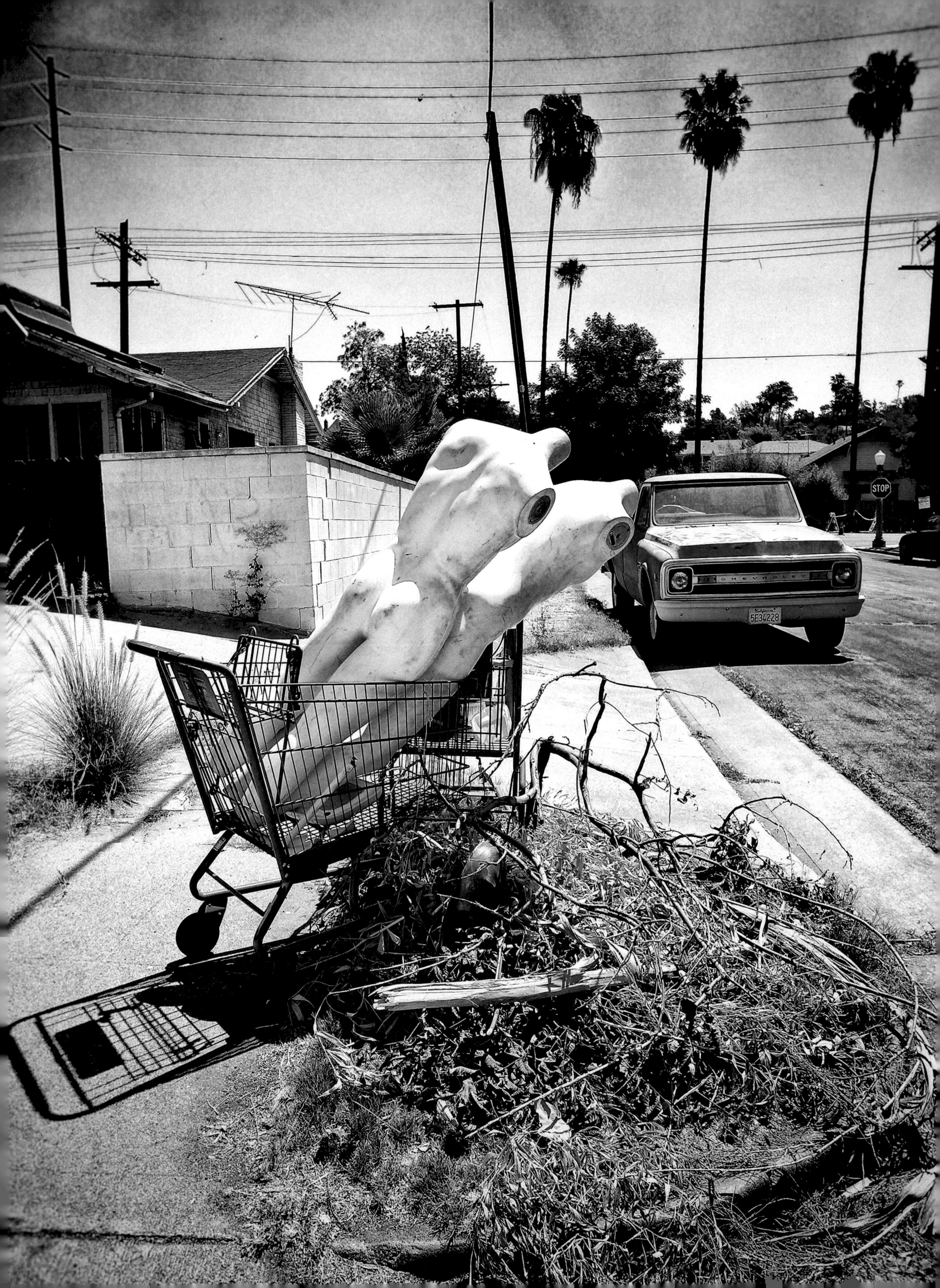
STOP
CHEVROLET
5E34228

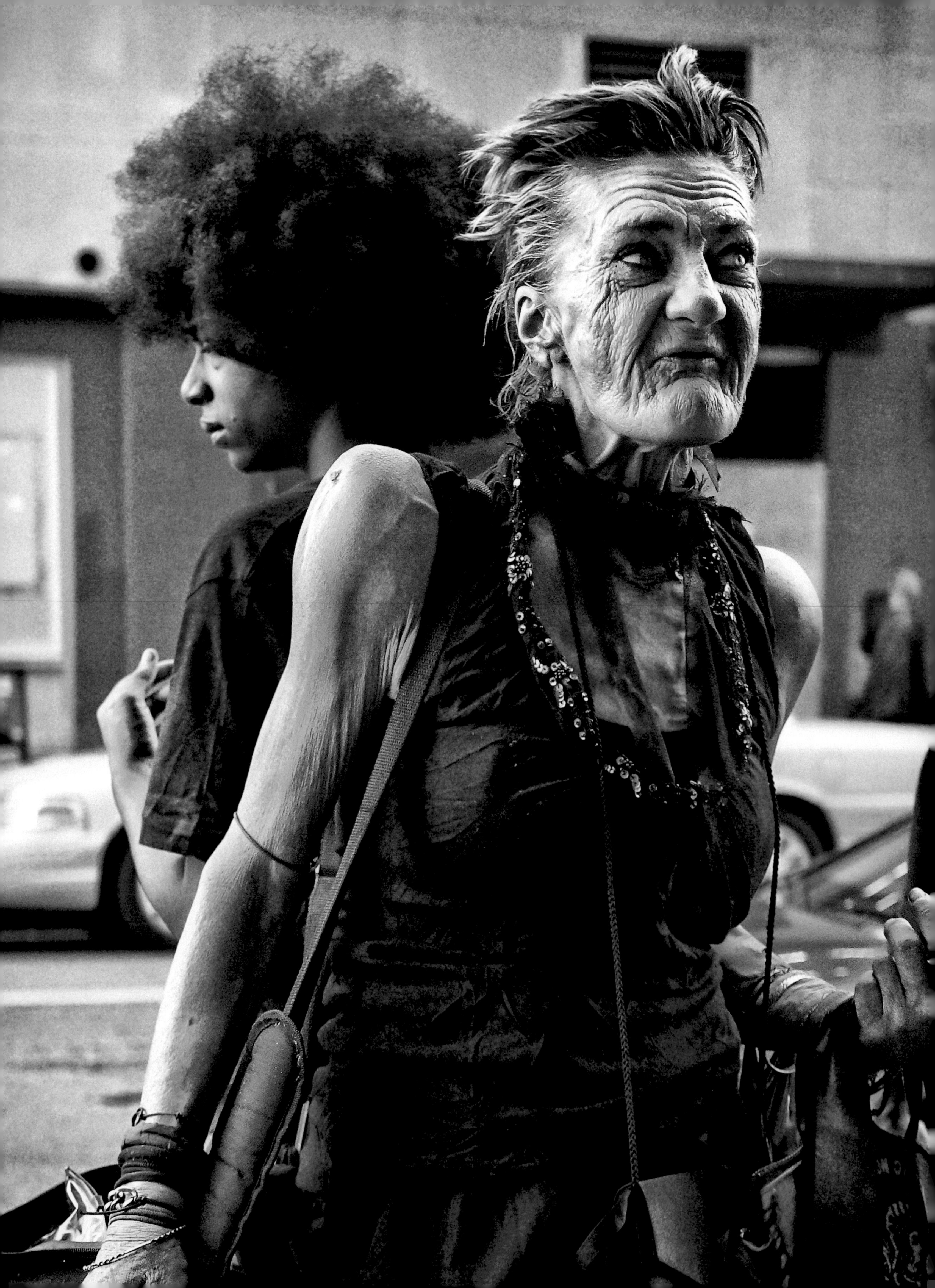

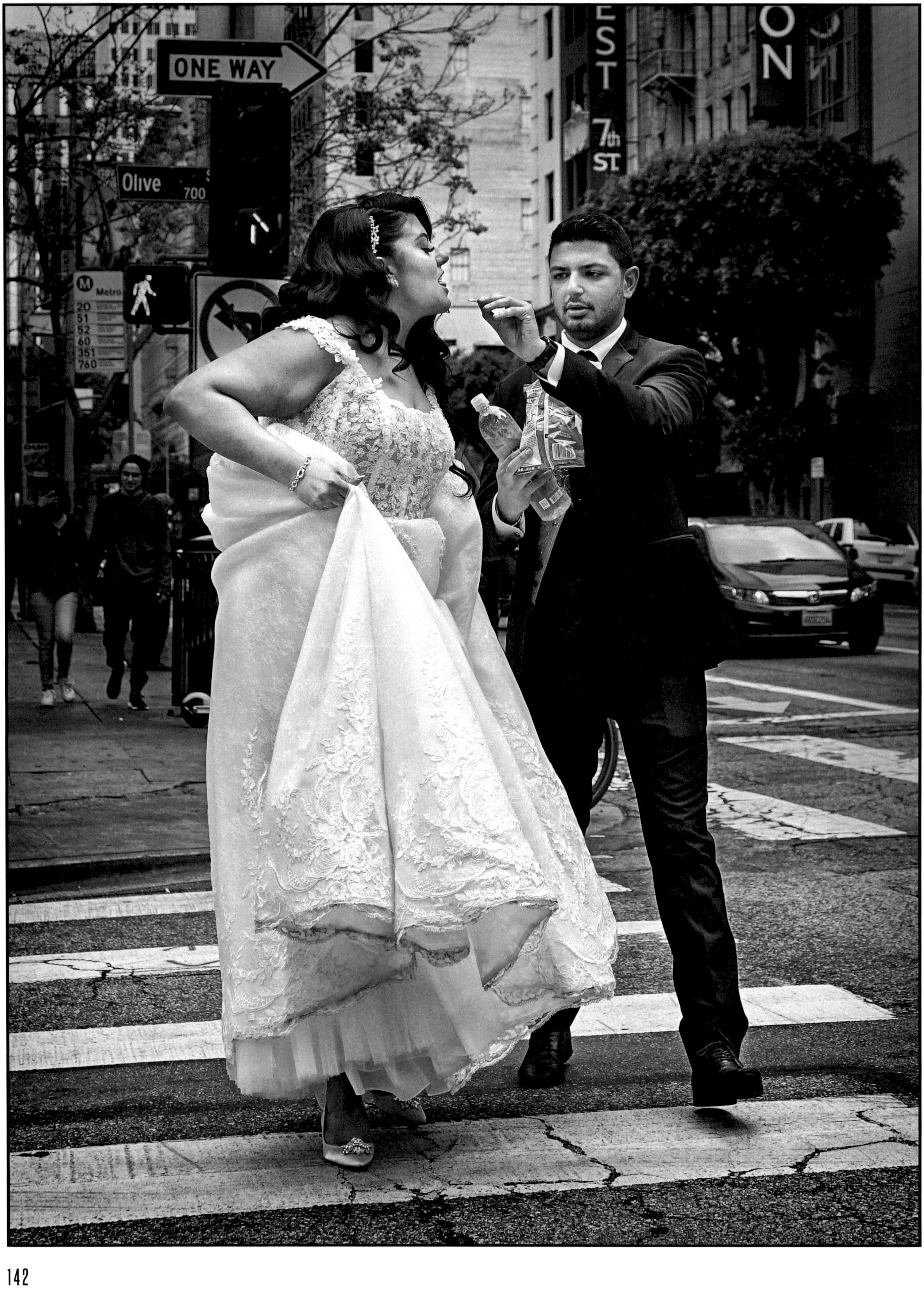
ONE WAY
Olive
700
EST
7th
ST.
ON
Metro
20
51
52
60
351
760

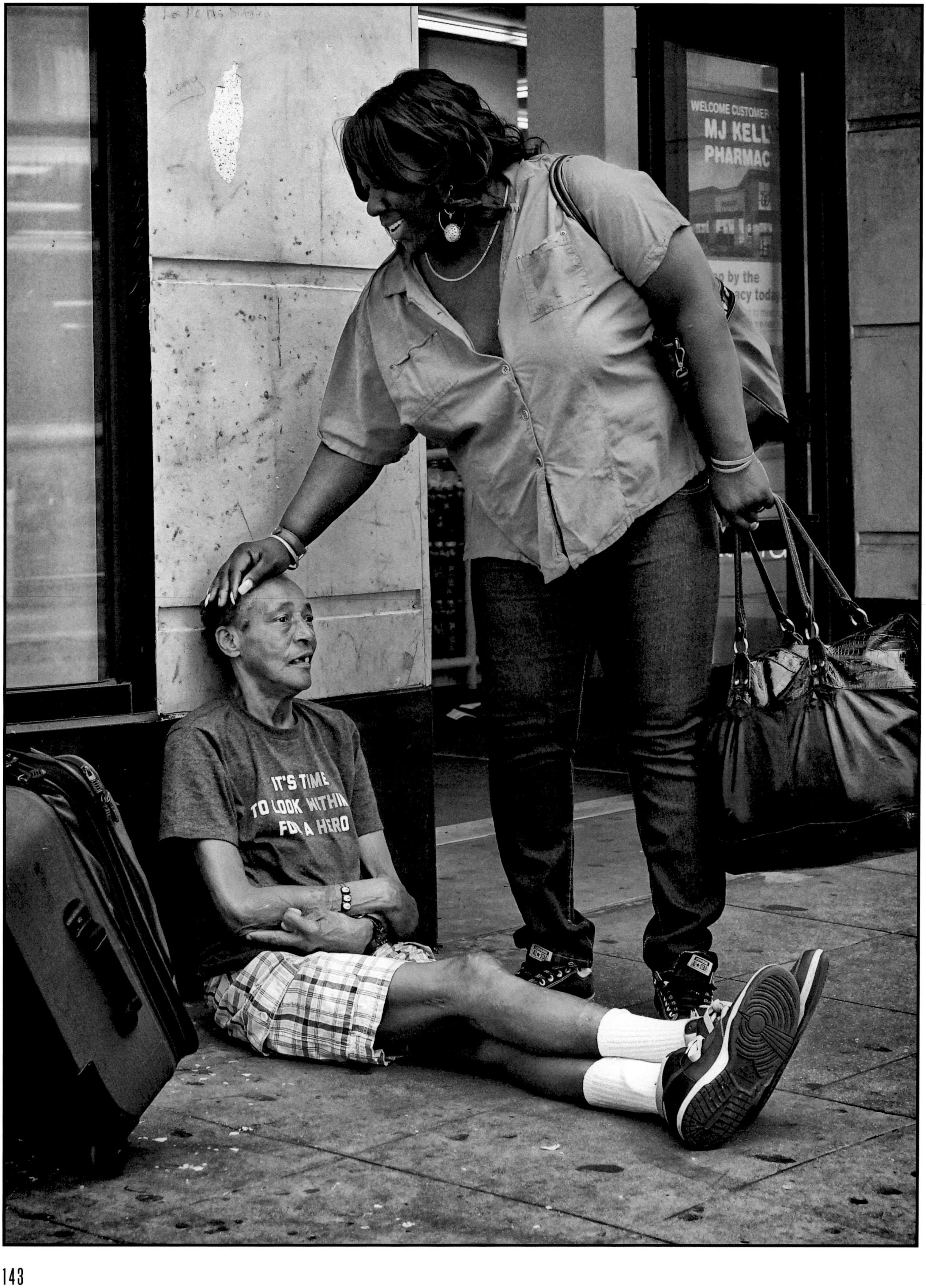
WELCOME CUSTOMER
IT'S TIME

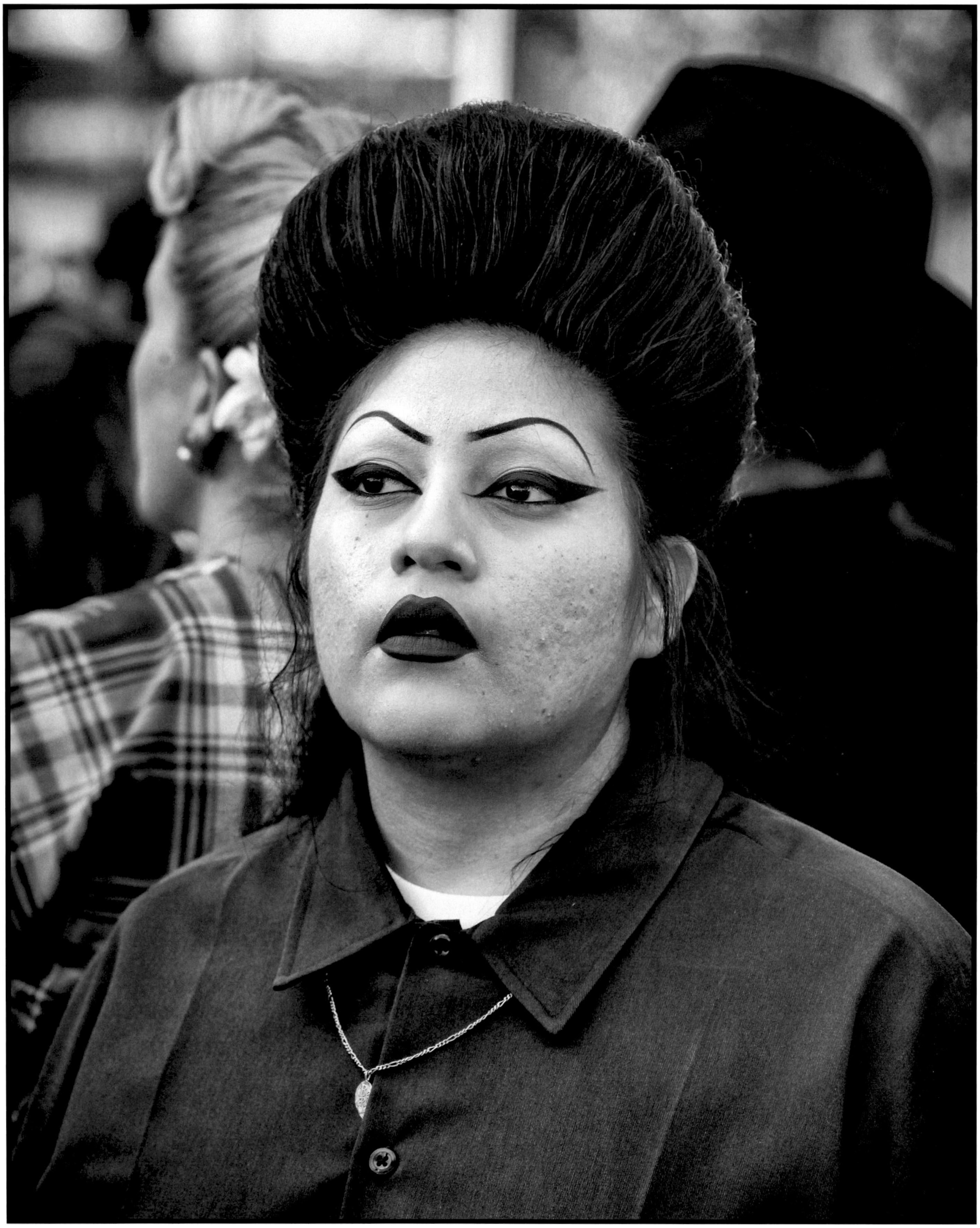

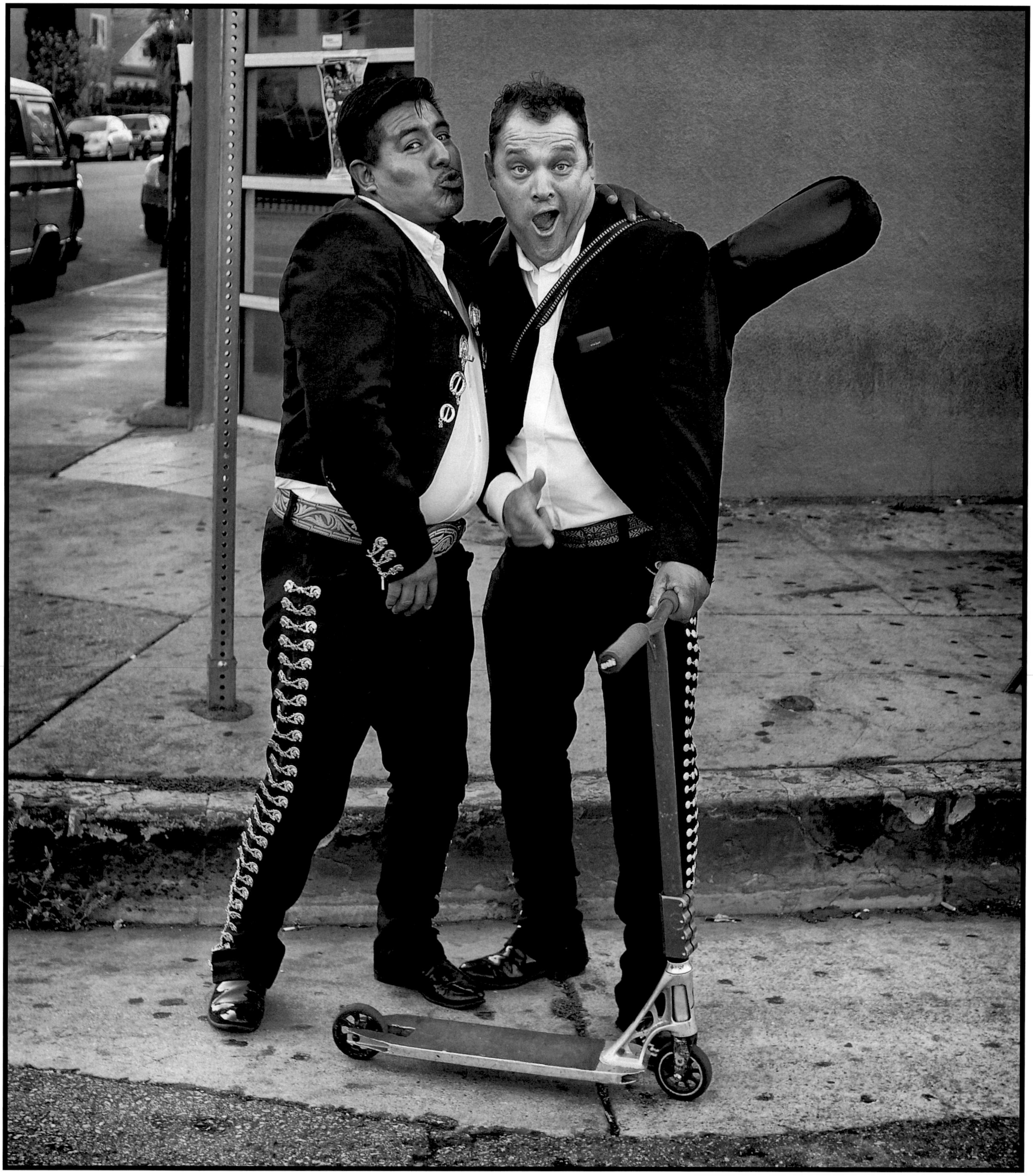

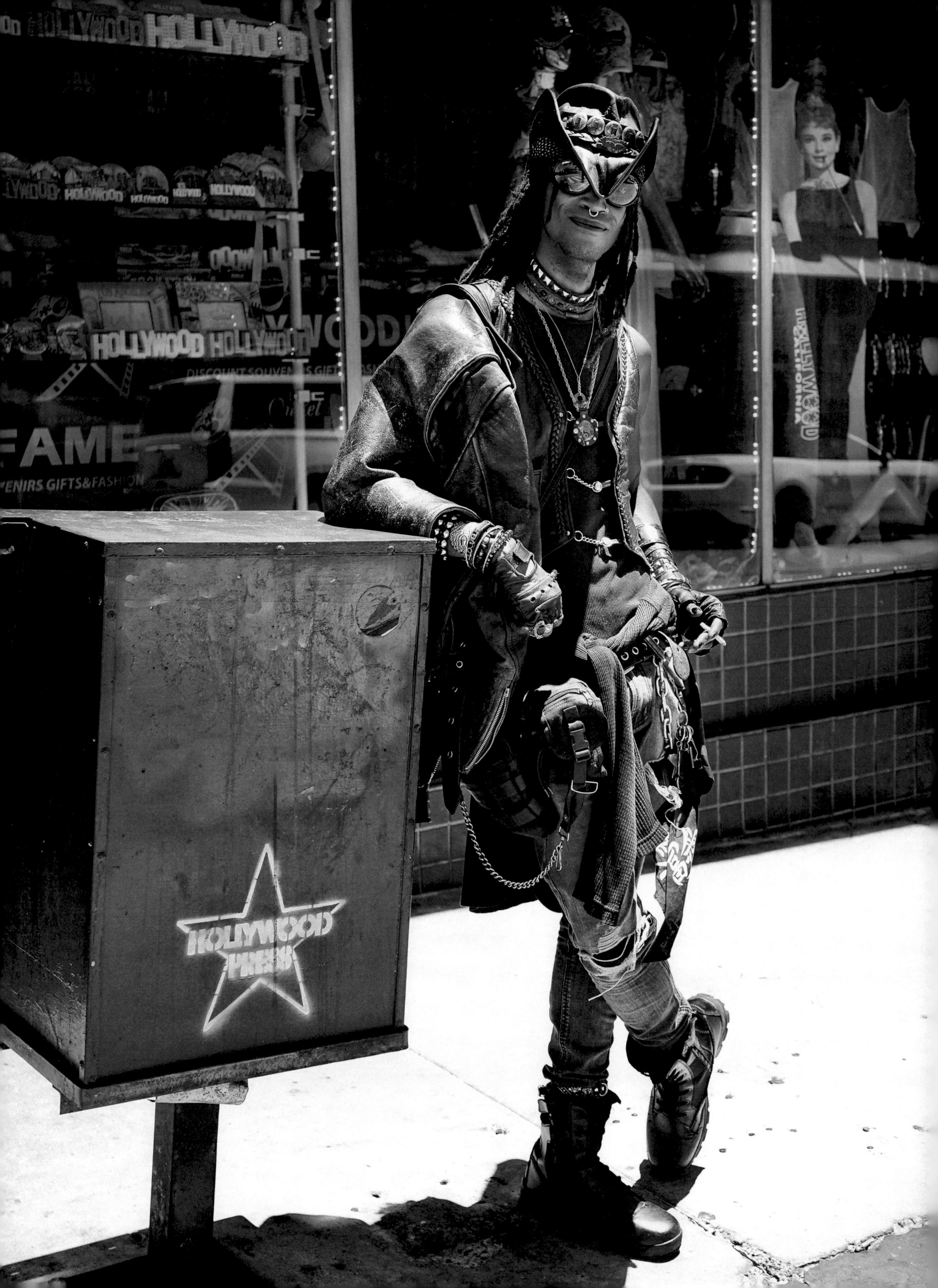
HOLLYWOOD HOLLYWOOD
HOLLYWOOD HOLLYWOOD
FAME
ENIRS GIFTS&FASHION
HOLLYWOOD
PRESS

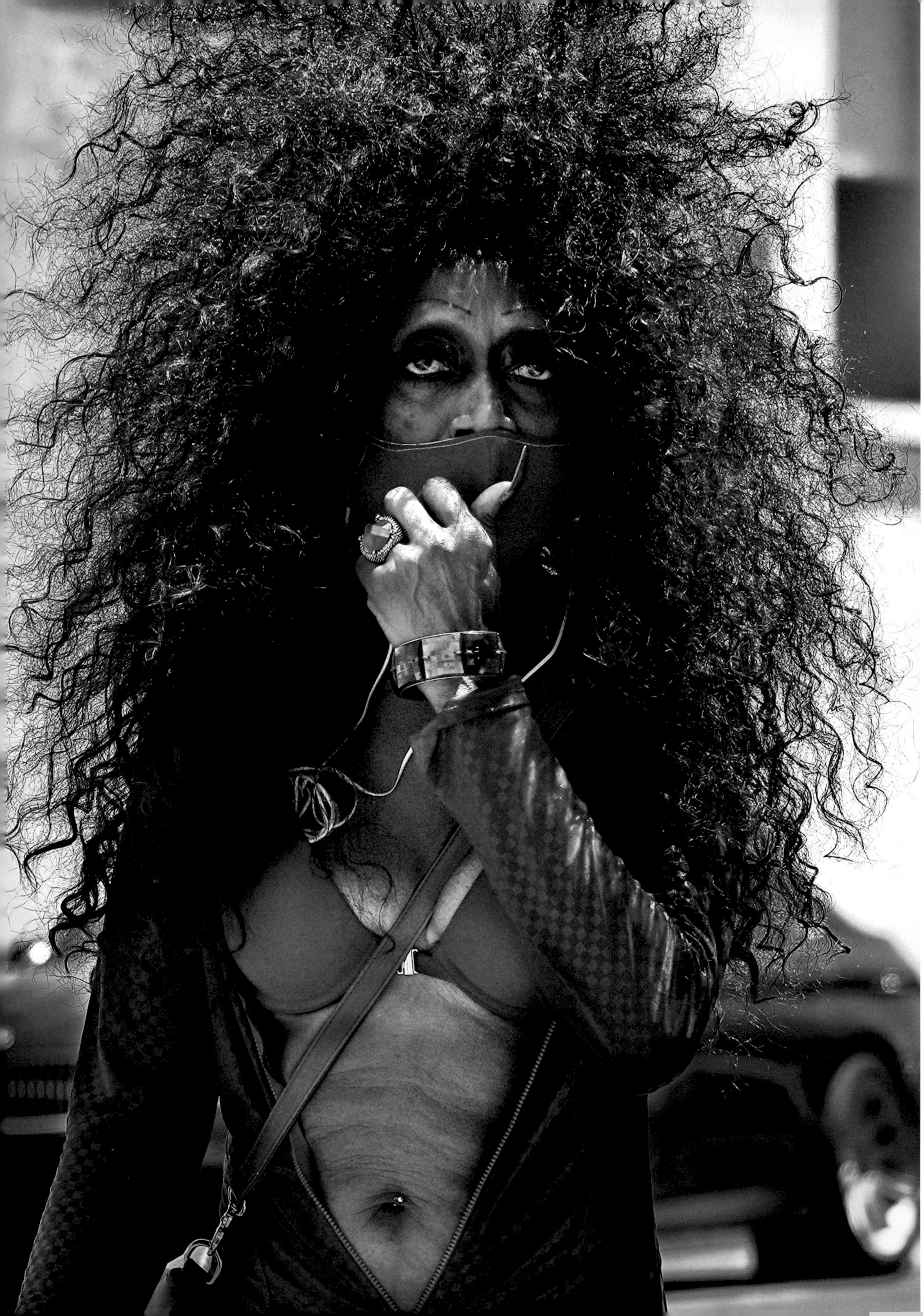

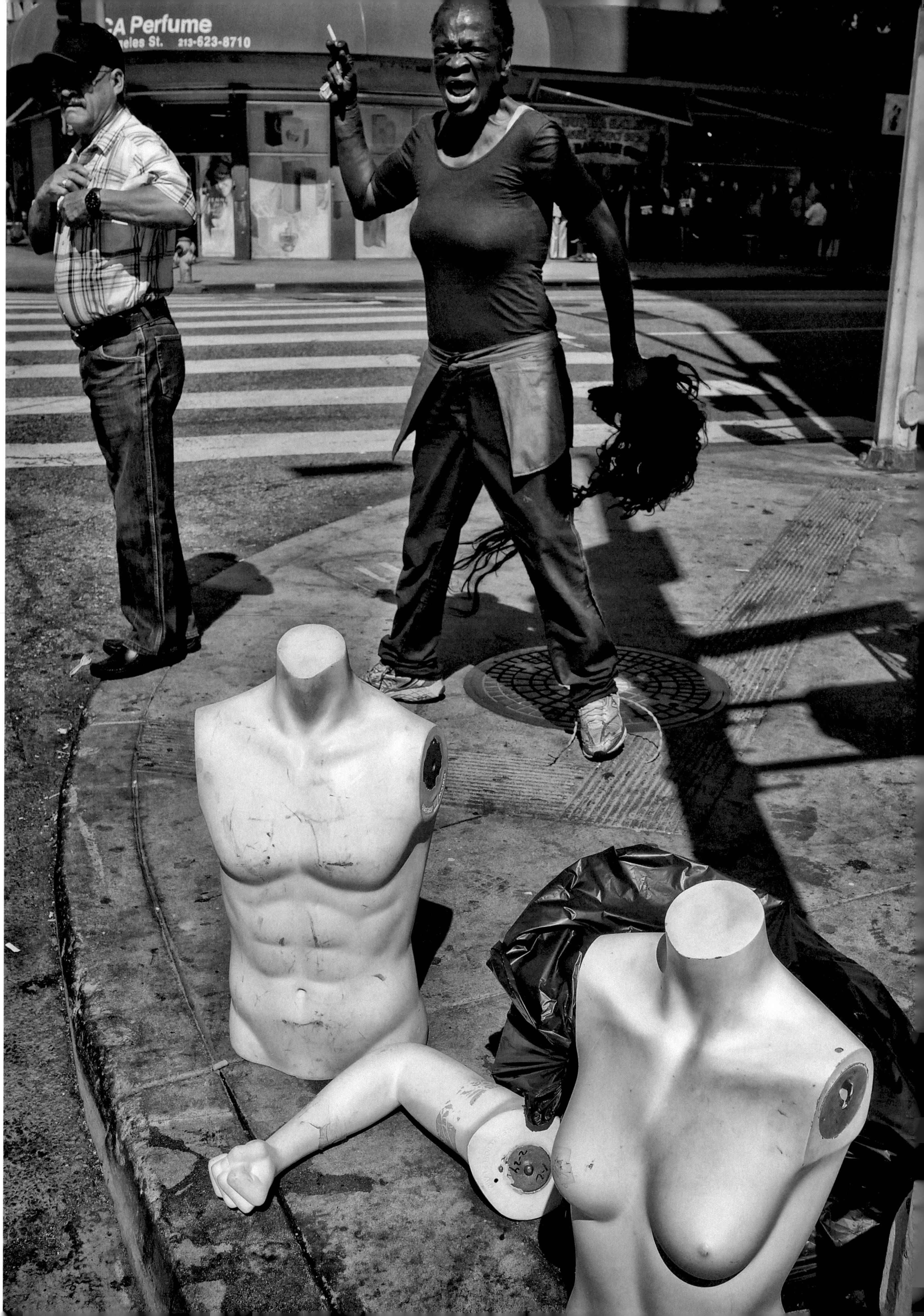
CA Perfume
213-623-8710

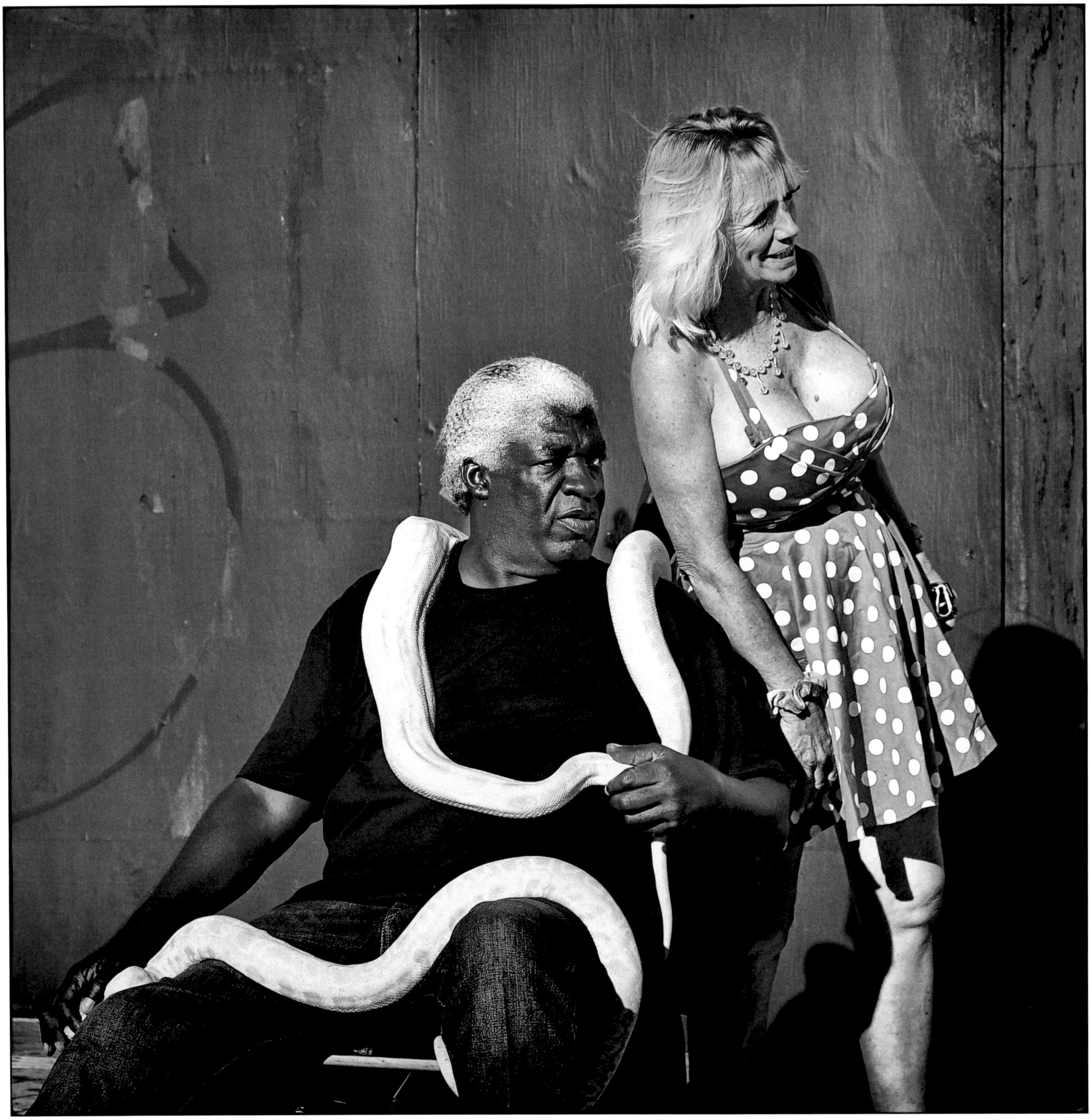

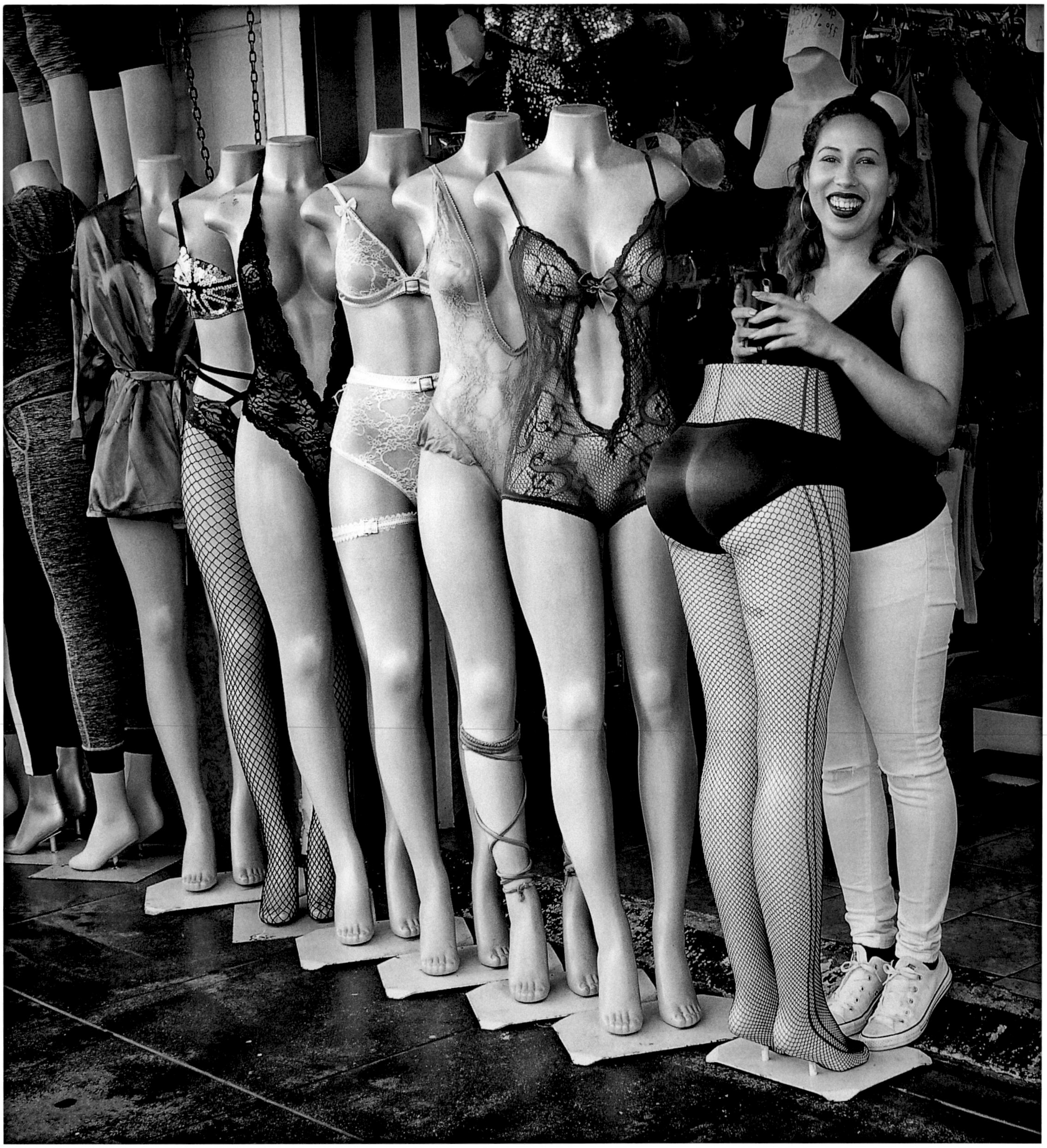

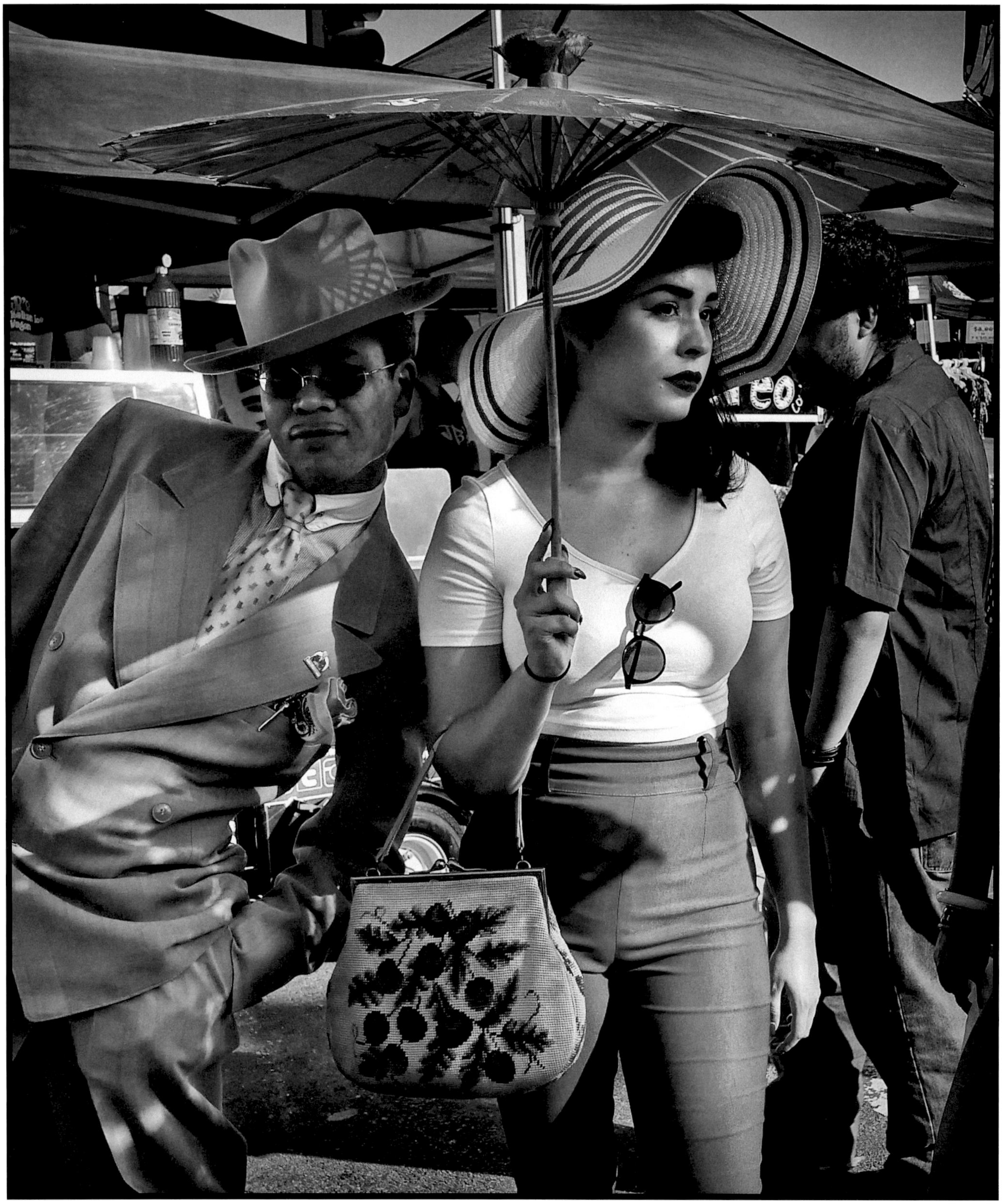

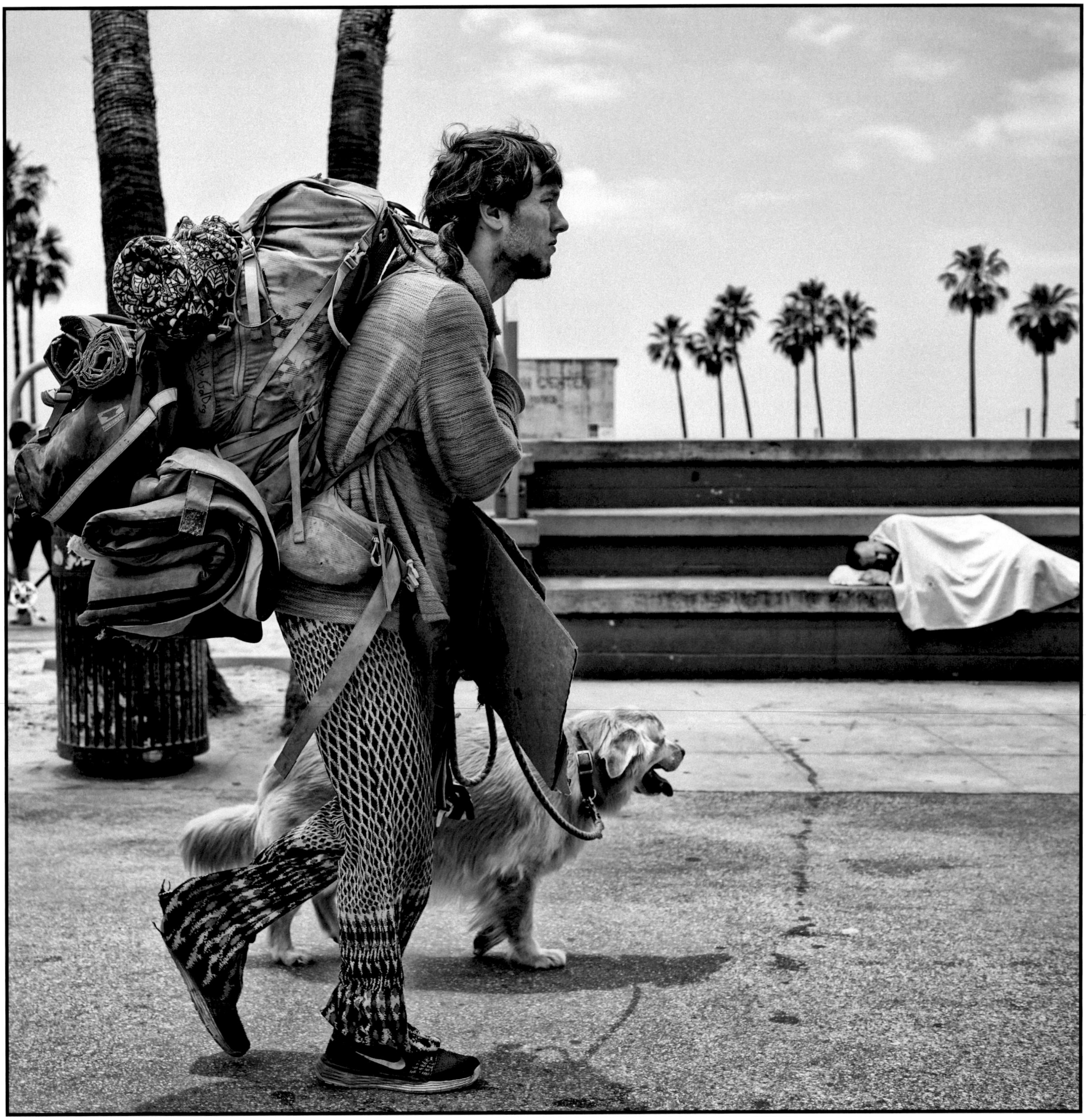

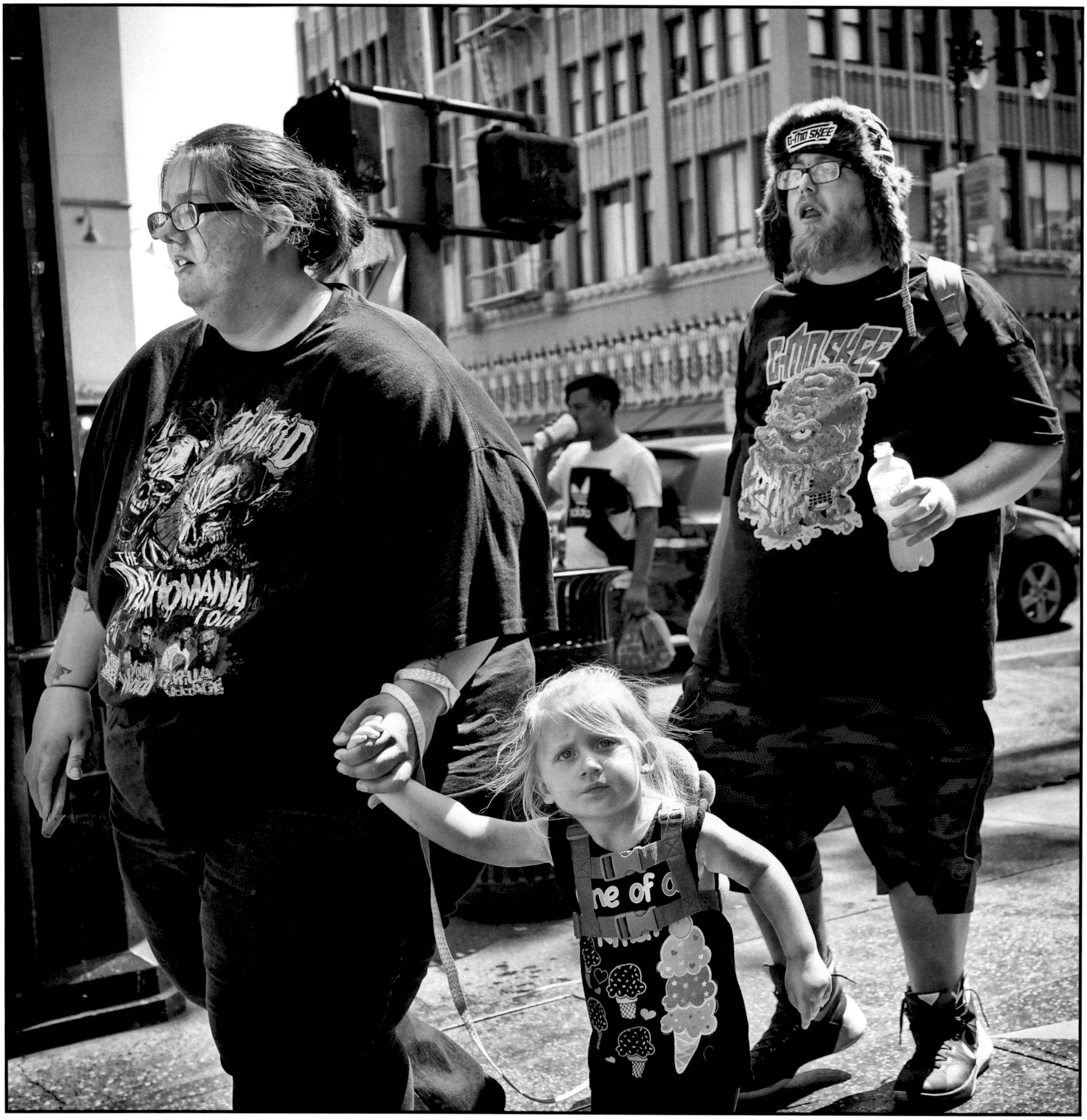
G-MO SKEE
G-MO SKEE

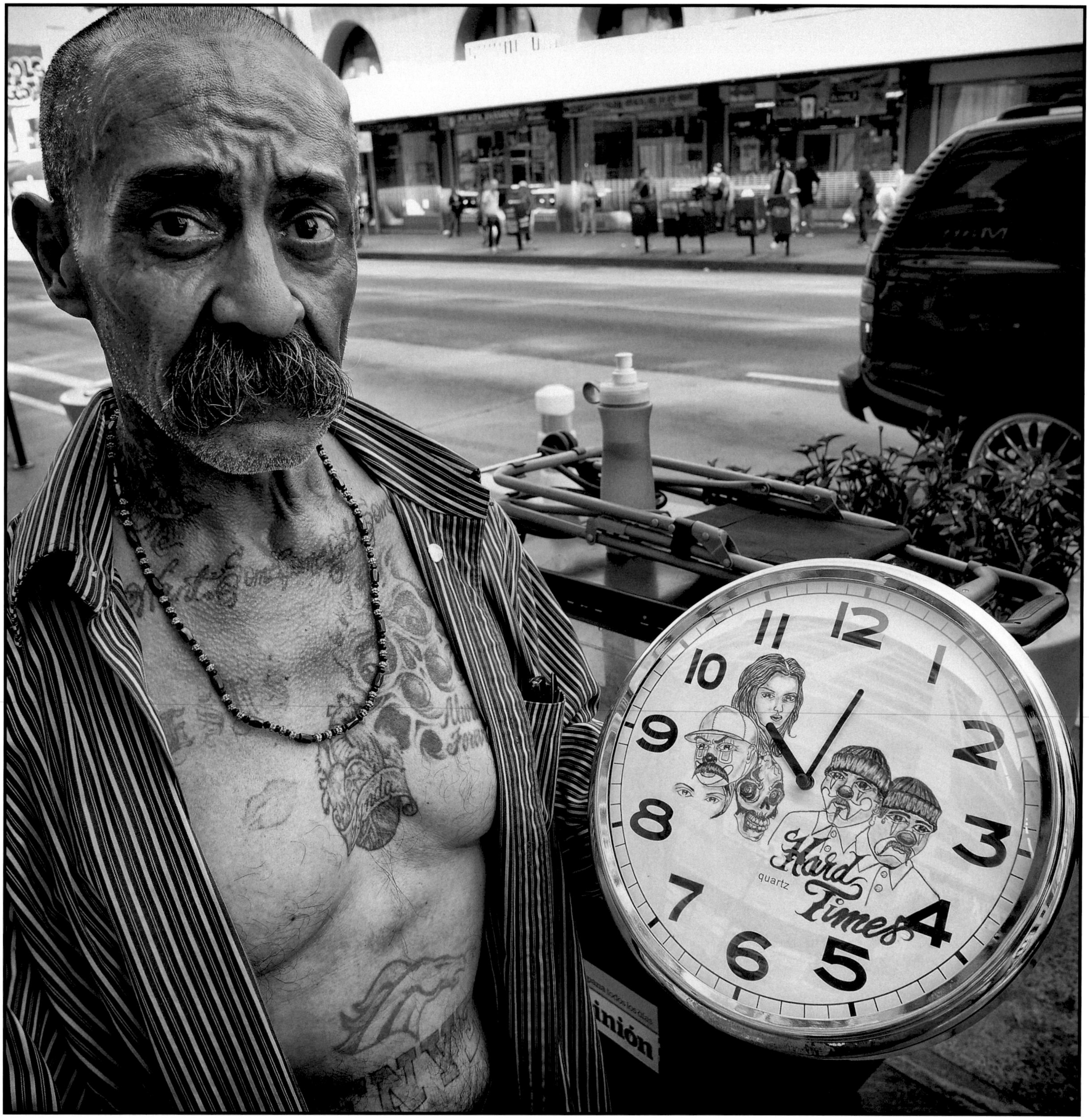
Hard Times
quartz

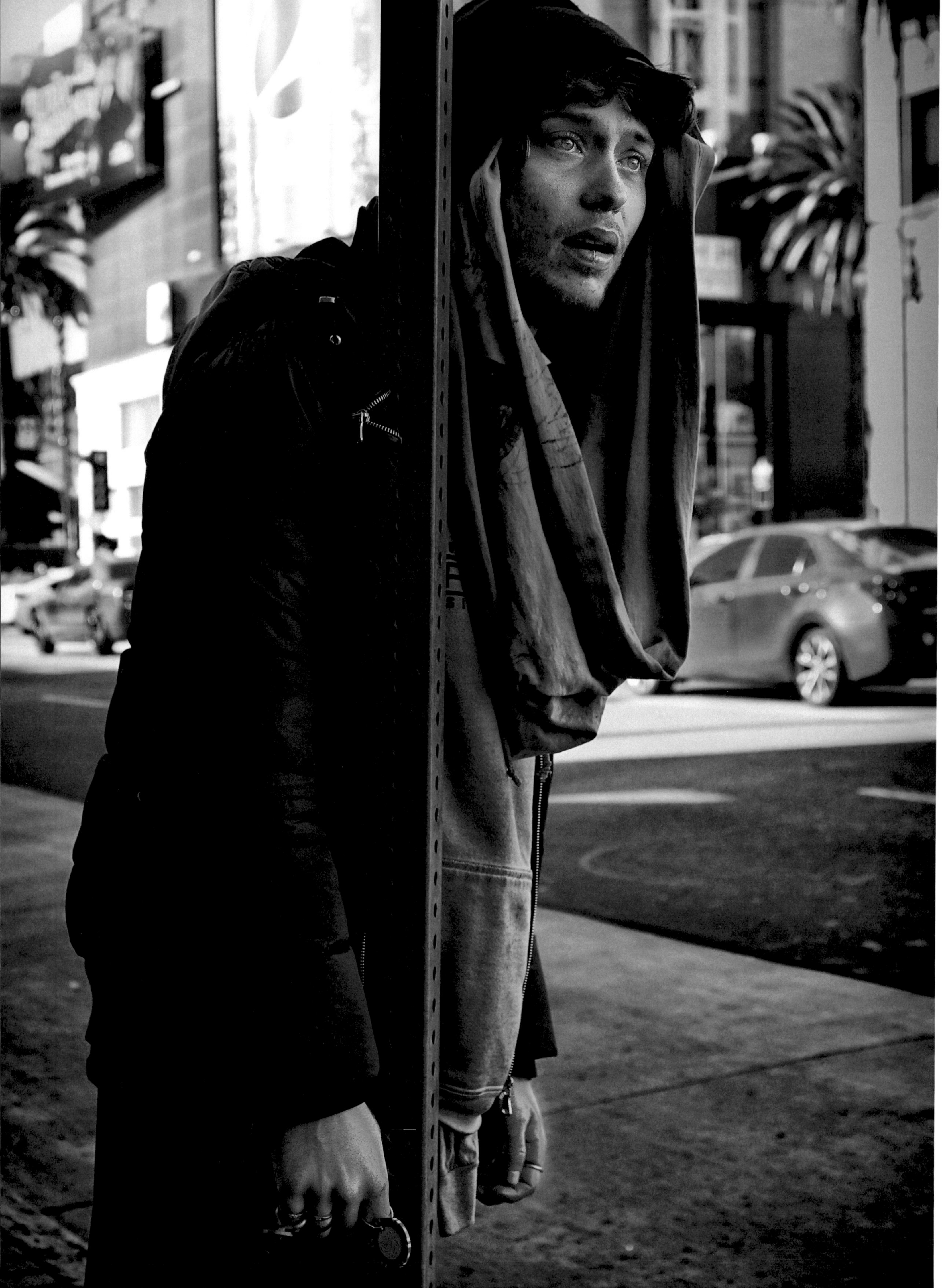

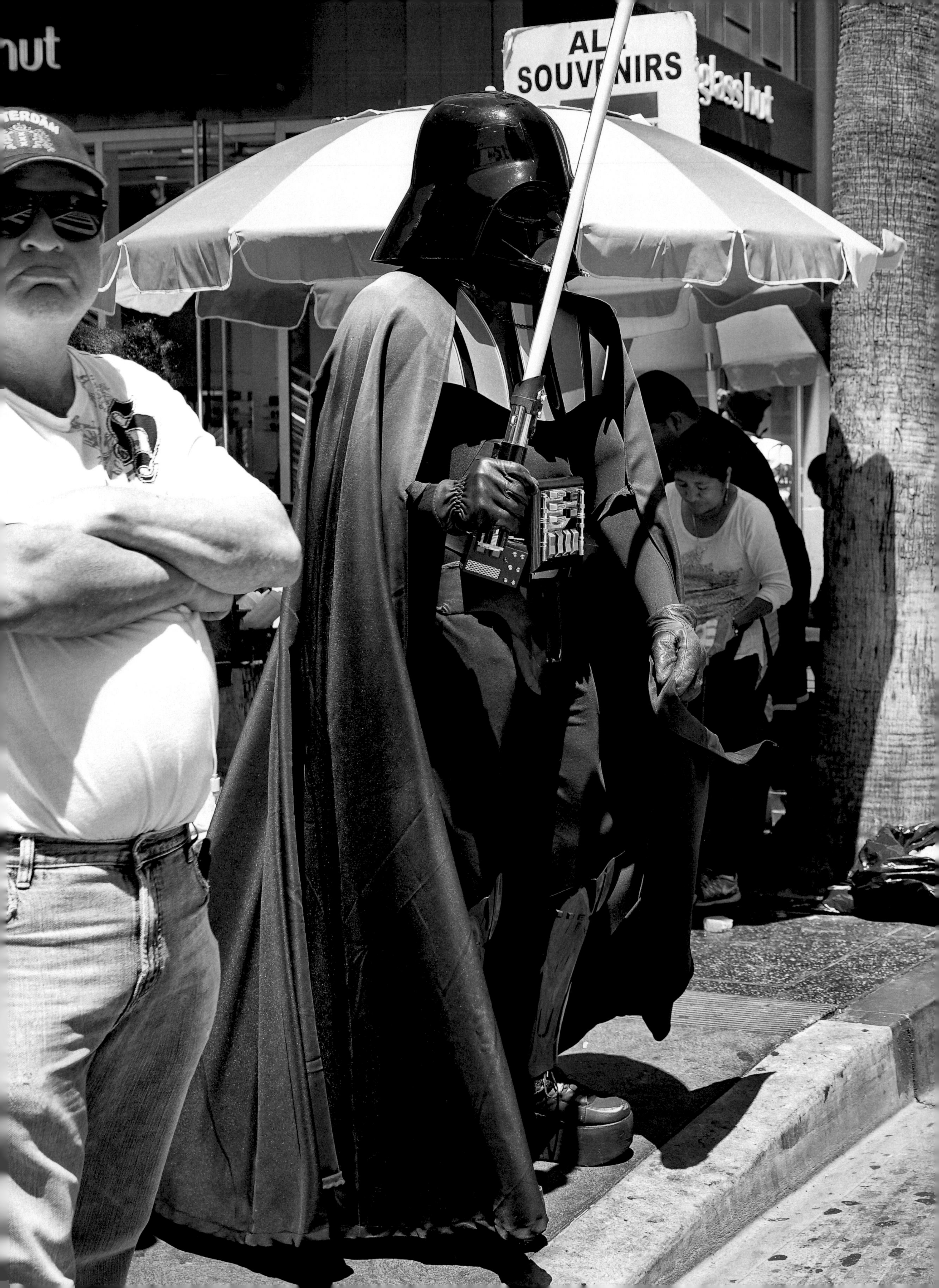
ALL
SOUVENIRS
glass hut

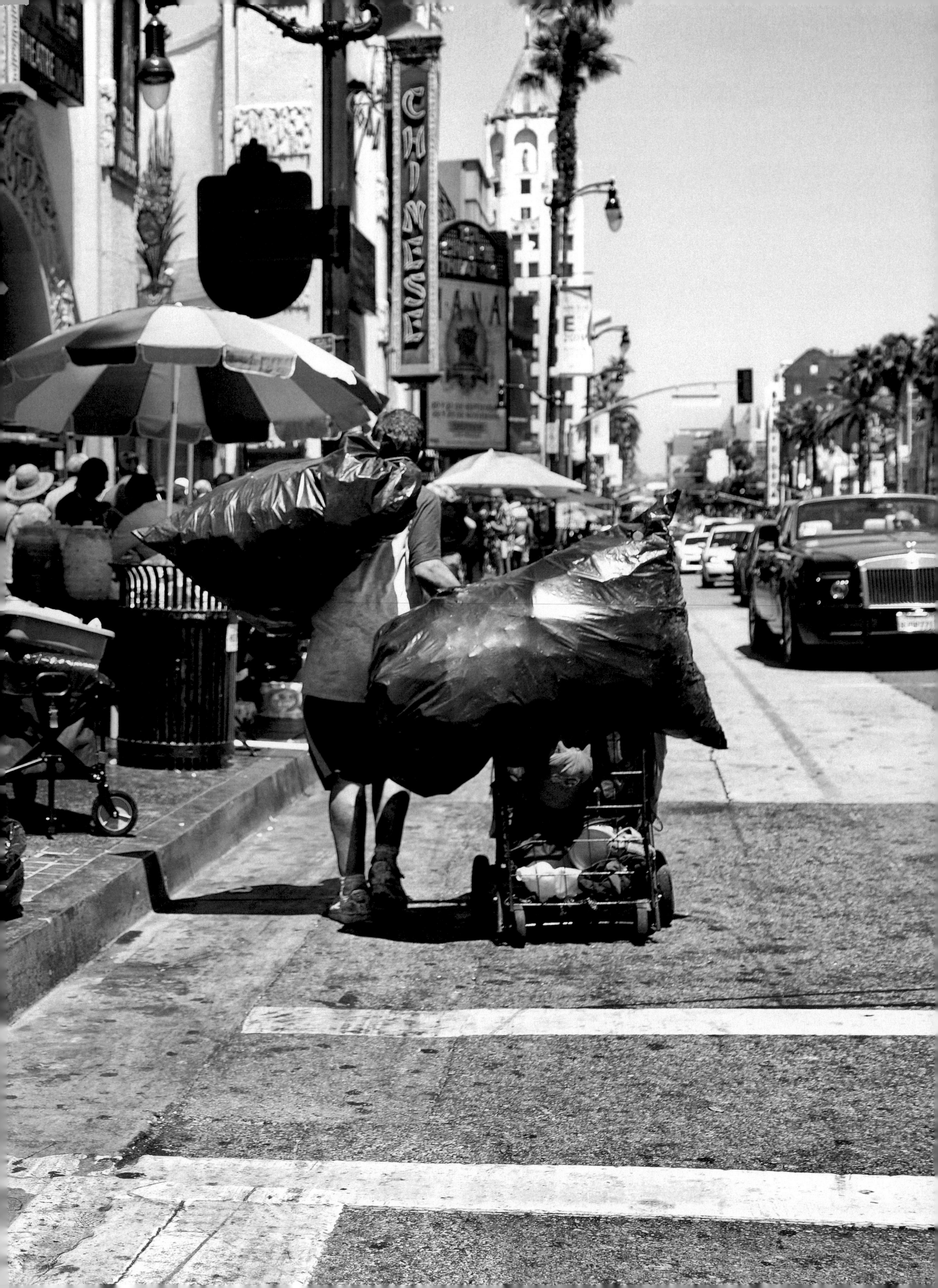
CHINESE

"The entrance to the Underworld is in Los Angeles."

Rick Riordan

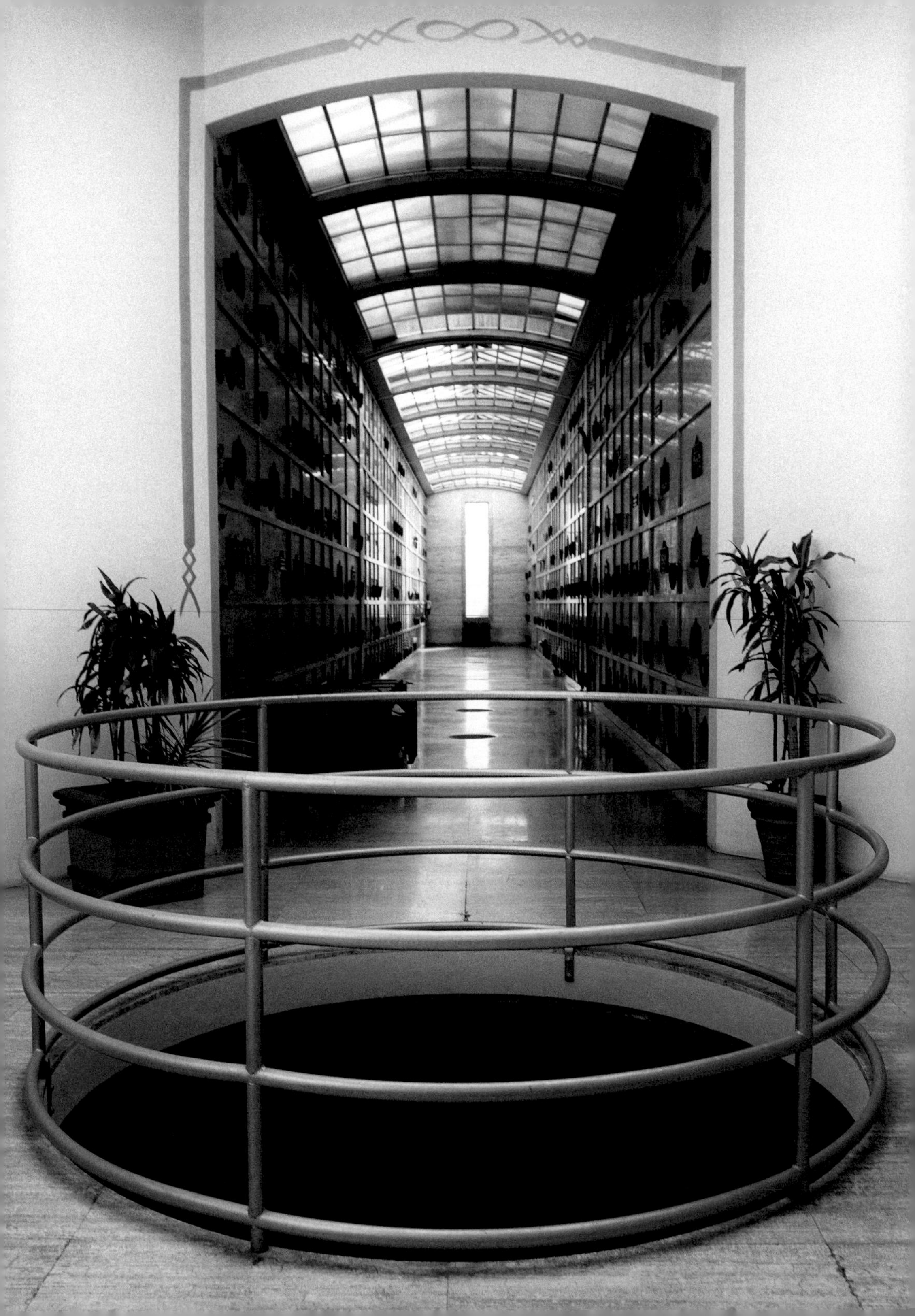

Everyday Empathy in the Photographs of Michael Dressel

A Conversation with F. Scott Hess

Born in 1958, Michael Dressel grew up behind the Iron Curtain in East Berlin obsessed with film and desiring to be a painter. In attempting to escape the Worker's Paradise he was captured climbing the Wall and spent two years in a Stasi prison, years he calls "the most awful, important and formative" of his life. In 1986 he washed ashore in Los Angeles, where he has spent thirty years editing sound for movies. Michael Dressel never stopped making visual art, and he recently took time to answer a few questions about his new photographs.

FSH The recent photographs I've seen of yours capture people "in the moment," going through their daily lives. They are profoundly human and remarkable because their moment seems so fleeting. When you go out do you have a camera constantly before your eye?

MD Sometimes I say jokingly "I am a camera." Even without carrying one, I'm constantly scanning my surroundings for constellations that make meaningful images. Jack Delano said, "What impels me to click the shutter is not what things look like, but what they mean." I feel just that. Henri Cartier-Bresson talks about the "decisive moment." I'm striving to be ready for that moment and catch it. A whole archive of images, taken seconds after what I tried to capture had passed, proves the difficulty. This kind of photography forces me to be always aware, and I see awareness as a key to experiences and joy in life.

FSH These works strike me as connecting to an earlier era of photography. How do past masters influence you?

MD The more you work yourself the more you see in, and learn from, the work of others. I admire Edward Steichen, Jacques-Henri Lartigue, and Cartier-Bresson. I keep looking at the work of Gregory Crewdson, Josef Koudelka, and Rudi Meisel. Also James Nachtwey, whose images are extremely painful and exhilarating but best enjoyed in small doses. One of my favorites is Tazio Secchiaroli. Federico Fellini formed the main character of *La Dolce Vita* after him. His photos from the set of *8½* are some of my favorites ever.

FSH You are the product of two cultures, Berlin and Hollywood. What do each of these bring to your art?

MD I spent my formative years in Berlin. German art is what I'm rooted in. Coming to LA at tweny-seven felt like a great liberation, artistically. When I arrived, art didn't seem to matter here. Hollywood reigned supreme. Art was more of a New York thing. So I felt like I didn't have to live up to anything. I could just do whatever, because nobody cared anyway. The LA-Berlin theme is still a large part of my work.

FSH You've worked in Hollywood for years as a sound editor, with a list of films to your name that boggles the mind. Is there a connection between your sound work and photography?

MD LA and Hollywood have been very good to me, and I love them for it, warts and all. I got to work with great people on great films, including some of my early heroes like John Schlesinger, the director of *Asphalt Cowboy* and *Day of the Locust*. I'm especially proud of having worked on the last fourteen Clint Eastwood films. Quite a few films I worked on ended up winning Oscars and Golden Reels for the sound work we did on them. Hollywood didn't just provide me with a good living; it also opened the world of sound for me. I was always visually oriented and never thought I would end up making a living doing sound.

FSH Some of your previous photographic work was elaborately staged and highly produced, whereas this work is shot in the world "as is." What provoked the change?

MD Those staged works can be seen as my last attempts at painting. With the advent of digital photography I realized I could produce images that I didn't have the technical skills to do as paintings. Things changed once I realized how hard it is to shoot meaningful images of people in the real world. I used to feel inhibited about photographing people. It was hard to overcome this and develop an attitude that made possible the short but intimate encounter with strangers when photographing them. This challenge attracts me greatly because it goes way beyond photography. Every such encounter has the potential for friendly exchange or conflict. It is a fine line that requires tact and sensitivity toward the situation and the person. One learns a lot about oneself and others that way. Those images cannot be produced, only captured, and you have to be there and be ready when the moment comes. I don't know who said it, but I agree with the quote "What a good photographer needs more than a good camera is a good pair of shoes."

FSH Do you think many contemporary photographers avoid empathy for aesthetic or stylistic purposes? Is there a downside to work connecting too well to other human beings?

MD I think many aspiring and established artists are under pressure to produce work that is conforming to the art market in order to make a living. The market wants "new," and this kind of work has an old-fashioned feel. Another problem is that this kind of work isn't easily produced. It is easier to come up with some conceptual gimmick that doesn't require skills and isn't as time-consuming.

FSH These images point to your great empathy toward your fellow humans, but also a wicked joy you take in pointing out their flaws or weaknesses. Is this an accurate reading?

MD I always loved that Fellini could describe people in the most unflattering way without being condescending. It seemed he was laughing with us because deep down he knew he was as much a tragic joke as the rest of us. I wish to be like that. I do not have preconceived ideas about what I want to express. I am not religious or "spiritual." I could never even figure out what that is supposed to mean. But I do believe in magic. The magic that happens when I am pointing a camera at life and freeze a few hundredths of a second into an image. Afterwards that image turns into this thing that communicates what I think and feel about the world. This magic allows me to photograph myself into the world.

F. Scott Hess,
Artist and Associate Professor at Laguna College of Art + Design

Über die alltägliche Empathie in den Fotografien von Michael Dressel

Ein Gespräch mit F. Scott Hess

1958 geboren, wuchs Michael Dressel film- und kunstbesessen hinter dem Eisernen Vorhang in Ost-Berlin auf und wollte Maler werden. Beim Versuch, dem Arbeiter-und-Bauern-Paradies zu entkommen, wurde er beim Übersteigen der Mauer verhaftet und verbrachte zwei Jahre in einem Stasi-Gefängnis. Jahre, die er als »die schrecklichsten, wichtigsten und prägendsten« seines Lebens bezeichnet. 1986 verschlug es ihn nach Los Angeles, wo er dreißig Jahre lang den Ton für Filme bearbeitete. Michael Dressel hat nie aufgehört, bildende Kunst zu machen, und hat sich die Zeit genommen, ein paar Fragen zu seinen neuen Fotografien zu beantworten.

FSH Die letzten Fotos, die ich von dir gesehen habe, zeigen Menschen »im Moment«, wie sie ihren Alltag durchleben. Sie sind zutiefst menschlich und bemerkenswert, weil der Augenblick so flüchtig erscheint. Hast du beim Rausgehen ständig eine Kamera vor Augen?

MD Manchmal sage ich scherzhaft: »Ich bin eine Kamera«. Auch ohne eine zu tragen, scanne ich ständig meine Umgebung nach visuellen Konstellationen ab, die aussagekräftige Bilder ergeben könnten. Jack Delano sagte: »Was mich dazu bringt, auf den Auslöser zu drücken, ist nicht, wie die Dinge aussehen, sondern was sie bedeuten.« Ich fühle genau das. Cartier-Bresson spricht vom »entscheidenden Moment«. Ich bemühe mich, für diesen Moment bereit zu sein und ihn einzufangen. Ein ganzes Archiv von Bildern, aufgenommen nur Sekunden nachdem das, was ich einzufangen versuchte, bereits vorbei war, beweist, wie schwer es ist, diesen Moment zu erwischen. Diese Art der Fotografie zwingt mich, immer bewusst da zu sein, und ich sehe diese bewusste Wahrnehmung als Schlüssel zu Erfahrungen und Erfüllung im Leben.

FSH Die Arbeiten scheinen mir eine Verbindung zu einer früheren Ära der Fotografie zu sein. Wie beeinflussen dich große Fotografen der Vergangenheit?

MD Je mehr man selbst arbeitet, desto mehr sieht man in der Arbeit anderer und lernt von ihnen. Ich bewundere Edward Steichen, Lartigue und Cartier-Bresson. Ich schaue mir immer wieder die Arbeiten von Crewdson, Koudelka und Rudi Meisel an. Auch Nachtwey, dessen Bilder äußerst schmerzhaft und eindrucksvoll sind und die man am besten nur in kleinen Dosen genießt. Einer meiner Favoriten ist Tazio Secchiaroli. Fellini formte nach ihm die Hauptfigur in *La dolce vita*. Seine Fotos vom Set des Fellini Films *8 ½* gehören zu meinen Lieblingsbildern überhaupt.

FSH Du bist das Produkt zweier Kulturen, Berlin und Hollywood. Welche Rolle spielen diese beiden Seiten in deiner Kunst?

MD Meine prägenden Jahre habe ich in Berlin verbracht. Ich bin in der deutschen Kunst verwurzelt. Mit 27 Jahren nach LA zu kommen fühlte sich künstlerisch wie eine große Befreiung an. Als ich ankam, schien Kunst hier kaum eine Rolle zu spielen. Hollywood dominierte alles. Kunst war eher eine New-York-Sache. Ich musste also keine Erwartungen erfüllen. Ich konnte einfach alles machen, weil es sowieso niemanden interessierte. Das Thema LA–Berlin ist immer noch ein wichtiger Bestandteil meiner Arbeit.

FSH Du hast jahrelang in Hollywood als Sound Editor an einer beeindruckend langen Liste von großen Hollywoodfilmen gearbeitet. Gibt es eine Verbindung zwischen deiner Tonarbeit und der Fotografie?

MD LA und Hollywood waren sehr gut zu mir und ich liebe sie dafür. Ich habe mit großartigen Leuten an großartigen Filmen gearbeitet, darunter einige meiner frühen Helden wie John Schlesinger, dem Regisseur von *Asphalt Cowboy* und *Tag der Heuschrecke*. Besonders stolz bin ich darauf, an den letzten vierzehn Clint-Eastwood-Filmen mitgewirkt zu haben. Nicht wenige Filme, an denen ich gearbeitet habe, gewannen Oscars und Golden Reels für unsere Soundarbeit. Hollywood hat mir nicht nur einen guten Lebensunterhalt ermöglicht, es hat mir auch die Welt des Tons eröffnet. Ich war immer visuell orientiert und hätte nie gedacht, dass ich mal meinen Lebensunterhalt mit Sound verdienen würde.

FSH Einige deiner früheren fotografischen Arbeiten wurden aufwendig inszeniert, während die Fotografien in diesem Buch die Welt zeigen, wie sie ist. Was hat die Veränderung ausgelöst?

MD Diese inszenierten Arbeiten können als meine letzten Malversuche angesehen werden. Mit dem Aufkommen der digitalen Fotografie wurde mir klar, dass ich Bilder machen konnte, die meine malerischen Fähigkeiten übertrafen. Als ich jedoch merkte, wie schwer es ist, aussagekräftige Bilder von realen Menschen in der realen Welt zu machen, änderte dies einiges. Früher hatte ich Hemmungen, Menschen zu fotografieren. Es fiel mir schwer, diese zu überwinden und eine Haltung zu entwickeln, die die kurze, aber intime Begegnung mit Fremden beim Fotografieren ermöglichte. Diese Herausforderung reizt mich immer noch, weil sie weit über die Fotografie hinausgeht. Jede solche Begegnung birgt das Potenzial für freundschaftlichen Austausch oder Konflikt. Es ist ein schmaler Grat, der Fingerspitzengefühl und Sensibilität für die Situation und die Person erfordert. So lernt man viel über sich selbst und andere. Diese Bilder können nicht produziert, sondern nur festgehalten werden, und man muss anwesend und bereit sein, wenn der Moment kommt. Ich weiß nicht, wer es gesagt hat, aber ich stimme dem Zitat »Was ein guter Fotograf mehr braucht als eine gute Kamera, sind gute Schuhe« zu.

FSH Glaubst du, dass viele zeitgenössische Fotografen Empathie aus ästhetischen oder stilistischen Gründen vermeiden? Gibt es einen Nachteil, sich mit seiner Arbeit zu sehr auf die menschliche Begegnung einzulassen?

MD Ich denke, viele aufstrebende und etablierte Künstler stehen unter dem Druck, kunstmarktkonforme Arbeiten zu produzieren, um ihren Lebensunterhalt zu verdienen. Der Markt will »neu« und meine Art von Fotografie hat eine altmodische Anmutung. Ein weiteres Problem ist, dass diese Art von Arbeit nicht einfach zu produzieren ist. Es ist einfacher, sich ein konzeptionelles Gimmick auszudenken, das keine besonderen Fähigkeiten erfordert und nicht so zeitaufwendig ist.

FSH Diese Bilder weisen auf deine große Empathie gegenüber deinen Mitmenschen hin, sind aber auch spöttisch, wenn du ihre Fehler oder Schwächen entblößt. Sehe ich das richtig?

MD Ich fand es immer großartig, dass Fellini Menschen auf die wenig schmeichelhafteste Art und Weise beschreiben konnte, ohne dabei herablassend zu sein. Es schien, als würde er mit uns lachen, denn tief in seinem Inneren wusste er, dass er genauso ein tragischer Witz war wie der Rest von uns. So möchte ich sein. Ich habe keine vorgefassten Meinungen darüber, was ich ausdrücken möchte. Ich bin weder religiös noch »spirituell«. Ich konnte mir nie vorstellen, was das auch nur bedeuten soll. Aber ich glaube an Magie, an Magie, die entsteht, wenn ich eine Kamera auf das Leben richte und ein paar Hundertstelsekunden in ein Bild einfriere. Danach verwandelt sich das Bild in etwas, das vermittelt, was ich über diese Welt denke und fühle. Diese Magie ermöglicht es mir, mich in die Welt hinein zu fotografieren.

F. Scott Hess,
Künstler und Professor am Laguna College of Art + Design

All photographs in this book
were taken in Los Angeles County
between 2014 and 2020.

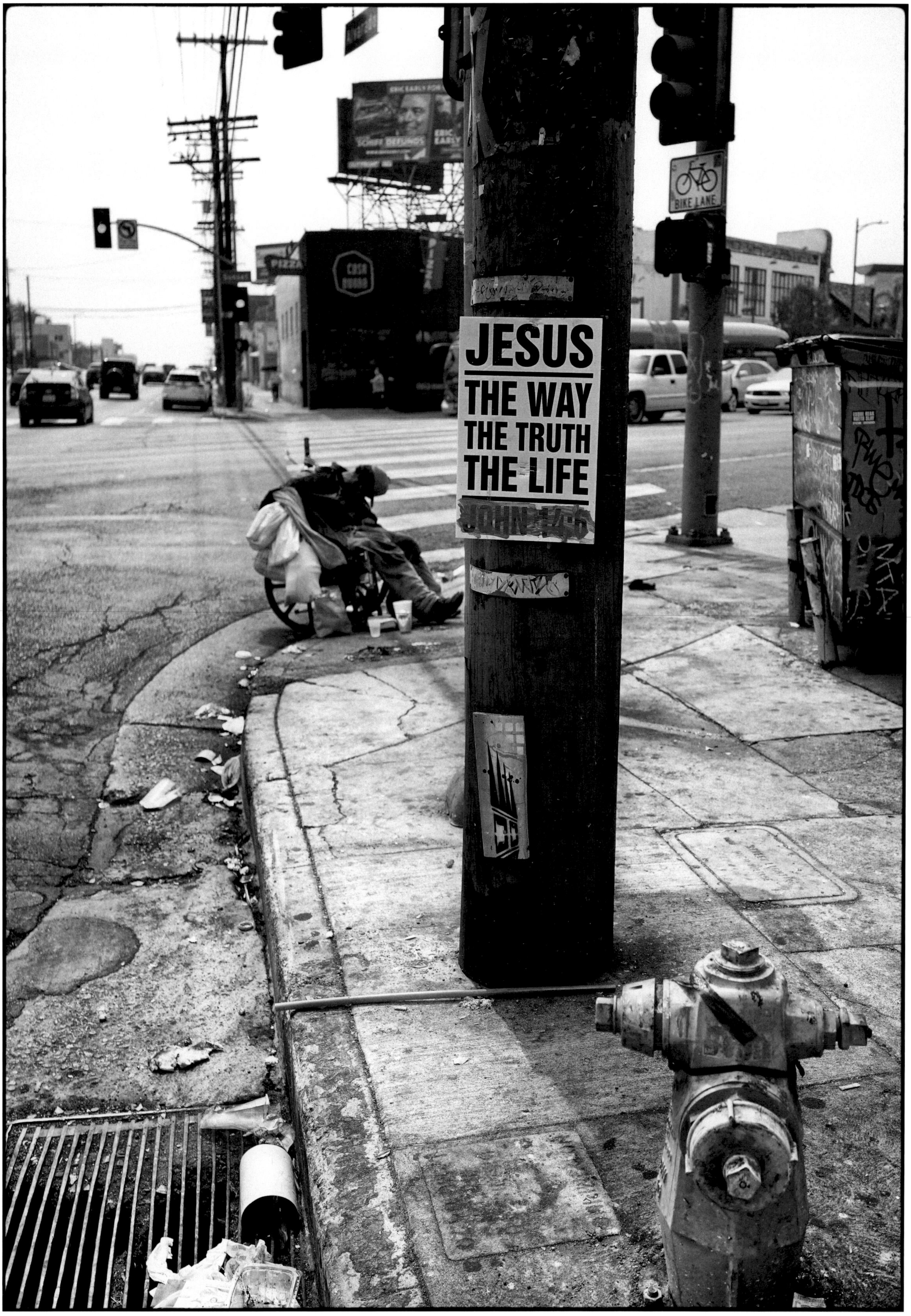
JESUS
THE WAY
THE TRUTH
THE LIFE
BIKE LANE
PIZZA

A World Theater with Different Casts

Michael Dressel confronts us with fleeting encounters with people who most of us prefer to ignore in everyday life on the streets, including many homeless, aggressive, or confused people. It takes a lot of courage to approach and portray them. Instead of using a zoom lens, Dressel stands face to face with people and is also perceived by the protagonists of this visual world theater. The photographer takes his counterparts seriously, and people feel it—which is probably the ticket for his unusual portrait journey through the urban jungle of Los Angeles.

Dressel was born in Berlin, at a time when that city was not as hip as it is today, and—what's more—on the "other side" of the now-gone Iron Curtain, in East Berlin. He wanted to get away, no matter what the cost, but his attempt to escape from East Germany failed, and Dressel ended up in prison like many others trying to break out. He eventually made it to West Berlin, became a taxi driver, and soon traveled on to Los Angeles. When Dressel tells his East-West life story it sounds like it could be an intense movie. Parallel to his main job in the Hollywood film business, he has been photographing unknown people in the streets for many years. What began as an ambitious private mission has grown into an autonomous and professional occupation that includes publications and museum exhibitions.

Dressel's working style is an attentive and intuitive reaction to the situation at hand, accompanied by sometimes superficial, sometimes more intense communications with the people he happens to meet on his wanderings through this sunburned metropolis. Sometimes his subjects seem to turn into accomplices. Everything becomes a stage here—you just have to look carefully and be able to react quickly. Dressel scans the situation that presents itself to him at lightning speed; he anticipates, and sometimes provokes, always looking for the appropriate image. He seems to be less interested in what the subjects of his pictures—mostly people—look like than what they mean in a certain context. Many of those whom Dressel portrays in the streets of Hollywood, Venice Beach, or Downtown LA once came full of hope to this desired place, which after a while became a trap for them. They simply couldn't earn enough for such an expensive place, and some ended up losing their jobs and homes. For the homeless, practically all social lifelines have been torn; they have been rejected by our fast-paced, profit-oriented society. The dualism of rich and poor, beautiful and ugly, and healthy and sick coexists in many metropolises, but in Los Angeles these extremes seem to be especially obvious.

After living in Los Angeles for over thirty years, Dressel is socially integrated and has nevertheless retained the outsider's view of this glittering and illusory world. Here, like the legendary Weegee, he shows us the pure, sometimes brutal reality of the street, which he also turns into a stage. Occasionally he relies on symbolic situations such as when a decorated pig walks through the streets or a middle-aged man portrays himself with a selfie stick in front of an S-M lingerie shop. In this way, he lets us take part in this never-ending street theater. His sometimes challenging, sometimes empathic photography is a paraphrase of classical, humanistic street photography, which was initiated by Henri Cartier-Bresson in Paris and had many followers and variants in the United States and elsewhere. Cartier-Bresson also introduced the catchphrase "decisive moment" into photo history: you simply have to be in the right place at the right time and then be able to react quickly—with the camera functioning as a kind of sketch pad. Dressel adds to this famous image strategy from the 1950s a modern, harsher variety, "Decisive Moment 2.0," as it were. He cites not only Cartier-Bresson, but also Tazio Secchiaroli as a source of inspiration: the "first paparazzo" later became notorious as a film character in Federico Fellini's *La Dolce Vita*.

The "gentlemen paparazzi" of the first hour combined ingenuity and speed, chutzpah and perseverance to supply international magazines with the coveted shots of the jet set. These factors can also be found in Dressel's way of working, even though his perception of the world tends to result in anti-celebrity photography. He does not have to submit these recordings to an editor, nor does he have to market them; in this respect he remains independent and can visualize his interpretations of everyday human life without compromise. Nevertheless, we can feel the empathy and interest of the German-American photographer for his fellow humans in his photos. While always allowing them to retain their dignity, Dressel also makes us into voyeurs. When looking at his images, we can take a closer look at things we would probably avoid in real life. Dressel has neither reservations nor hesitations about observing and photographing dropouts and the destitute as well as lovers and role-players in the streets. He, too, lost everything as a young man and reinvented himself in California, far from home. In this respect, he could recognize kindred spirits in some people who live on the street but might find their way back into society. We can learn a lot from his *Los(t) Angeles* project, which is a work in progress: about social tipping points and crashes into parallel worlds, about the often overlooked face in the crowd of a metropolis—and ultimately about ourselves with regard to our own prejudices.

Whether observed or posed, all portraits are quite individual. Dressel often puts the protagonists at the center of the compositions, accompanied by visual comments from the immediate environment, for example, in the picture of a young black homeless man who looks grimly into the camera at a bus stop in Los Angeles while a whiskey advertisement in the background caters to a middle-class clientele. In this context, the combination creates a bitter contrast, because the symbolic image reveals the cynical reality of life in our society today. All in all, although the clashing world designs in Dressel's pictures may confuse and disturb us, they are less about the opposition or togetherness of privileged and underprivileged than about all of us being powerless against the social or health disasters that can befall all of us out of the blue at any given moment. The series of images thus becomes a mirror of our existence, perhaps even a distorting mirror. Dressel confronts us with a reality that is sometimes difficult to bear, which connects him with the German photographer Miron Zownir.

When leafing through this publication, we also encounter the loud, shrill, self-celebrating life that gives us renewed hope. People dress up in the streets of Hollywood to be seen by others. There are moments when the photographer flirts with his counterpart in order to take the perfect, magical picture, for example, that of a young saleswoman in Los Angeles who is putting underwear on female headless mannequins. She shows Dressel her most beautiful smile for her portrait. The woman remains anonymous and yet completely herself. In other shots we meet Batman and Catwoman, drag queens, and men covered in large tattoos; they all move freely in public space, and some of them may hope to meet someone by chance, who will invite them to a casting, and ultimately to get involved in a film production. Here, on this playground of vanities, privacy does not seem to exist. Seen as a sequence of images, Dressel's curious observations are transformed into a contemporary study of society in the backyard of Hollywood, and his lyrical and analytical photographs leave a long-lasting impression.

Matthias Harder
Director of the Helmut Newton Foundation, Berlin

Ein Welttheater in unterschiedlicher Besetzung

Es sind flüchtige Begegnungen, mit denen uns Michael Dressel konfrontiert, mit Menschen, die die meisten von uns im Straßenalltag lieber ignorieren, darunter viele Obdachlose, aggressive oder verwirrte Menschen. Es gehört schon eine große Portion Mut dazu, sich ihnen so zu nähern und sie zu porträtieren. Dressel verwendet keine Teleoptik, er steht den Menschen vielmehr jedes Mal von Angesicht zu Angesicht gegenüber und wird von den Protagonisten dieses visuellen Welttheaters ebenfalls wahrgenommen. Der Fotograf nimmt sein Gegenüber ernst; das spüren die Leute und das ist vermutlich die Eintrittskarte für seine ungewöhnliche Porträtreise durch den Straßendschungel von Los Angeles.

Dressel ist in Berlin geboren, allerdings zu einer Zeit, als die Stadt noch nicht so hip war wie heute, und überdies auf der »anderen Seite« des inzwischen verschwundenen Eisernen Vorhangs, also in Ost-Berlin. Von dort wollte er weg, koste es, was es wolle. Doch der Fluchtversuch aus der DDR scheiterte, und Dressel landete wie so manch anderer »Republikflüchtling« im Gefängnis. Schließlich kam er doch nach West-Berlin, wurde Taxifahrer und reiste bald weiter nach Los Angeles. Seine Ost-West-Lebensgeschichte könnte verfilmt werden, so spannend klingt sie, wenn Dressel sie erzählt. Seit vielen Jahren fotografiert er parallel zu seinem Hauptjob im Hollywood-Filmgeschäft unbekannte Menschen auf den Straßen. Was als ambitionierter Selbstauftrag begann, entwickelte sich langsam und stetig zu einer autonomen und professionellen Beschäftigung inklusive Publikationen und Museumsausstellungen.

Dressels Arbeitsstil entspricht einem aufmerksamen und intuitiven Reagieren auf die vorgefundene Situation, begleitet von einer mal belanglosen, mal intensiveren Kommunikation mit den Menschen, denen er zufällig auf seinen ziellosen Streifzügen durch die taghelle Stadt begegnet. Manchmal scheinen seine Subjekte zu Komplizen zu werden. Alles wird hier zur Bühne, man muss nur genau hinschauen und schnell genug reagieren können. Dressel scannt die Situation – die sich ihm bietet – blitzschnell; er antizipiert sie, mitunter provoziert er sie auch, stets auf der Suche nach dem adäquaten Abbild.

Dabei scheint es ihn weniger zu interessieren, wie der Bildgegenstand – zumeist sind es Menschen – aussieht, sondern was dieser in einem bestimmten Kontext bedeutet. Viele, die Dressel in den Straßen von Hollywood, Venice Beach oder Downtown LA porträtiert, kamen einst voller Hoffnung an diesen Sehnsuchtsort, der für sie nach einer Weile zur Falle wurde. Sie verdienten schlicht zu wenig für ein so teures Pflaster, manche verloren schließlich Job und Wohnung. Für die Obdachlosen sind fast alle sozialen Rettungsseile gerissen, sie sind von unserer schnelllebigen, profitorientierten Gesellschaft gewissermaßen ausgespuckt worden. Der Dualismus von Arm und Reich, Schön und Hässlich, von Gesund und Krank existiert in vielen Metropolen, aber ganz besonders in Los Angeles, als gehörte das eine zum anderen Extrem.

Dressel lebt selbst seit über 30 Jahren in Los Angeles, ist gesellschaftlich integriert und hat sich gleichwohl den Blick des Außenseiters auf diese Glitzer- und Scheinwelt bewahrt. Hier zeigt er uns wie einst der legendäre Weegee die pure, mitunter schonungslose Realität auf der Straße, die auch er immer wieder zur Bühne umwidmet. Gelegentlich setzt er auf symbolhafte Situationen, wenn etwa ein geschmücktes Schwein durch die Straßen läuft oder ein Mann mittleren Alters sich mit einem Selfie-Stick vor einem SM-Dessous-Laden selbst porträtiert. So lässt er uns teilhaben an diesem endlosen Straßentheater. Seine mal herausfordernde, mal empathische Fotografie ist eine Paraphrase der klassisch-humanistischen Street Photography, die unter anderem einst von Henri Cartier-Bresson in Paris initiiert wurde und auch in den USA viele Nachfolger fand und Varianten hervorbrachte. Cartier-Bresson führte auch das Schlagwort des »decisive moment« in die Fotogeschichte ein: Man müsse schlicht zum richtigen Zeitpunkt am richtigen Ort sein und dann schnell reagieren können – und die Kamera fungiere dabei als eine Art Skizzenblock. Dressel stellt dieser berühmten Bildstrategie aus den 1950er-Jahren eine moderne, härtere Spielart an die Seite, gleichsam »decisive moment 2.0«. Er nennt nicht nur Cartier-Bresson, sondern auch Tazio Secchiaroli als Inspirationsquelle: Jener erste »Paparazzo« wurde als Filmfigur in

Federico Fellinis *La dolce vita* bekannt – und später berüchtigt. Die »Gentlemen-Paparazzi« der ersten Stunde verbanden Erfindungsreichtum und Schnelligkeit, Chuzpe und Beharrlichkeit, um für die internationalen Magazine die gewünschten Bilder des Jetsets liefern zu können. Diese Faktoren finden sich auch in der Arbeitsweise Dressels wieder, wenngleich seine Weltwahrnehmung eher zu einer Anti-Celebrity-Fotografie führt. Er muss diese Aufnahmen keinem Redakteur vorlegen, er muss sie nicht vermarkten; insofern bleibt er unabhängig und kann ohne Kompromisse seine Interpretationen des menschlichen Alltags visualisieren.

Gleichwohl spüren wir immer die Empathie und das Interesse des deutsch-amerikanischen Fotografen für seine Mitmenschen. Dressel lässt ihnen stets ihre Würde. Er macht uns aber auch zu Voyeuren. Beim Betrachten seiner Bilder können wir genauer hinschauen, obwohl wir vor Ort wohl eher wegsehen würden. Dressel hat weder Berührungsängste noch Bedenken, die Mittellosen und Aussteiger, aber auch die Liebespaare und Rollenspieler in den Straßen zu beobachten und zu fotografieren. Auch er hat als junger Mann alles verloren und sich in Kalifornien, weit weg von der Heimat, gleichsam neu erfunden. Insofern könnte er in manchen Menschen, die auf der Straße leben, Geistesverwandte erkennen, die möglicherweise wieder den Weg zurück in die Gesellschaft finden. Aus seinem noch nicht abgeschlossenen Projekt *Lost Angeles* können wir eine Menge lernen: über gesellschaftliche Kippeffekte und Abstürze in Parallelwelten, über das häufig übersehene Gesicht in der Masse einer Millionenmetropole – und nicht zuletzt über uns selbst hinsichtlich etwaiger Vorurteile.

Ob Beobachtung oder Pose – alle Porträts bleiben letztlich sehr individuell. Dressel rückt die einzelnen Protagonisten häufig ins Zentrum der Kompositionen, begleitet von visuellen Kommentaren aus dem unmittelbaren Umfeld, etwa im Bild eines jungen schwarzen Obdachlosen, der an einer Bushaltestelle in Los Angeles grimmig in die Kamera schaut, während im Hintergrund eine Whiskey-Werbung auf die Aufmerksamkeit einer bürgerlichen Klientel abzielt. In diesem Kontext sorgt die Kombination für einen bitteren Kontrast, denn das Symbolbild offenbart die zynische Lebensrealität unserer heutigen Gesellschaft. Insgesamt verwirren, ja verstören uns die aufeinanderprallenden Weltentwürfe in Dressels Bildern, doch geht es hier weniger um das Gegen- oder Miteinander von privilegierten und verlorenen Menschen, sondern vielmehr um unser aller Machtlosigkeit gegenüber den gesellschaftlichen oder gesundheitlichen Abgründen des Lebens, die mit einem Schicksalsschlag plötzlich eintreten können. So wird seine Bildserie zu einem Spiegel unserer Existenz, vielleicht sogar zu einem Zerrspiegel. Dressel konfrontiert uns mit einer Realität, die manchmal nur schwer zu ertragen ist. Das verbindet ihn mit seinem deutschen Kollegen Miron Zownir.

Doch beim Blättern in dieser Publikation begegnet uns ebenfalls das laute, schrille, sich selbst feiernde Leben, das uns wieder hoffen lässt. Menschen verkleiden sich auf den Straßen Hollywoods wie in Deutschland für den Karneval, auch für die Blicke der anderen. Und es gibt Momente, in denen der Fotograf mit seinem Gegenüber geradezu flirtet, um das entsprechende – möglichst magische – Bild zu machen, etwa mit einer jungen Verkäuferin in Los Angeles, die gerade weiblichen kopflosen Schaufensterpuppen Unterwäsche anzieht. Sie zeigt Dressel für sein Porträt ihr schönstes Lächeln. Die Frau bleibt anonym und doch ganz sie selbst. In anderen Aufnahmen treffen wir auf Batman und Catwoman, auf Dragqueens und Männer mit großflächigen Tattoos; sie alle bewegen sich ungeniert im öffentlichen Raum, und manche von ihnen hoffen mit Sicherheit auf eine zufällige Begegnung mit jemandem, der sie zu einem Casting einlädt, und schließlich auf ein Engagement für eine Filmproduktion. Privatheit scheint hier, auf dieser Spielwiese der Eitelkeiten, nicht zu existieren. Dressels neugierige Beobachtungen verwandeln sich als Bildsequenz in eine zeitgenössische Gesellschaftsstudie im Hinterzimmer Hollywoods. Und seine poetisch-analytischen Aufnahmen wirken lange nach.

Matthias Harder
Direktor der Helmut Newton Stiftung, Berlin

Special Thanks to:

Liz Stewart

Johnny Lieberman

Lucas Reiner and Maud Winchester

F. Scott Hess

Michael and Sonja Jastram

Manfred Carpentier

Christian Rothmann

Matthias Harder

Florian Günther

Hans Peil

Vera Mercer

Peter Böthig

Patrizia Rossi

Rudi Meisel

Benjamin Wolbergs

Angelika and Markus Hartmann

English copyediting: Tas Skorupa
German copyediting: Monika Reutter
Graphic design: Benjamin Wolbergs, Berlin
Typefaces: GT Sectra, Rama Gothic

Stock: Gardapatt Kiara, 135 g/m²
Color separation: Carsten Humme, Leipzig
Printing and binding: DZA Druckerei zu Altenburg GmbH

First edition November 2021

Published by

Hartmann books

Hartmann Books
Breitscheidstr. 48
70176 Stuttgart, Germany
www.hartmann-books.com

ISBN 978-3-96070-071-5

Hartmann Books is the publishing arm of Hartmann Projects, a company promoting artists, curating and organizing exhibitions, and publishing books.

Copublished for the Americas by

GINGKO PRESS

Gingko Press
2332 4th Street, Suite E
Berkeley, CA 94710
USA

ISBN 978-1-58423-771-6

Printed in Germany